Roane County, Tennessee

Marriages

1856 – 1875

Byron and Barbara Sistler

JANAWAY PUBLISHING, INC.
2013

Roane County, Tennessee, Marriages 1856-1875

Copyright © 1988 by Byron Sistler

Originally printed, Nashville, 1988

Reprinted
by

Janaway Publishing, Inc.
732 Kelsey Ct.
Santa Maria, California 93454
(805) 925-1038
www.JanawayPublishing.com

2007, 2013

Permission to reproduce in any form
must be secured from the publisher.

ISBN: 978-1-59641-075-6

Made in the United States of America

ROANE COUNTY, TN MARRIAGES
1856-1875

Where two dates appear on an entry, the first one is the date license was issued, the second (in parentheses) the date marriage was solemnized. If only one date, it usually means that the date of execution was the same as the date of license issuance.

Sometimes the execution of the marriage was not reported to the courthouse, and occasionally the clerk failed to note in the marriage book that the license was returned. We would usually make a notation in the entry to indicate the non-execution of a marriage if the book so stated.

The marriages are arranged alphabetically, the first half of the book by groom--the second by bride.

The records included in this book were transcribed by us directly from microfilmm of the original marriage books. Error, where it occurs, may be attributed to us, or to the clerks of the period, many of whom did an appallingly sloppy job of entering the information.

If the bride and groom were black, a B is placed at the end of the entry.

It should be remembered that this and other marriage books we have prepared are indexes, and do not include all the information to be found in the original marriage book. Such data as names of bondsmen, ministers, justices of the peace, churches, etc., are omitted. Often such information is helpful to the researcher. Consequently the serious researcher, to obtain this additional information as well as to check on the accuracy of the transcriber, should examine the original marriage record if at all possible.

Byron Sistler
Barbara Sistler

Nashville, TN
January 1988

Roane County Grooms

Abbot, Dewitt C. to Melvina Fitts 7-28-1857 (7-30-1857)   [Ro]
Abbott, D. C. H. to Letitia Johnson 10-5-1870 10-6-1870   [Ro]
Abbott, L. L. to Martha J. Johnson 9-15-1868 (9-17-1868)   [Ro]
Abels, Geo. W. to F. M. Robbs 6-22-1867 (6-23-1867)   [Ro]
Ables, Wm. to Sarah Hichew? 10-6-1874 (10-8-1874)   [Ro]
Abner, James to Nancy Huffland 7-20-1867 (7-21-1867)   [Ro]
Absten, Charles to Ann Devaney 5-19-1857   [Ro]
Absten, Joseph to Caroline Ladd 4-28-1856 (not executed)   [Ro]
Abstent, Stephen B. to Louisa Roberts 1-7-1861 (1-9-1861)   [Ro]
Abston, William to Jane Clark 8-5-1873 (8-7-1873)   [Ro]
Acuff, D. M. to Mary E. Kendrick 12-23-1868 (12-24-1868)   [Ro]
Acuff, Samuel J. to Leatha M. Kindrick 8-1-1859   [Ro]
Adams, Asa to Elizabeth Narramore 11-18-1861   [Ro]
Adams, J. H. to Mary C. Ragh 9-20-1865   [Ro]
Adams, Newton A. to Seraphina Parmley 6-24-1862   [Ro]
Adams, Robert W. to Rachel S. Harrison 12-26-1860   [Ro]
Adkins, Calaway to Elizabeth Hill 12-5-1864 (12-6-1864)   [Ro]
Adkins, Willis to Misorina England 5-25-1861 (5-28-1861)   [Ro]
Adkisson, W. B. to Nancy A. Walker 4-28-1870   [Ro]
Adkisson, Wilkerson to Emaline Greene 7-7-1866 (7-8-1866)   [Ro]
Adkisson, Yerby to Nancy J. Underwood 3-24-1857 (3-26-1857)   [Ro]
Agee, Wm. J. to Cynthia L. Wilson 12-15-1859   [Ro]
Aiken, Thomas to Sarah Thomas 11-1-1866 (11-7-1866)   [Ro]
Alexander, Jefferson to MSary Everrett 11-19-1859 (11-24-1859)   [Ro]
Alexander, Robert H. to Nancy C. Munger 12-10-1866 (12-13-1866)   [Ro]
Alger, Ezera J. to Nancy Bever 3-24-1857   [Ro]
Aliston, Lewis F. to S. C. Tedder 1-13-1872 (1-14-1872)   [Ro]
Allen, James to Catherine Clark 3-5-1864 (3-6-1864)   [Ro]
Allen, Jas. P. to Ellen C. Duff 10-2-1869 10-10-1869   [Ro]
Allen, Jason to Mary E. Tindle? 2-17-1869 (2-18-1869)   [Ro]
Allen, Richard to Johanna C. Martin 8-24-1865   [Ro]
Allen, Richard to Mary Washington Hart 2-10-1858 (2-11-1858)   [Ro]
Allen, Wm. C. to Mary Wright 12-27-1856 (1-25-1857)   [Ro]
Alley, David to Elizabeth Cole 8-1-1856   [Ro]
Alley, Seth to Mary J. Demming 12-24-1860   [Ro]
Allison, R. E. to Martha Lowery 7-11-1863 (7-12-1863)   [Ro]
Allison, Uriah S. to Mary E. Burnett 3-5?-1864 (3-7-1864)   [Ro]
Ambrose, David C. to Eliza J. Johnson 9-18-1856 (9-19-1856)   [Ro]
Ambrose, James to Jane Ambrose 7-8-1864 (7-10-1864)   [Ro]
Ambrose, John T. to Margaret A. Claibourn 6-1-1857   [Ro]
Amos, David W. to Elizabeth Harvey 9-12-1867   [Ro]
Amos, John to Sarah E. Long 6-28-1867 (6-30-1867)   [Ro]
Amos, Wesley to Elizabeth Moreland 12-17-1856 (12-18-1856)   [Ro]
Amos, Zachariah to Margaret J. Fuller 6-13-1866   [Ro]
Anderson, John to Isabella Hotchkiss 4-30-1867 (5-2-1867)   [Ro]
Anderson, Robert R. to Emily J. Huff 10-13-1859   [Ro]
Anderson, Samuel to Margaret Huff 4-27-1867 (4-28-1867)   [Ro]
Anderson, Simeon W. to Orleans E. Hedgecock 7-12-1873 (7-13-1873)   [Ro]
Andrew, Francis to Mary A. Sparks 1-18-1869   [Ro]
Anthony, George to Susan Williams 8-22-1860   [Ro]
Apperson, F. E. to Margaret E. Gamble 12-27-1865   [Ro]
Arndel, Daniel to Metilda Frazier 10-26-1859 (10-27-1859)   [Ro]

Roane County Grooms

Arnett, Wm. G. to Pheby L. Smith 6-6-1857 (6-7-1857) [Ro]
Asbury, D. F. to Mary Ann Holmen 10-24-1871 (10-29-1871) [Ro]
Asbury, David F. to Mary J. Bacon 2-13-1860 (2-23-1860) [Ro]
Atwood, C. M. to Martha Surrett 8-8-1874 (8-9-1874) [Ro]
Atwood, J. B. to Elizabeth McCulley 12-28-1864 (12-29-1864) [Ro]
Aughinbaugh, W. A. to Elizabeth Devaney 12-7-1869 [Ro]
Aytes, Jas. M. to Eliza C. Millican 8-17-1867 (8-18-1867) [Ro]
Babb, Hiram to Margaret Wright 6-23-1857 [Ro]
Babb, Jas. A. to Rebecca C. Lunsford 6-18-1869 (6-19-1869) [Ro]
Babb, Willis J. to Mary Jane Johnson 11-16-1869 11-18-1869 [Ro]
Bacon, A. S. to S. K. Crowder 5-16-1868 [Ro]
Bacon, C. C. to Elizabeth Matlock 9-18-1857 (9-24-1857) [Ro]
Bacon, G. P. to Melissa Harner 2-25-1870 2-27-1870 [Ro]
Bacon, J. H. to Lucinda Breeden 4-27-1874 [Ro]
Bacon, John H. to Hannah J. Breeden 11-19-1867 [Ro]
Bacon, John H. to Jane Haggard 4-7-1859 (4-10-1859) [Ro]
Bacon, John W. to Mary M. Boyd 4-12-1871 [Ro]
Bacon, Josiah J. to Rutha C. Hines 12-29-1864 (1-1-1864?) [Ro]
Bacon, Langston to Mary E. Robbs 10-9-1858 (10-10-1858) [Ro]
Bacon, Wm. A. to Amelia J. Crowder 5-24-1865 (5-25-1865) [Ro]
Bagwell, T. J. to N. E. Millican 7-15-1869 7-16-1869 [Ro]
Bagwell, William to Eveline Ambrose 9-17-1856 (9-19-1856) [Ro]
Bagwell, Wm. D. to Hariet Cofer 8-6-1870 8-11-1870 [Ro]
Bailey, A. J. to Susan A. Lewis 7-29-1869 8-1-1869 [Ro]
Bailey, Henry to Rebecca Rich 2-20-1866 (2-22-1866) [Ro]
Bailey, Hiram to Elizabeth Miller 4-17-1861 [Ro]
Bailey, Hiram to Mary Tuterrow 5-3-1871 [Ro]
Bailey, John E. to Sarah F. Isham 10-4-1866 [Ro]
Bailey, Samuel J. to Frances C. Diggs 5-21-1867 (5-23-1867) [Ro]
Bailey, T. F. to E. F. Brackett 9-2-1870 9-4-1870 [Ro]
Baily, John to Jane Carter 11-28-1865 (11-29-1865) [Ro]
Baily, Samuel to Rachel Qualls 9-13-1869 9-19-1869 [Ro]
Baily, W. F. to Laura Fisher 8-11-1868 (8-13-1868) [Ro]
Bainbridge, Saml. to Mary Nicholson 7-21-1865 [Ro]
Baird, James S. T. to Sarah L. Abbott 8-17-1857 (8-19-1857) [Ro]
Baker, David A. to Rebecca Hester 11-1-1869 11-3-1869 [Ro]
Baker, James H. to E. A. Silvey 4-14-1874 (4-16-1874) [Ro]
Baker, James M. to Cyntha C. Butler 2-10-1862 (2-13-1862) [Ro]
Baldwin, John T. to Elizabeth Whitlock 12-16-1873 [Ro]
Baldwin, R. T. to Rhoda E. Campbell 5-16-1873 [Ro]
Bales, E. M. to Maggie E. Tarwater 5-19-1874 (5-27-1874) [Ro]
Balew, George W. to Matilda Waller 9-24-1862 [Ro]
Ball, Calvin to Elizabeth Hacker 3-23-1864 (3-24-1864) [Ro]
Ball, George W. to Mary H. Sellars 1-31-1867 [Ro]
Ball, Saml. G. to Rachel Jane Clowers 1-10-1860 [Ro]
Ball, Samuel G. to Rachel J. Clowers 1-10-1860 [Ro]
Ball, William H. to Ann Andes 1-18-1858 (1-19-1858) [Ro]
Ballard, Saml. S. to Mary E. Williams 4-24-1860 [Ro]
Ballard, Washington to Harriet Oliphant 4-6-1857 (4-9-1858?) [Ro]
Bane, Charles M. to Rebecca J. Holland 6-27-1874 (6-28-1874) [Ro]
Bane?, J. S. E. to Martha Finch? 12-16-1859 [Ro]
Barbour, William D. to Mariah? Parmley 6-21-1856 (6-22-1856) [Ro]
Barger, Julian F. to Fanny Williams 9-18-1868 (9-20-1868) [Ro]

Roane County Grooms

Bargers, Z. T. to Elizabeth Sullins 12-21-1870 12-22-1870 [Ro]
Barley, George P. to Christina Hester 8-5-1859   [Ro]
Barnard, George W. to Melinda C. Crowder 1-5-1857 (1-8-1857) * [Ro]
Barnard, J. M. to R. A. D. Weese 12-21-1870 12-22-1870 [Ro]
Barnard, James J. to Margaret Crowder 4-1-1869 (4-4-1869) [Ro]
Barnett, James D. to De Annah Crow 2-22-1859 (2-23-1859) [Ro]
Barnett, Samuel H. to Rebecca A. Whitlock 10-31-1859 (11-8-1859)   [Ro]
Barnette, William to Ann E. Nixon 5-22-1862   [Ro]
Barnwell, Wetherford G. to Minerva Cristian ;12-1-1856   [Ro]
Bartonett, Lewis W. to Martha J. Gray 3-29-1869   [Ro]
Basket, J. R. to Lizzie McPeters 6-13-1868   [Ro]
Basket, John E. to Frances C. Moreland 2-21-1865   [Ro]
Bates, Francis M. to Delilah Estes 5-1-1867 (5-5-1867) [Ro]
Bates, J. C. to Martha McCollister 8-3-1869 8-4-1869 [Ro]
Bauer, C. F. to M. C. Wineter 3-8-1873 (3-9-1873) [Ro]
Bauer, Charles to Elizabeth S. Gillem 7-18-1872   [Ro]
Bazel, Saml. to Lydia Miles 9-3-1874   B [Ro]
Beale, Augustus W. to Mary A. Prater 1-30-1866 (2-21-1866)   [Ro]
Beard, Hugh L. to Melvisa Powell 8-4-1865 (8-5-1865) [Ro]
Bearden, Charles to Adaline Crutchfield 9-18-1873   [Ro]
Bearden, George to Margaret Hartley 11-24-1869 11-25-1869 [Ro]
Beaver, J. J. to Rachel M. Pratt 12-19-1868 (12-3?-1868)   [Ro]
Beaver, R. A. to Caroline Fritts 7-20-1869   [Ro]
Beeler, James to Susan Easter 3-14-1863   [Ro]
Belamy, Thomas J. to Serena C. Long 5-30-1870 6-1-1870 [Ro]
Belew, George W. to Sarah E. Freelds 7-25-1863   [Ro]
Belew, James P. to Mary E. Belew 10-22-1867   [Ro]
Belew, John to Catharine Copeland 8-4-1862   [Ro]
Belew, John D. to Sarah Ann Copeland 8-15-1865   [Ro]
Belew, William to Lurina J. Devers 5-7-1857   [Ro]
Bell, D. J. to L. J. Winters 6-28-1872 (6-29-1872) [Ro]
Bell, D. M. to Eliza Underwood 5-1-1874   [Ro]
Bell, George to Eliza J. Bell 6-18-1870   [Ro]
Bell, Luke to Barbara Hardbarger 3-18-1872 (3-21-1872) [Ro]
Bell, Samul H. to Martha Giles 1-7-1873 (1-9-1873) [Ro]
Bell, Wm. T. to Martha N. Monday 11-29-1873 (11-30-1873) [Ro]
Belvin, William F. to Elizabeth M. Perry 3-26-1859 (3-27-1859)   [Ro]
Benegyr, Chas. to Mary McCart 9-17-1867 (9-18-1867) [Ro]
Benge, William A. to Susan Gallimore 5-4-1863   [Ro]
Bennett, James to Mary Malinda Penix 6-2-1865   [Ro]
Bennett, John to Susan Rainey 5-24-1862   [Ro]
Benton, Mordicai S. to Lou E. Baker 10-6-1856 (10-7-1856) [Ro]
Berry, George W. to Nancy J. Lovelace 5-17-1873   [Ro]
Bett, James to Nancy Ann Fondered 7-31-1865   [Ro]
Bilderback, James N. to Lucinda Jane True 3-8-1856 (3-12-1856)   [Ro]
Billings, Bayless W. to Rachel M. Cooley 8-27-1873 (8-31-1873)   [Ro]
Billings, Jasper to Eliza Jane Fox 1-28-1868 (1-30-1868) [Ro]
Billingsley, Jas. H. to N. J. Walker 8-24-1869   [Ro]
Billingsley, John H. to Sarah R. Byrd 1-16-1869 (1-17-1869) [Ro]
Billingsly, Benj. F. to Eliza J. McDuffee 12-23-1856 (12-24-1856)   [Ro]
Billingsly, J. A. to Mary C. Wilson 11-28-1868 (11-29-1868) [Ro]
Bink, Robert A. to Sarah E. McCully 4-24-1861 (4-25-1861) [Ro]
Bishop, Benj. F. to Hannah L. Lewis 5-12-1863 (5-14-1863) [Ro]

Roane County Grooms

Bishop, George W. to Mary M. Young 4-14-1873 (4-17-1873) [Ro]
Bishop, James to Nancy Loveless 11-21-1866 (11-23-1866) [Ro]
Bisplinghoff, Charles to Margaret Stolling 7-22-1858 (7-23-1858) [Ro]
Bivens, James P. to Nancy J. Hopkins 10-6-1871 (10-8-1871) [Ro]
Bivins, Joseph to Clori S. Guffey 3-3-1871 (3-4-1871) [Ro]
Black, James to Margaret Fouse 1-11-1865 (1-12-1865) [Ro]
Blackburn, Wm. to Catharine Soward 5-2-1871 (5-4-1871) [Ro]
Blackwell, Geo. W. to Martha J. Hickey 10-9-1856 [Ro]
Blair, Hugh to Nancy B. Johnson 8-30-1865 [Ro]
Blair, John to Amanda Huffman 2-7-1859 (2-10-1859) [Ro]
Blair, John J. to Mary C. Osborn 9-9-1861 (9-17-1861) [Ro]
Blair, Josiah to Eliza Lea 12-23-1868 (1-3-1869) [Ro]
Blair, N. L. to G. G. Williams 9-16-1864 (10-6-1864) [Ro]
Blair, S. P. to Mary Martin 8-31-1868 (9-1-1868) [Ro]
Blair, Samuel T. to Nancy Jolly 1-13-1858 (1-15-1858) [Ro]
Blankenbicker, J. M. to Margaret Miller 9-1-1865 (9-8-1865) [Ro]
Blevins, Thomas C. to Louisa J. Delosier 8-10-1867 (8-11-1867) [Ro]
Bly, James to L. C. Tapp 8-2-1873 (8-4-1873) [Ro]
Bodine, W. T. to M. J. East 8-11-1874 (8-13-1874) [Ro]
Bogart, Henry M. to Frances E. Freeman 1-7-1859 (1-9-1859) [Ro]
Bogart, Wm. W. to Nancy A. Cardwell 2-10-1870 [Ro]
Bolden, Hugh L. to Rachel C. Dever 7-9-1858 [Ro]
Boles, Rufus to Mary A. Jiles 10-3-1872 [Ro]
Boling, Thomas to Tennessee A. Ward 6-20-1874 (6-21-1874) [Ro]
Bolt, James M. to Isabella Breazeale 2-12-1856 [Ro]
Borum, Henry E. to Nancy Jane Martin 12-25-1858 (12-26-1858) [Ro]
Bowen, John to Mary E. Hicks 9-16-1860 (9-17-1860) [Ro]
Bowers, Casper F. to Sarah P. Myers 8-19-1871 (8-20-1871) [Ro]
Bowers, Samuel V. to Rebecca J. Allis 12-4-1869 12-5-1869 [Ro]
Bowles, David to Catharine Suvall 10-8-1864 [Ro]
Bowles, Jesse to Nancy Kizziah 2-19-1873 (2-20-1873) [Ro]
Bowles, John F. to Susan L. Monday 7-16-1870 7-31-1870 [Ro]
Bowlin, Stephen to Martha E. Millican 7-19-1856 [Ro]
Bowling, Henderson to Matilda Marney 10-31-1864 [Ro]
Bowling, Isaac to Phoebe Godsey 3-12-1874 (3-13-1874) [Ro]
Bowling, Joseph D. to Josie Furgerson 10-26-1872 (10-27-1872) [Ro]
Bowling, Thos. to Surrelda J. Belew 5-2-1868 (5-3-1868) [Ro]
Bowling, Wm. F. to Nancy Bacon 3-9-1865 (3-23-1865) [Ro]
Bowling, Z. T. to Nancy Leffew 3-5-1874 (3-4?-1874) [Ro]
Bowman, G. M. to Mary E. Giles 5-14-1864 (5-15-1864) [Ro]
Bowman, James L. to Jemima Edwards 11-3-1856 (11-6-1856) [Ro]
Bowman, John W. to Caroline Marney 12-21-1858 (1-4-1859) [Ro]
Boyd, D. M. to Sallie P. Smith 10-13-1869 [Ro]
Boyd, Fernando C. to Elizabeth J. Winchester 6-1-1860 [Ro]
Boyd, Thomas to Winney Davis 6-11-1865 (7-2-1865) [Ro]
Brackett, James to Mary C. Reeder 2-25-1861 (2-26-1861) [Ro]
Brackett, John to Melissa Baldwin 1-14-1857 (1-15-1857) [Ro]
Brackett, Joseph to Mahaley Ahart 4-13-1857 [Ro]
Brackett, Stephen to Eliza Brackett 6-13-1867 (6-16-1867) [Ro]
Brackett, Thomas to Linda Baldwin 7-23-1856 (7-25-1856) [Ro]
Bradham?, Joseph to Nancy C. Crace 6-30-1865 [Ro]
Bradley, James to Elizabeth Smith 4-4-1859 (4-7-1859) [Ro]
Bradley, Stephen to Amelia Gallaher 3-31-1870 4-3-1870 [Ro]

Roane County Grooms

Bradshaw, John H. to Sarah Sharp 8-13-1864 (9-1-1860?)   [Ro]
Brady, Smith to Harriet J. Sellers 1-29-1856 (1-30-1856)   [Ro]
Brandon, John to Nancy C. Lemons 1-17-1871 (1-19-18710   [Ro]
Brandon, Joseph to Mahaly A. Franklin 6-25-1873   [Ro]
Branham, George W. to Lucinda Dickson 11-11-1856   [Ro]
Brashears, Saml. to Delilah Mays 12-28-1863 (12-29-1863)   [Ro]
Brashers, William D. to Margaret F. Cox 7-12-1865 (7-13-1865)   [Ro]
Brazeale, William H. to Elizabeth E. Breazeale 11-12-1858 (11-14-1858)
Breazeale, James F. to Susanah Mongen 5-1-1866 (5-3-1866)   [Ro]
Breazeale, Jefferson to Elizabeth Kollock 1-30-1856 (1-31-1856)   [Ro]
Breazeale, Thomas B. to Nancy Young 10-11-1860 (10-14-1860)   [Ro]
Breeden, Rufus S. to Louisa Cox 8-26-1861 (8-27-1861)   [Ro]
Brewer, William to Polly A. McAlister 4-6-1867 (4-7-1867)   [Ro]
Briant, G. W. to M. J. Gladen 11-20-1874   [Ro]
Brice, John B. to Sarah A. Thompson 9-17-1866 (9-20-1866)   [Ro]
Briddle, John W. to Malinda J. Scarbrough 3-19-1874 (3-22-1874)   [Ro]
Brient, John to Susan W. Ellis 9-28-1865 (9-29-1865)   [Ro]
Briggs, John R. to Lucinda Bullen 10-14-1868 (10-15-1868)   [Ro]
Briggs, Samuel T. to Malinda Cox 11-2-1870 11-3-1870   [Ro]
Britt, Canady to Elizabeth Martin 7-31-1857 (8-2-1857)   [Ro]
Brock, James H.? to Mary Wilson 9-25-1861 (9-26-1861)   [Ro]
Brock, John to Rachel R. Philips 9-28-1865   [Ro]
Brock, John h. to Winney Johnson 6-4-1866 (6-19-1866)   [Ro]
Brock, Larkin to Mary A. Walls 12-14-1872 (12-15-1872)   [Ro]
Brogden, Elkany to Lucinda J. Murphy 10-17-1868 (10-18-1868)   [Ro]
Brogdon, James to Amanda C. Carroll 3-23-1858 (3-16-1858)   [Ro]
Brogdon, William to Melinda C. Selvage 3-17-1860   [Ro]
Bronson, James to Elizabeth Roberts 7-31-1872 (8-1-1872)   [Ro]
Brooks, Asbury to Rebecca Martin 12-18-1856   [Ro]
Brooks, Moses to Martha Jane Amos 11-4-1861 (11-10-1861)   [Ro]
Browder, Darius to Caroline Haynes 2-11-1856 (2-14-1856)   [Ro]
Browder, John F. to Sarah E. Gallaher 3-11-1862 (3-12-1862)   [Ro]
Browder, Samuel to Mary Ann Smith 1-18-1858 (1-21-1858)   [Ro]
Brown, Alex. H. to Margaret Narramore 9-23-1869   [Ro]
Brown, C. H. W. to Nancy A. Mayton 2-8-1869 (2-11-1869)   [Ro]
Brown, Calvin M. to Eliza Furgerson 11-19-1872 (11-21-1872)   [Ro]
Brown, David to Mary Gurly 9-7-1868   [Ro]
Brown, E. K. to Jane Russell 6-27-1866 (6-28-1866)   [Ro]
Brown, Ephraim H. to Ann E. Carter 8-30-1865   [Ro]
Brown, F. M. to Mary Morgan 6-17-1874   [Ro]
Brown, Houston to Sarah E. Burnett 11-4-1861 (11-12-1861)   [Ro]
Brown, James S. to Hester V. Blount 6-27-1870 6-28-1870   [Ro]
Brown, Jeremiah to Rebekah Peatt 3-3-1864 (3-4-1864)   [Ro]
Brown, John to Elizabeth Peatt? 7-6-1867 (11-7-1867)   [Ro]
Brown, Joseph to Rebecca Roberts 10-10-1868 (10-11-1868)   [Ro]
Brown, Rufus B. to Eliza C. Phifer 11-3-1865 (11-19-1865)   [Ro]
Brown, S. C. to S. M. Sharp 2-2-1875   [Ro]
Brown, Thomas J. to Martha A. Owings 12-11-1867 (12-12-1867)   [Ro]
Brown, William to Esther Weaver 12-28-1867 (1-2-1868)   [Ro]
Brown, Wm. to Matilda Usra 7-28-1866   [Ro]
Brown, Wm. F. to Charlotte M. Stevens 5-6-1873 (5-18-1873)   [Ro]
Browning, Joseph M. to Sarah J. Scott 5-23-1871 (5-24-1871)   [Ro]
Bruce, John to Catharine Jones 8-4-1866 (8-9-1866)   [Ro]

Roane County Grooms

Brumett, Wm. R. to Sarah E. Kitchen 3-18-1868 [Ro]
Buckland, James to Annis Rentfro 4-22-1857 (4-30-1857) [Ro]
Buckner, Allen to Mary J. Cooley 1-2-1868 (1-5-1868) [Ro]
Bullen, J. C. to Dora A. Smith 4-12-1871 [Ro]
Bullen, William C. to Eleanor Borum 1-2-1858 (1-3-1858) [Ro]
Buller, Hiram J. to Elizabeth Roberts 10-24-1859 [Ro]
Bulling, Benjamin G. to Elly M. Miller 1-16-1867 (1-21-1867) [Ro]
Buns?, Joseph E. to Barbara J. Shackelford 9-12-1862 [Ro]
Burchfield, Frank to Clementine Blankenbicker 5-9-1874 (5-10-1874) [Ro]
Burchfield, Willis to Mary Johnson 4-9-1872 (4-19-1872) [Ro]
Burell, W. J. to Margaret T. Knox 10-1-1869 10-3-1869 [Ro]
Buren?, James H. to Elizabeth Morse 5-24-1861 (5-25-1861) [Ro]
Burgess, Lemuel to Theodocia Cunningham 7-6-1870 7-10-1870 [Ro]
Burke, James to Eliza Burke 2-20-1873 [Ro]
Burnett, James to Catharine Frith 11-24-1858 [Ro]
Burnett, James to Martha Jane Branham 6-5-1858 [Ro]
Burnett, John to Elisabeth Stout 10-22-1874 (8?-22-1874) [Ro]
Burnett, John L. to Sarah J. Monger 5-29-1869 (5-30-1869) [Ro]
Burnett, M. J. to Clarissa J. Burnett 6-8-1872 (6-10-1872) [Ro]
Burnett, W. C. to Eliza J. Kyle 12-24-1870 12-25-1870 [Ro]
Burnett, Wm. to Martha Howard 6-22-1870 6-24-1870 [Ro]
Burns, Benjamin B. to Adaline Bruister 2-27-1866 (3-1-1866) [Ro]
Burns, Henry to E. E. Williams 3-4-1865 (3-5-1865) [Ro]
Burns, Henry W. to Permelia F. May 9-20-1860 [Ro]
Burns, John to Pricilla Hacker 8-8-1860 (8-10-1860) [Ro]
Burns, M. V. to M. C. Cundiff 3-3-1871 (3-5-1871) [Ro]
Burns, Smith P. to Rebecca A. Roberts 9-3-1860 (9-6-1860) [Ro]
Burton, George to Sarah Griffis 10-24-1874 (10-25-1874) [Ro]
Bush, Yocum C. to Lucinda Hart 5-1-1866 (5-3-1866) [Ro]
Bussell, C. P. to Julia Ann Malinda Leeper 2-5-1862 [Ro]
Butler, Geoge to Melia Freels 9-17-1870 [Ro]
Butler, J. J. to Martha A. Littleton 4-13-1869 (4-15-1869) [Ro]
Butler, John H. to Margaret S. Deavenport 9-1-1857 [Ro]
Butler, Moses to Caroline Gillespie 5-23-1868 B [Ro]
Butler, W. H. to Martha A. Millions 1-26-1865 (1-29-1865) [Ro]
Butler, Wm. L. to Margaret Qualls 12-23-1856 (1-31-1856?) [Ro]
Byram, John W. to Rebecca A. McClanahan 9-11-1868 (9-15-1868) [Ro]
Byrd, G. W. to Amanda Talent 9-22-1869 [Ro]
Byrd, Geo. W. to Mary Sylvey 1-31-1865 [Ro]
Byrd, George G. to Roena Hassler 10-24-1861 [Ro]
Byrd, John H. to Mary A. Ballard 12-21-1867 (12-26-1867) [Ro]
Byrd, Robert K. to Mary K. _____ 7-23-1861 [Ro]
Byrd, Thomas B. to Savanah E. Margrave 3-6-1856 [Ro]
Byrd, Wm. P. to Rebecca E. Breashears 10-1-1873 (10-2-1873) [Ro]
Byrum, John to Lucinda Rich 10-13-1858 (10-16-1858) [Ro]
Cables, Freeman to Louisa M. Hampton 12-17-1864 (12-18-1864) [Ro]
Cagan, Michael to Nancy Rayder 2-3-1866 (3-3-1866) [Ro]
Cameron, Andrew to Margaret Breazeale 11-13-1856 (11-23-1856) [Ro]
Camp, James to L. S. Hess 6-7-1873 (6-12-1873) [Ro]
Campbell, Columbus to Sarah J. Locke 11-3-1869 11-4-1869 [Ro]
Campbell, James to Mary Brogden 2-7-1863 (2-8-1863) [Ro]
Campbell, Jesse P. to Tempy McEwen 3-7-1859 (3-29-1859) [Ro]
Campbell, John B. to Mariah King 7-21-1866 (7-25-1866) [Ro]

Roane County Grooms

Campbell, Moses T. to Mary Jane Robinson 9-9-1858 (9-10-1858) [Ro]
Campbell, Robt. to Arminda Dennis 12-19-1865 (12-24-1865) [Ro]
Campbell, William H. G. to Mary Ann Jane Soward 4-5-1857 (4-6-1857) [Ro]
Capps, A. M. to M. H. Hamilton 3-27-1867 (4-4-1867) [Ro]
Capps, Gideon to Sarah Jane Tinel 1-17-1867 [Ro]
Capps, M. B. to Susan Massey 3-30-1867 (3-31-1867) [Ro]
Carden, A. O. to Margaret E. Murray 1-11-1866 (1-15-1866) [Ro]
Carden, John N. to Mary Rector 1-1-1856 [Ro]
Cardin, Daniel J. to Malinda Wade 2-28-1862 (3-2-1862) [Ro]
Cardon, G. W. to Sophia Ladd 8-22-1867 [Ro]
Cardwell, Anthony W. to Sarena E. Carter 5-18-1857 (5-20-1857) [Ro]
Cardwell, John H. to Mary A. Brown 11-11-1871 (11-12-1871) [Ro]
Cardwell, Joseph N. to Mary C. Waller 3-25-1871 (3-26-1871) [Ro]
Cardwell, Robert to Nancy Underwood 8-6-1860 [Ro]
Carmichael, John to Sarah Gitgood 5-13-1859 (6-3-1859) [Ro]
Carmichal, Georg W. to Mary T. Simons? 10-24-1868 (10-25-1868) [Ro]
Carnell, Wiley to Angeline Taylor 6-27-1856 [Ro]
Caroway, W. R. to Cynthi J. Sharp 9-12-1868 (9-15-1868) [Ro]
Carr, Samuel to Malinda Jane Bice 8-15-1865 (8-17-1865) [Ro]
Carroll, Dennis to Malinda Eaton 4-30-1870 5-1-1870 [Ro]
Carroll, George to Matilda Mullins 1-20-1866 [Ro]
Carroll, Hiram H. to Malinda Fapp 6-16-1870 [Ro]
Carroll, J. T. to Caroline Huffine 12-2-1874 (12-3-1874) [Ro]
Carroll, James M. to Polly Gooden 2-4-1868 (2-6-1868) [Ro]
Carroll, James M. to Sarah Ann Crabtree 6-28-1859 [Ro]
Carroll, Jas. E. to Arty J. Fortner 7-11-1864 (7-24-1864) [Ro]
Carroll, John C. to Lucinda Robinson 8-25-1865 (8-30-1865) [Ro]
Carroll, John W. to Ann E. Parks 9-25-1873 (9-28-1873) [Ro]
Carroll, William to Mary A. Farner 4-19-1856 [Ro]
Carroll, William to Sarah Bevens 1-30-1858 (1-31-1858) [Ro]
Carter, Andrew to Cyntha Belew 7-3?-1862 (7-6-1862) [Ro]
Carter, Daniel M. to Nancy E.(Mary?) Cooley 4-30-1864 (5-1-1864) [Ro]
Carter, Genl. T. to Elizabeth Watt 10-28-1864 (10-30-1864) [Ro]
Carter, J. D. to Sue R. Tutterrow 3-2-1869 (3-11-1869) [Ro]
Carter, James to Amanda Wilson 11-20-1874 (11-21-1874) [Ro]
Carter, Joshua A. to Amanda Eaton 11-23-1864 [Ro]
Carter, Martin B. to Lizzie Leeper 2-8-1866 (2-21-1866) [Ro]
Carter, Rawlings to Elizabeth J. Eaton 12-19-1865 [Ro]
Carter, Rufus M. to M. J. Saunders 12-22-1868 (12-27-1868) [Ro]
Carter, Samuel C. to Elizabeth Coker 4-3-1858 (4-4-1858) [Ro]
Carter, Samul W. to Mary E. Billingsley 9-29-1868 (10-1-1868) [Ro]
Carter, William to Amanda Hillsman 5-3-1869 (5-6-1869) [Ro]
Carter, Wilson to Sarah Jane Robinson 3-30-1866 [Ro]
Casey, John to Eliza Kirkland 8-4-1874 (8-23-1874) [Ro]
Casey, John to Sarah A. Talor 12-25-1856 [Ro]
Cash, Andrew T. to Sarah J. Dyer 10-18-1865 [Ro]
Cash, Benjamin to Rebecca Wilkey 3-19-1872 [Ro]
Cash, John S. to Sarah Murray 9-11-1865 [Ro]
Cassady, Jas. A. to Mary Sellars 12-21-1867 (12-22-1867) [Ro]
Cate, Daniel to Nancy Jane Miller 5-19-1865 (5-21-1865) [Ro]
Cate, G. W. to Mary Green 5-9-1872 [Ro]
Cate, John to Mary C. Miller 9-21-1863 [Ro]
Cate, Thomas J. to Mary B. Turnbill 11-30-1864 (not executed) [Ro]

Roane County Grooms

Cate, Thos. J. to Matilda Wilkerson 2-22-1865 (3-31-1865)   [Ro]
Cates, Edward to Margaret R. Scarbrough 12-21-1871   [Ro]
Cates, Harvey to Sarah Hood 9-27-1873 (10-2-1873)   [Ro]
Cates, John to Emaline Horner 2-8-1860   [Ro]
Cates, John to Linda Bouling 9-19-1868 (9-20-1868)   [Ro]
Cates, Samuel to Mary Qualls 1-7-1856   [Ro]
Cates, William to Caroline Miller 12-29-1859   [Ro]
Celp, James to Dorcas Herring 9-20-1865 (9-21-1865)   [Ro]
Center, Franklin K. to Sarah W. Crow 11-21-1859   [Ro]
Center, Thomas C. to Joanna C. McEwen 8-31-1857 (9-1-1857)   [Ro]
Chambers, Henry A. to Laura Senoir? 1-25-1867 (1-13?-1867)   [Ro]
Chaney, Joseph to R. E. Freeman 8-15-1874 (8-16-1874)   [Ro]
Chaney, Wm. H. to Sarah L. Girley 9-2-1872 (9-5-1872)   [Ro]
Chapman, F. B. to Caroline Cook 9-4-1862   [Ro]
Chapman, Thomas A. to Loriet Short 6-20-1857 (6-22-1857)   [Ro]
Cheatham, A. J. to Louisa Sylvey 5-10-1873 (5-11-1873)   [Ro]
Chester, Moses to Mary Thomas 1-11-1868 (1-12-1868)   [Ro]
Childress, A. I. to Mary Niece 4-16-1870 4-17-1870   [Ro]
Childress, John B. to Mary G. Childres 10-27-1870   [Ro]
Childress, William T. to Mary S. Marney 3-24-1858 (3-25-1858)   [Ro]
Childs, John to Jane Sharp 3-13-1869 (3-17-1869)   [Ro]
Chiles, Pleasant to Amanda Rector 4-3-1857   [Ro]
Chiles, Taylor to Mary E. Cooper 7-11-1871 (7-17-1871)   [Ro]
Choat, Edward to Julia Ann Land 8-2-1866   [Ro]
Christian, James M. to Mary Rear 11-13-1860   [Ro]
Christian, John to Elizabeth Cooly 11-27-1856 (11-13-1857?)   [Ro]
Christian, Wiley M. to Julia M. D'Armand 3-20-1866   [Ro]
Chumney, J. J. to Elizabeth Cook 1-28-1860 (2-12-1860)   [Ro]
Clack, Francis M. to Mary V. Freeh 7-25-1856   [Ro]
Clak?, Joseph to Martha Peirce 12-5-1874 (12-6-1874)   [Ro]
Clark, Allen to Sarah Jordan 10-10-1857 (10-12-1857)   [Ro]
Clark, B. W. to Sarah E. Proffitt 8-9-1867 (8-11-1867)   [Ro]
Clark, David to Artis McChristian 10-31-1864 (11-1-1864)   [Ro]
Clark, Geo. W. to Martha J. Reader 12-7-1867 (12-8-1867)   [Ro]
Clark, J. C. to Margaret Harless 2-13-1874   [Ro]
Clark, James to Cynthia J. Everett 11-14-1856   [Ro]
Clark, John C. to Margaret E. Allison 2-21-1860   [Ro]
Clark, John M. to Nancy A. Walker 11-21-1870 11-24-1870   [Ro]
Clark, R. E. D. to Julinda Carroll 12-23-1872   [Ro]
Clark, Robt. to Caroline Campbell 6-14-1864 (7-12-1864)   [Ro]
Clark, William to Mary Carroll 8-5-1872 (8-8-1872)   [Ro]
Clark?, J. N. to Elizabeth Harrison 8-23-1867 (8-25-1867)   [Ro]
Claybrooks, Richard to Jane Teller 8-20-1863 (8-23-1863)   [Ro]
Clemens, William A. to Mary J. England 3-17-1860   [Ro]
Clifton, Amos B. to Nancy C. Thompson 12-14-1874 (12-17-1874)   [Ro]
Clough, Chas. E. to Mary E. Scarbrough 12-5-1874 (12-6-1874)   [Ro]
Clough, James M. to Mahala D. Scarbrough 7-31-1872 (8-1-1872)   [Ro]
Clough, Wm. H. to Telitha Stubbs 9-2-1871 (9-3-1871)   [Ro]
Clower, Daniel N. to Nancy L. Deatherage 5-7-1859 (5-8-1859)   [Ro]
Clower, JSames L. to Thena Rucker 8-14-1868 (8-16-1868)   [Ro]
Clower, James L. to Nancy Reed 5-3-1856 (5-4-1856)   [Ro]
Clower, Jasper to Elizabeth Burdine 2-16-1856 (2-17-1856)   [Ro]
Clower, Joseph to Margaret Guffey 12-26-1868 (12-27-1868)   [Ro]

Clowers, James to Elizabeth Fuller 10-19-1865 (10-29-1865)   [Ro]
Cluff, George W. to Mary Copeland 12-26-1866 (1-27-1866?)   [Ro]
Coaker, Geo. W. to Martha J. Seibor 12-17-1867 (12-19-1867)   [Ro]
Coalman, Brice to Eliza L. Johnson 11-10-1866 (11-11-1866)   [Ro]
Coalman, D. J. to Margaret Deatherige 12-21-1870 12-22-1870   [Ro]
Cobb, Jacob M. to Mary E. Temple 6-14-1867 (6-23-1867)   [Ro]
Cockam, Wiley to Nancy J. Gallimore 2-6-1861 (2-7-1861)   [Ro]
Cofer, Lewis to Catharine Tedder 12-28-1872 (12-29-1872)   [Ro]
Cofer, Wm. J. to M. J. Cooper 5-26-1869 (5-27-1869)   [Ro]
Cofer, Zachrih to Eliza Jane Crow 8-17-1868 (8-20-1868)   [Ro]
Coker, Daniel T. to Nancy M. Stinecipher 10-10-1874 (10-11-1874)   [Ro]
Coker, John to Lidia M. Roberts 2-7-1865 (2-16-1865)   [Ro]
Coker, Seth to Nancy A. Lockett 10-19-1868 (10-22-1868)   [Ro]
Cole, George W. to Mary J. Robertson 7-20-1861 (7-25-1861)   [Ro]
Cole, James to Sarah E. Montgomery 12-27-1862   [Ro]
Cole, Samuel L. to Margaret L. Willson 11-26-1856   [Ro]
Coleman, John H. to Rachel Brown 5-5-1856 (5-6-1856)   [Ro]
Coley, James M. to Emiline Nicholson 8-15-1867   [Ro]
Collet, John to Mary A. Ingram 11-14-1871 (11-16-1871)   [Ro]
Collet, Thomas to Charity Ann Henson 11-26-1867 (11-28-1867)   [Ro]
Collet, Wm. M. to Mary Pool 8-2-1873 (8-7-1873)   [Ro]
Collier, John to Nancy Ambrose 12-27-1863 (12-28-1863)   [Ro]
Collins, D. J. to Mary E. Ramsy? 7-31-1867   [Ro]
Collins, Hugh to Nancy J. Cates 12-6-1866 (12-13-1866)   [Ro]
Collins, Jas.? to Elizabeth Shahan 1-16-1868   [Ro]
Collins, John to Elizabeth Carol 6-10-1869 (6-13-1869)   [Ro]
Comly, E. G. to Sophia Allen 2-4-1864   [Ro]
Conly, John to Malinda Crawford 6-3-1874 (6-4-1874)   [Ro]
Conner, Caleb to Jane Davis 7-16-1859   [Ro]
Cook, Alfred to Dicey Dodson 12-18-1856 (12-19-1856)   [Ro]
Cook, Alfred to Sarah Carrimore 8-5-1859   [Ro]
Cook, Bruce to Frances Hall 10-13-1868 (10-15-1868)   [Ro]
Cook, David to Elizabeth Collet 7-24-1865 (7-25-1865)   [Ro]
Cook, Francis to Mary E. Bracket 1-8-1868 (1-9-1868)   [Ro]
Cook, Frank to Malinda Easter 3-21-1873 (3-27-1873)   [Ro]
Cook, George to Mary Collet 5-31-1871 (6-1-1871)   [Ro]
Cook, J. H. to Sarah E. Ahart 12-22-1871 (12-4?-1871)   [Ro]
Cook, Jacob M. to Nancy Reed 11-11-1861 (11-14-1861)   [Ro]
Cook, James to Mary Jane Moore 11-20-1858 (11-21-1858)   [Ro]
Cook, James H. to Susan E. Walker 8-24-1861 (8-25-1861)   [Ro]
Cook, Jas. M. to Tabitha M. Peters 2-14-1865   [Ro]
Cook, John Y. to Sarah Vann 2-26-1873 (2-27-1873)   [Ro]
Cook, L. H. to Martha E. Hart 12-16-1869   [Ro]
Cook, Peter to Monarcky Kidd 3-11-1858   [Ro]
Cook, Riley to Elzena Abbott 3-13-1862   [Ro]
Cook, Robert to Malinda Stowers 8-22-1858 (8-26-1858)   [Ro]
Cook, Samuel B. to Florentha J. Fuller 7-25-1856 (7-31-1856)   [Ro]
Cook, Samuel H. to Mildridge F. Johnson 9-5-1859 (9-8-1859)   [Ro]
Cook, William to Josephine Hall 10-23-1872   [Ro]
Cook, Wm. A. to Hannah C. Ellis 12-20-1865 (12-24-1865)   [Ro]
Cooke, M. L. to Mary Easter 4-6-1867 (4-7-1867)   [Ro]
Cooley, J. J. to Margaret Johnson 2-8-1865 (2-9-1865)   [Ro]
Cooley, James P. to Mary Jenkins 7-13-1871   [Ro]

Roane County Grooms

Cooley, Joshua to Matilda A. Farmer 12-28-1869   [Ro]
Cooley, Josiah to Elizabeth Woody 11-3-1862   [Ro]
Cooly, Jesse to Martha C. Cooley 9-4-1868   [Ro]
Cooper, Absalom to Elizabeth C. Brashears 9-30-1868 (10-1-1868)   [Ro]
Cooper, Lawson to Lucinda Guffee 8-6-1867 (8-18-1867)   [Ro]
Cooper, Thos. W. to Bridget Odonall 5-5-1864 (5-6-1864)   [Ro]
Copeland, James K. to Catharine Qualls 2-8-1869 (2-11-1869)   [Ro]
Copeland, John H. to Mary A. Davidson 10-2-1866 (10-4-1866)   [Ro]
Copland, William to Rutha Seiber 8-27-1860   [Ro]
Cormany, Silvester F. to Caroline Carter 5-18-1857 (6-9-1857)   [Ro]
Cornwell, Wm. H. to Mary E. Hope 6-15-1867 (6-16-1867)   [Ro]
Corry, James A. to Caroline P. Smith 2-13-1861 (2-14-1861)   [Ro]
Costen, Thos. to Margaret A. E. Susir? 9-18-1860 (9-20-1860)   [Ro]
Coward, Dodson to Elizabeth Lacey 12-19-1867 (12-22-1867)   [Ro]
Coward, Isaac to Sarah C. Walls 1-22-1869 (1-24-1869)   [Ro]
Cox, Abraham to Martha Childress 12-22-1864   [Ro]
Cox, Gains R. to Sarah J. Cassady 3-5-1856 (3-8-1856)   [Ro]
Cox, James to Susannah Currin 8-24-1860   [Ro]
Cox, John to Nancy A. Thrailkill 5-11-1870 5-12-1870   [Ro]
Cox, Martin to Fanny Farmer 12-12-1860   [Ro]
Cox, Richard to Jane Melton 12-11-1865 (9?-12-1865)   [Ro]
Cox, Rufus to Malinda C. Wilson 10-6-1860 (10-7-1860)   [Ro]
Cox, W. M. to Susan Bowman 2-25-1873   [Ro]
Crabtree, C. C. to M. L. Cade 10-1-1873 (10-5-1873)   [Ro]
Crabtree, Calvin to Mary Emaline Fuller 8-4-1858   [Ro]
Crabtree, George W. to Nancy Jones 10-5-1859 (10-8-1859)   [Ro]
Crabtree, Jasper to Sarah E. Hinds 8-21-1872 (8-22-1872)   [Ro]
Crabtree, Jefferson to Tempy Reed 8-28-1862   [Ro]
Crabtree, John H. to M. J. Amos 2-13-1872 (2-15-1872)   [Ro]
Crabtree, Wm. to Sarah Wade 3-3-1866 (3-4-1866)   [Ro]
Craigmile, Pryor L. to Mary V. Grant 4-22-1858 (4-27-1858)   [Ro]
Crase, Jacob to Sarah Jones 1-2-1867 (1-31-1867)   [Ro]
Crawford, Isaac G. to Marcella Oliver 8-18-1873 (8-19-1873)   [Ro]
Crawford, T. J. to Laura E. Sherwood 4-15-1874   [Ro]
Crawford, William to Naomia C. Nipper 10-17-1857 (10-18-1857)   [Ro]
Crenshaw, Samul T. to Susan Wilkey 12-19-1868   [Ro]
Crockett, David R. to Sarah G. Galyon 9-19-1870 9-19-1870   [Ro]
Crockett, David R. to Tempy Gallyan 8-2-1860   [Ro]
Crockett, Wm. S. to Mary A. Frees 5-11-1865 (5-14-1865)   [Ro]
Crook, Pinckney F. to Nancy A. McConnhell 6-19-1860 (6-20-1860)   [Ro]
Cross, Daniel to Elizabeth Thralekill 9-1-1870   [Ro]
Cross, William to Johanna Long 6-7-1872   [Ro]
Croswood, Saml. J. to Sarah M. Carter 6-3-1869 (6-5-1869)   [Ro]
Crow, James R. to Armeda A. Hassler 5-18-1867   [Ro]
Crow, James R. to Margaret (Mrs.) White 10-23-1871 (10-25-1871)   [Ro]
Crow, Saml. H. to Margaret Roberts 11-7-1872   [Ro]
Crow, Samuel W. to Margaret E. Farmer 7-9-1870 7-10-1870   [Ro]
Crow, Wm. A. to Joann M. Graves 9-18-1873 (9-19-1873)   [Ro]
Crowder, J. E. to Rachel A. Anderson 4-6-1867 (4-7-1867)   [Ro]
Crowder, James M. to Rebecca C. Hanecey 10-27-1866 (11-1-1866)   [Ro]
Crowder, Joseph to Jane Howard 2-20-1868   [Ro]
Crowder, William S. to Susan B. Harvey 10-5-1857   [Ro]
Crudgington, Elijah to Winney C. Finder? 10-7-1856   [Ro]

Roane County Grooms

Crudgington, Robt. to Elizabeth Nicely 7-27-1859   [Ro]
Crumley, William to Angaline McConnell 7-4-1860   [Ro]
Cully, John M. to Lois L. Mathis 12-13-1856 (12-14-1856)   [Ro]
Culvahouse, Edward F. to Sarah W. Miller 1-17-1868 (1-19-1868)   [Ro]
Culveyhouse, Edward to Keziah Minton 5-10-1869 (5-11-1869)   [Ro]
Cundiff, William R. to Mary M. Garland 10-27-1858 (10-28-1858)   [Ro]
Cunningham, Jas. to Lucinda Stinecipher 9-21-1874 (9-24-1874)   [Ro]
Cunningham, John B. to Lucretia McAnally 12-29-1866 (12-30-1866)   [Ro]
Cunningham, Samuel O. to M. H. Pyatt 9-10-1874 (9-12-1874)   [Ro]
Cunningham, W. H. to Eliza J. Underwood 7-12-1872 (7-14-1872)   [Ro]
Curd, Abraham to Louisa Stephens 3-17-1866 (3-18-1866)   [Ro]
Curd, James to Jane Mathis 4-10-1866   [Ro]
Curnier?, Benjamin to Nancy J. Turpin 3-12-1867 (3-14-1867)   [Ro]
Currier, Edward W. to Serilda J. Selvey 2-12-1864 (2-14-1864)   [Ro]
Currier, James to Elizabeth Thacker 9-19-1866 (9-20-1866)   [Ro]
Currier, Richard to Dice Yarber 3-3-1873 (3-4-1873)   [Ro]
D'Armond, John to Caladonia Bowers 10-28-1863 (10-29-1863)   [Ro]
Dail, Harvey N. to Margarett Babb 1-11-1859   [Ro]
Dail, S.? W. to Catharine Bradley 10-24-1865   [Ro]
Dail, Stephen to Lucretia J. Heath 9-19-1868 (9-27-1868)   [Ro]
Dalton, A. C. to Sarah C. Bowers 9-18-1856   [Ro]
Dalton, Walter B. to Caroline Crow 9-22-1857   [Ro]
Dalton, Walter B. to Sarah L. Childress 10-13-1863   [Ro]
Daniel, James A. to Mary C. Adkisson 2-7-1860   [Ro]
Daniels, Samuel A. to Martha E. Duncan 5-26-1866 (5-27-1866)   [Ro]
Dannels, N. F. to Sarah A. M. Hudson 10-2-1871 (10-4-1871)   [Ro]
Darhuty, John to Mary E. Martin 9-17-1868 (10-4-1868)   [Ro]
Davies, Thomas to Elizabeth Robinson 9-3-1870   [Ro]
Davis, Evan to Nancy Evans 4-24-1869 (5-11-1869)   [Ro]
Davis, Henderson to Martha Howard 4-16-1870 4-17-1870   [Ro]
Davis, Hesekiah to Sarah F. McKinney 4-6-1865   [Ro]
Davis, J. H. to Frances Thompson 4-26-1872 (5-5-1872)   [Ro]
Davis, James to Elizabeth Walls 9-24-1866 (9-25-1866)   [Ro]
Davis, James to Malinda Dixon 1-22-1857   [Ro]
Davis, James D. to Mary E. Duff 3-10-1858 (3-11-1858)   [Ro]
Davis, James R. to Cinda E. Coker 2-22-1862   [Ro]
Davis, John W. to Margaret A. Seiber 10-25-1874 (10-29-18740   [Ro]
Davis, Joseph S. to Mary Davis 5-16-1872   [Ro]
Davis, Lewis to Lydia May 2-2-1869 (2-5-1869)   [Ro]
Davis, Robert W. to Margaret A. Duff 11-22-1858 (11-23-1858)   [Ro]
Davis, Rufus A. to Misouri A. Pierce 5-12-1870 5-4-1870?   [Ro]
Davis, Samuel A. to Elizabeth J. Copeland 1-23-1871 (1-26-1871)   [Ro]
Davis, Spencer to Sarafine Wilson 9-10-1874 (9-11-1874)   [Ro]
Davis, Wm. C. to Caroline C. Cox 9-26-1866 (9-30-1866)   [Ro]
Davis, Wm. H. to Missouri C. Burnum 9-22-1869 9-26-1869   [Ro]
Day, James L. to Sarah Minton 7-7-1865 (6-8-1865)   [Ro]
De Konnoritz, Oscar to Maria Reileo 5-1-1872 (5-3-1872)   [Ro]
Dearmond, Samuel J. to Margaret A. Yost 1-30-1858 (1-31-1858)   [Ro]
Deatherage, Alexander to Catherine Hornsby 6-2-1860 (6-5-1860)   [Ro]
Deatherage, Allen to Martha S. Kindricks 5-6-1872 (5-9-1872)   [Ro]
Deatherage, Henderson to Elizabeth Walker 2-19-1863   [Ro]
Deatheridge, John M. to Sarah C. Norman 2-17-1868 (2-20-1868)   [Ro]
Deatherige, Wm. J. to Eliza Norman 5-11-1871 (5-14-1871)   [Ro]

Roane County Grooms

Deathridge, William to Rebeca D. Hall 5-28-1868 [Ro]
Debary, T. M. to Elizabeth Chumley 9-16-1865 (9-17-1865) [Ro]
Delaney, S. P. to Martha Cook 5-15-1869 (5-16-1869) [Ro]
Delany, John to Mary Jane Hacker 7-4-1865 (7-6-1865) [Ro]
Delosier, Geo. H. to Savannah Cofer 12-4-1867 (12-5-1867) [Ro]
Demars, Flaven to Charlotte Short 5-5-1870 5-8-1870 [Ro]
Denham, Crabtree to Ann McKinley 2-9-1874 [Ro]
Denham, William to Louisa Benfield 9-29-1873 [Ro]
Denney, R. M. to M. A. Lea 8-31-1868 [Ro]
Dennis, Gideon M. to Sarah P. Crockett 11-3-1865 (11-5-1865) [Ro]
Dennis, Henry H. to Sarah J. Gage 2-11-1870 2-13-1870 [Ro]
Derossett, Andrew L. to Rebecca E. Qualls 5-30-1856 (6-1-1856) [Ro]
Derossett, J. H. to Elizabeth F. Bates 10-23-1869 10-25-1869 [Ro]
Devaney, Ellis M. to Martha E. Dail 10-8-1868 [Ro]
Devoux, T. M. to Elizabeth Chumley 9-16-1866 [Ro]
Dewitt, Willson N. to Sarah Jane Sparks 9-23-1856 (9-25-1856) [Ro]
Dickey, David D. to Martha J. Vann 5-28-1860 (5-29-1860) [Ro]
Dickey, Philip R. to Nancy E. Hendrixon 1-9-1867 (1-10-1867) [Ro]
Dickinson, Isaih to Rebecca Stalcup 4-19-1866 (4-22-1866) [Ro]
Dixon, John to Emelin Chrisp 10-17-1868 (10-18-1868) [Ro]
Dixon, Samuel L. to Martha L. Mathis 6-21-1872 (6-23-1872) [Ro]
Dodd, William to Polly Ann Martin 5-31-1856 (6-1-1856) [Ro]
Dodson, Barton to Sarah Carroll 2-19-1875 [Ro]
Doherty, John to Matilda Price 4-11-1865 [Ro]
Doke, James W. to Elizabeth Recror? 9-29-1865 [Ro]
Donaldson, William to Nancy F. Taylor 1-14-1858 (3-2-1858) [Ro]
Donelson, Thos. A. to Annie E. Williams 9-22-1868 (9-23-1868) [Ro]
Doran, Saml. to Martha Cooley 6-17-1870 6-19-1870 [Ro]
Doremus, P. J. to Maggie J. Porter 8-14-1866 (8-16?-1866) [Ro]
Doss, Nathaniel to Louisa Hinds 5-10-1873 [Ro]
Dotson, Joel to Elizabeth N. Shelton 12-6-1860 [Ro]
Doughty, Wm. L. to Rachel J. Hood 10-10-1866 (10-11-1866) [Ro]
Downer, Charels L. to Caroline Brown 3-10-1864 [Ro]
Driskill, Richard to Mary Rayborn 3-29-1866 [Ro]
Duff, J. W. to Sarah J. Eblen 7-25-1866 (8-1-1866) [Ro]
Duff, James A. to Martha Ann Gibson 1-20-1858 [Ro]
Duff, John H. to Margaret E. Philpot 12-21-1867 (12-29-1867) [Ro]
Duff, Rufus to Elizabeth Van 9-4-1862 (9-18-1862) [Ro]
Duggan, A. M. to Elizabeth l Marcum 12-12-1856 (12-14-1856) [Ro]
Duggan, John to Caroline Getgood 12-27-1864 (12-28-1864) [Ro]
Dugger, Saml. to Mary Underwood 4-12-1860 [Ro]
Dulton, Wm. A. to Elizabeth Mathis 5-12-1860 (5-15-1860) [Ro]
Duncan, Columbus M. to Adaline Breazeale 10-19-1859 [Ro]
Duncan, Columbus M. to Martha Mourfield 1-17-1857 (1-18-1857) [Ro]
Duncan, E. L. to Sarah K. Pickel 10-14-1865 (10-17-1865) [Ro]
Duncan, Henry C. to Sarah A. C. Clark 3-12-1866 (3-15-1866) [Ro]
Duncan, James W. to Mary Ann McDonald 1-30-1866 (2-1-1866) [Ro]
Duncan, John to Anna Grant 9-6-1873 [Ro]
Dunham, John E. to Louisa C. Pulham no dates (with 9-1864) [Ro]
Dunlston?, William to Jane Christenbury 8-25-1857 [Ro]
Dunn, Samuel to Nancy Bazel 6-26-1874 [Ro]
Dunn, Wm. to Ellen Adamson 11-6-1865 (11-9-1865) [Ro]
Dupee, Robert to Sarah Underwood 9-23-1862 [Ro]

Roane County Grooms

Dupre, James M. to Mary Elizabeth Absten 4-24-1858 (4-25-1858)   [Ro]
Durham, C. C. to Mary A. Deatherage 4-22-1863   [Ro]
Durham, James S. to Columbia A. Harmon 12-20-1873 (12-25-1873)   [Ro]
Durham, John M. to Margaret E. Grimsley 1-20-1866 (1-21-1866)   [Ro]
Dyke, James H. to Margaret D. Hinds 12-18-1865   [Ro]
Dyke, Wm. H. to Maria P. Boyd 12-16-1867 (12-19-1867)   [Ro]
Early, Thos. J. to Sarah B. Byerly 10-20-1856 (10-23-1856)   [Ro]
East, Samuel H. to Sarah A. Holloway 12-22-1874 (12-24-1874)   [Ro]
Easter, G. W. to Lucinda P. Forguson 9-7-1860 (9-20-1860)   [Ro]
Easter, James M. to Mary Jane Campbell 8-31-1865 (9-3-1865)   [Ro]
Easter, John to Margaret A. Furgerson 8-20-1868 (9-24-1868)   [Ro]
Easter, John M. to Elizabeth McCart 2-28-1868 (3-1-1868)   [Ro]
Easter, John P.? to Cynthia Wooten 3-9-1872   [Ro]
Easter, M. M. to Martha A. Bales 2-4-1874 (2-5-1874)   [Ro]
Easter, M. M. to Mary C. Bales 5-8-1868 (5-10-1868)   [Ro]
Easter, Peter P. to Mary A. Ward 2-19-1872 (2-20-1872)   [Ro]
Easter, William H. to Mary C. Russell 3-25-1873 (3-27-1873)   [Ro]
Eastwood, Wm. to Susan E. Hamilton 4-3-1874 (4-9-1874)   [Ro]
Eaton, John to Alsa Staples 11-9-1865   [Ro]
Eaton, Simeon to Martha Campbell 2-16-1871 (2-17-1871)   [Ro]
Eblen, B. M. to Eva Montgomery 9-30-1874 (10-1-1874)   [Ro]
Eblen, Isaac N. to Nancy J. Crowder 9-14-1857 (9-15-1857)   [Ro]
Eblen, Newton to Mary M. Lawhorn 10-17-1857   [Ro]
Eblen, Thos. A. to Ann E. Reagan 2-18-1867 (2-19-1867)   [Ro]
Eblin, Samuel to Elizabeth J. Raybourn 9-23-1863 (9-25-1863)   [Ro]
Edgmond, Jonathan to Ruth Crumpley 10-21-1871 (10-22-1871)   [Ro]
Edgwood, J. P. to Sarah E. A. M. Kelsay 10-4-1870   [Ro]
Edmonds, I. M. to Elizabeth Russell 2-28-1870   [Ro]
Edmonds, J. B. to P. A. Price 6-30-1869 (7-1-1869)   [Ro]
Edmondson, Wm. L. to Lucinda C. Evans 1-20-1866 (1-21-1866)   [Ro]
Edwards, Arthur to Mary J. Davis 2-8-1873 (4-13-1873)   [Ro]
Edwards, George to Susan Ann Sylvey 11-20-1869 11-23-1869   [Ro]
Edwards, Henry to Nancy Melton 2-18-1865 (3-5-1865)   [Ro]
Edwards, Ivy? to Polly Branson 9-24-1856 (9-25-1856)   [Ro]
Edwards, William B. to Julia Ann Wilson 10-13-1858   [Ro]
Edwards, Wm. J. to Sarah J. Wilson 2-21-1868 (2-23-1868)   [Ro]
Effingham, George W. to Susan Philips 4-5-1856   [Ro]
Eldridge, Jasper to Rebecca Scales 5-14-1869 (5-16-1869)   [Ro]
Eldridge, R. B. to Margaret Bogart 3-15-1869 (3-18-1869)   [Ro]
Ellis, Abraham to Eliza Haywood 3-25-1873 (3-26-1873)   [Ro]
Ellis, Caleb J. to Sarah Wakefield 8-30-1871 (8-14-1871)   [Ro]
Ellis, Charles to Mary Haggard 7-21-1871 (7-24-1871)   [Ro]
Ellis, George W. to Martha J. Smith 8-26-1856 (10-21-1856)   [Ro]
Ellis, John to Mary E. Patton 10-15-1866 (10-16-1866)   [Ro]
Ellis, John to Parthena Haggard 11-2-1864 (11-3-1864)   [Ro]
Ellis, W. O. to Enarcha W. Delezin 7-7-1859 (7-21-1859)   [Ro]
Ellis, Jr., Benjamin to Etherlinda Leffew 2-28-1870 3-3-1870   [Ro]
Ellit, Ben to Rebecca Stewart 2-29-1868 (3-1-1868)   [Ro]
England, Thomas to Mary Cole 7-24-1860   [Ro]
Enoch, William A. to Jane Henry 8-25-1870 8-25-1870   [Ro]
Enocks, William A. to Mary E. Rodgers 1-18-1859 (1-20-1859)   [Ro]
Erskins, Joseph L. to Rhoda McSherman 2-8-1870   [Ro]
Ervin, Jackson to Adaline Carter 12-27-1869 12-28-1869   [Ro]

Roane County Grooms

Ervin, John to Martha A. Wallace 10-19-1860   [Ro]
Ervin, Wm. to Sarah E. Walker 12-9-1864 (12-12-1864)   [Ro]
Erving, Arthur C. C. to Sarah F. Barnard 3-22-1858 (3-25-1858)   [Ro]
Erving, Wm. J. to Annie Moore 8-28-1874 (8-30-1874)   [Ro]
Erwin, James A. to Barbara Lea 11-3-1857   [Ro]
Erwin, Tho. T. to Margaret Butram 3-10-1870   [Ro]
Eskridge, Samuel B. to M. E. McDaniel 12-26-1866 (12-27-1866)   [Ro]
Estes, Fielding to Visey Ann Cook 12-18-1872 (12-19-1872)   [Ro]
Estes, John to Eliza J. Cook 9-14-1871   [Ro]
Estes, Preston C. to Martha Norman 9-7-1859 (9-11-1859)   [Ro]
Estes, W. A. G. to Martha L. Mathis 8-14-1874 (8-16-1874)   [Ro]
Estes, William A. to Anna M. Ketchenn 12-6-1870 12-25-1870   [Ro]
Evans, A. J. to Catharine Ragles 12-26-1866 (12-27-1866)   [Ro]
Evans, Hugh to Mary Ann Davis 4-20-1872   [Ro]
Evans, Patrick W. to Mary E. Bowers 10-3-1866 (10-4-1866)   [Ro]
Evans, S. P. to Emma R. Godby 12-26-1868 (12-27-1868)   [Ro]
Evans, Tho. R. to Betsey A. Robinson 2-22-1869 (3-2?-1869)   [Ro]
Everett, Jesse to Farley Ann Cooley 7-17-1857 (7-19-1857)   [Ro]
Everitt, Samel J. to Sarah J. Everitt 12-2-1868 (12-6-1868)   [Ro]
Evins, Evan to Julia A. Williams 2-17-1869 (2-18-1869)   [Ro]
Evins, G. W. to Martha Hensley 5-17-1864 (5-19-1864)   [Ro]
Ewell, John to Parthena M. Carroll 8-6-1873 (8-7-1873)   [Ro]
Ewings, Jacob M. to Mary McPhearson 9-19-1859 (9-29-1859)   [Ro]
Fain?, John S. to M. M. Lee 6-7-1863 (6-9-1863)   [Ro]
Fanscher, Lewis H. to Fanny Birchfield 1-17-1872 (1-18-1872)   [Ro]
Faris, Calvin F. to Martha A. Williams 1-20-1869 (1-21-1869)   [Ro]
Farmer, D. J. to Hester A. Wells 10-10-1874 (10-11-1874)   [Ro]
Farmer, James to Mary Moss 2-14-1866 (2-18-1866)   [Ro]
Farmer, John to Phebe Raney 4-17-1857 (4-19-1857)   [Ro]
Farmer, S. W. to M. A. Abbott 10-4-1873 (10-5-1873)   [Ro]
Farris, T. J. to Malinda Garner 9-23-1869   [Ro]
Farris, William to Frances Sane? 3-6-1860   [Ro]
Faulkner, George to Malinda Rutor? 5-1-1858 (5-3-1858)   [Ro]
Felts, Calaway H. to Mary J. Baker 12-2-1868 (12-3-1868)   [Ro]
Fender, Daniel W. to Sarah A. Cole 2-6-1856   [Ro]
Fender, James H. to Elizabeth Stark 3-28-1859 (4-6-1859)   [Ro]
Fentral, James to Margaret Bennett 5-4-1870 5-5-1870   [Ro]
Fentral, Noah to Sarafina Edwards 4-24-1869 (4-25-1869)   [Ro]
Fergerson, John to Polly Durrett 4-24-1869 (4-25-1869)   [Ro]
Ferguson, F. H. to Mary E. Burke 11-8-1871 (11-9-1871)   [Ro]
Fields, Benjamin T. to Mary C. Lockett 8-16-1871 (8-20-1871)   [Ro]
Fields, J. S. to Nancy A. Brooks 11-12-1867 (11-13-1867)   [Ro]
Fields, Mumford to Susan M. Wooten 9-23-1876 (9-24-1876)   [Ro]
Finchum, Samuel to Amanda Thompson 10-9-1867 (10-13-1867)   [Ro]
Findly, Richard to Rachel West 1-23-1868 (crossed out)   [Ro]
Fisher, Francis M. to Louisa Sharp 12-25-1858 (12-28-1858)   [Ro]
Fisher, William to Sarah Nichol 12-14-1866 (12-20-1866)   [Ro]
Fisher, Wm. to Elizabeth Minton 8-28-1865   [Ro]
Fitch, George W. to Martha J. Garland 10-19-1861   [Ro]
Fitch, Samuel to Mary E. Jones 11-18-1857 (11-19-1857)   [Ro]
Fitsgerald, Coleman to Harriet Keeling 5-4-1869 (5-6-1869)   [Ro]
Fitts, Arch to Elender Moreland 2-2-1857 (2-3-1857)   [Ro]
Fleming, Michael to Juiley? Coons 3-23-1865 (3-24-1865)   [Ro]

Roane County Grooms

Fleming, W. W. to Sarah M. Davis 3-7-1866   [Ro]
Flinn, John W. to Sarah J. Nipper 7-28-1869 7-29-1869 [Ro]
Flinn, William G. to Candis Ann McCall 2-2-1856 (2-3-1856)   [Ro]
Ford, A. E. to Mary E. Cundiff 11-8-1873 (11-9-1873)   [Ro]
Ford, John to Martha J. Price 7-10-1874 (10-4-1874)   [Ro]
Forrester, Marshall H. to Rachel M. Wilkey 10-5-1865   [Ro]
Forrester, Marshall H. to Rachel M. Wilkey 10-5-1865   [Ro]
Forrister, George L. to Mary E. Moore 5-31-1856 (6-3-1856)   [Ro]
Forrister, Marshall H. to Martha Jordan 5-4-1859   [Ro]
Fortner, Henry to Lucy A. Estes 10-20-1860   [Ro]
Fortner, Josiah to Caroline E. Estrige 5-2-1861 (5-4-1861)   [Ro]
Foster, Simpson to MSary Deputy 5-17-1858   [Ro]
Foust, Jacob W. to Mary A. Cynthia(last name?) 1-20-1875   [Ro]
Fox, James W. to Esther T. Walker 3-1-1869   [Ro]
Frady, James to Mary Coward 7-16-1859   [Ro]
France, Ephraim to Nancy L. Wilson 11-16-1873 (11-23-1873)   [Ro]
France, William to Mary Jane Toney 3-20-1857 (3-23-1857)   [Ro]
Francis, William to Mary J. Toney 5-15-1861 (5-16-1861)   [Ro]
Frank, D. H. to Emaline Andes 11-5-1856   [Ro]
Frank, George to Mary Weece 5-14-1868   [Ro]
Frank, John to Catherine Whitlock 10-4-1860 (10-6-1860)   [Ro]
Frank, Wm. H. to Narcissa E. Spurling? 8-27-1867 (8-28-1867)   [Ro]
Frazier, Geo. W. to Nancy R. Short 11-7-1860   [Ro]
Freels, Alexander to Elizabeth A. Billingsly 10-30-1867 (10-31-1867)   [Rc
Freels, Isaac M. to Bethilda A. Pickel 11-3-1866 (11-15-1867?)   [Ro]
Freels, William S. to Susan C. Rather 8-10-1870] 8-11-1870   [Ro]
Freeman, James P. to Nancy A. Littleton 9-19-1871   [Ro]
Freeman, Jas. R. to Alice E. Maloy 10-10-1868   [Ro]
French, Samuel to Louisa Wallace 11-12-1866 (11-15-1866)   [Ro]
French, Wayne to Mary A. Coward 7-11-1866 (7-12-1866)   [Ro]
Friar, Jeremiah R. to Addie E. King 2-14-1868 (2-20-1868)   [Ro]
Fritts, Benjamin to Martha Moses 3-1-1871   [Ro]
Fritts, Geo. to Vina E. Lee 1-2-1864? (1-3-1865)   [Ro]
Fritts, George W. to Louisa Rich 1-17-1866 (1-19-1866)   [Ro]
Fritts, Henry to Sarah A. E. Been 10-29-1856 (10-30-1856)   [Ro]
Fritts, J. N. to M. C. Bell 9-26-1868 (9-27-1868)   [Ro]
Fritts, Jacob to Anna Nicholson 2-12-1874   [Ro]
Fritts, Jasper to Rebecca O.? Fritts 11-20-1860   [Ro]
Fritts, Jeremiah to Sarah Powell 8-17-1859   [Ro]
Fritts, John to Eliza Billingsly 4-23-1864   [Ro]
Fritts, John to Jane Coker 6-3-1863 (6-4-1863)   [Ro]
Fritts, John C. to Rhoda C. McDaffro? 10-4-1859   [Ro]
Fritts, John H. to Lorena E. Stalcup 10-9-1866 (10-11-1866)   [Ro]
Fritts, John W. to Milly Bailey 7-6-1858 (7-8-1858)   [Ro]
Fritts, Joseph to Eliza Sturgess 11-3-1863   [Ro]
Fritts, M. J. to F. J. Bunn 11-6-1863   [Ro]
Fritts, M. J. to Matilda A. Pierce 6-12-1869 (6-20-1869)   [Ro]
Fritts, Ransom to Nancy J. Powell 8-17-1859   [Ro]
Fritts, Silas to Dolly V. Beaver 5-29-1869   [Ro]
Fritts, William N. to Sarah J. Fritts 2-1-1860 (2-2-1860)   [Ro]
Fritts, Wm. to Nancy C. Rich 12-20-1865 (12-21-1865)   [Ro]
Frost, Hiram V. to Louisa Pyatt 7-26-1873   [Ro]
Fry, Henry to Mary E. Woody 12-22-1869 12-23-1869   [Ro]

Roane County Grooms

Fry, William to Hannah Aline? 3-24-1874 (3-26-1874) [Ro]
Fuller, George W. to Matilda F. Forister 12-22-1860 [Ro]
Fuller, George sr. to Mary McCulley 2-27-1867 (2-28-1867) [Ro]
Fuller, John to Mary Ann Griffin 8-21-1872 (8-22-1872) [Ro]
Fuller, John A. to Rebecca E. Retherford 8-5-1857 (8-16-1857) [Ro]
Fuller, O. B. to Martha Deatherage 11-26-1867 [Ro]
Fumbill?, James to Emaline Rich 12-5-1857 (12-16-1857) [Ro]
Furgerson, Jas. A. to Martha J. McInally 3-14-1867 [Ro]
Furry, William to Nancy C. Mee 4-29-1874 (5-3-1874) [Ro]
Gage, Francis M. to Delila McCulley 4-16-1856 (4-17-1856) [Ro]
Gallaher, W. T. to Ella C. Browder 10-16-1869 10-21-1869 [Ro]
Gallamore, George to Elizabeth Boyle 7-23-1864 (2-24-1864) [Ro]
Gallamore, Tandy to Susan Bazel 4-18-1864 (4-25-1864) [Ro]
Gallimore, George to Mary Ophatits 9-30-1858 [Ro]
Gallimore, James to Mary C. Williams 1-12-1871 [Ro]
Gallimore, John to Nancy Taylor 7-5-1860 [Ro]
Gallimore, Tobias to Adaline Gowings 10-8-1863 [Ro]
Galston, Wm. to Margaret E. Grammer 2-11-1871 (2-12-1871) [Ro]
Galyon, Eli M. to Elizabeth Easter 12-18-1857 (12-20-1857) [Ro]
Galyon, Francis to Nancy J. Rutherford 12-31-1868 [Ro]
Galyon, James M. to Nancy Temple 11-19-1866 (11-23-1866) [Ro]
Galyon, John to Emaline Barnett 1-2-1860 [Ro]
Galyon, Lea M. to Elizabeth Ambrose 1-19-1859 (1-20-1859) [Ro]
Gamble, Josiah N. to Eliza A. Apperson 11-30-1864 (12-1-1864) [Ro]
Gardener, John to Margaret H. Murray 12-14-1858 (12-25-1858) [Ro]
Gardner, John to M. E. White 6-30-1860 (7-1-1860) [Ro]
Garland, Lafayette to Sarah Ann Ray 1-11-1868 (1-12-1868) [Ro]
Geasland, Stephen A. to Frances Malvina Cofer 11-21-1858 (11-25-1858) [Ro]
Gentris, W. T. to M. J. Oneal 1-3-1865 (1-5-1865) [Ro]
George, Frank to Christena J. Cagley 8-4-1871 [Ro]
George, John to Nelli Woody 12-15-1860 [Ro]
Gerding, J. G. W. to Victoria Vaux 3-10-1863 (3-17-1863) [Ro]
Gersland, N. W. to Elizabeth Clark 2-25-1868 [Ro]
Ghormley, H. H. to Sarah C. Dosson 3-13-1860 (3-18-1860) [Ro]
Ghormley, John to Margaret M. Dosson 3-20-1860 [Ro]
Gibbs, James E. to Nancy C. Margrave 1-17-1860 [Ro]
Gibbs, Thomas R. to Sarah J. Buse 6-25-1870 [Ro]
Gibson, Eligah to S. I. Hutchison 2-23-1870 2-24-1870 [Ro]
Gibson, Harvey to Amanda E. Guy 7-14-1869 (7-16-1869) [Ro]
Gibson, Hiram to Mary Ann Wester 4-12-1860 [Ro]
Gibson, M. L. to Mary Jane Rogers 10-14-1865 (10-18-1865) [Ro]
Gibson, Smith to Josephine B. Hood 8-20-1872 (8-22-1872) [Ro]
Gibson, Thomas to Emily Dorm? 9-13-1864 [Ro]
Gideon, George W. to Margaret Tate 2-6-1866 (2-7-1866) [Ro]
Gideon, John A. to Martha Hughes 1-25-1868 (1-26-1868) [Ro]
Giles, Samuel M. to Sarah Rentrfro 9-19-1867 (9-22-1867) [Ro]
Giles, William to Nancy J. Minton 9-3-1860 (9-4-1860) [Ro]
Gilleland, Floyd to Harriet J. Keyton 6-11-1874 (6-19-1874) [Ro]
Gillespie, Geo. L. to Lucinda V. Brown 8-12-1863 (8-13-1863) [Ro]
Gipson, Thomas J. to Margaret McPherson 10-12-1867 (10-15-1867) [Ro]
Glass, Charles to Nancy Dunn 10-8-1872 (10-10-1872) [Ro]
Glover, J. P. to M. J. Evans 7-13-1867 (7-14-1867) [Ro]
Goddard, Thos. L. to Margaret Delozier 10-11-1860 [Ro]

Roane County Grooms

Goddard, Wiley Z. to Mary Wetherford 4-21-1859 [Ro]
Godsey, Anderson to Malinda E. Graham 11-5-1867 (11-7-1867) [Ro]
Goins, Claiborne to Lydda Underwood 4-21-1865 (4-22-1865) [Ro]
Goins, Elijah to Margaret D. Alexander 10-25-1865 (10-26-1865) [Ro]
Goldston, Wiley to Nancy Stringess 6-16-1862 (6-17-1862) [Ro]
Golston, James W. to Sarah E. Susey 11-20-1871 (11-23-1871) [Ro]
Good, Andrew J. to Eveline? Pickle 12-19-1859 (12-22-1859) [Ro]
Gooden, John D. to Mary J. Billingsley 1-2-1861 [Ro]
Goodin, Peter W. to America Waller 12-1-1856 (12-17-1856) [Ro]
Goodman, Abraham to Elizabeth C. Wetherford 11-15-1860 [Ro]
Goodwin, John to Sarah Harris 11-22-1856 (11-23-1856) [Ro]
Gorin, John C. to Mildred J. Boyd 8-19-1864 [Ro]
Gosset, Alexander to Margaret White 1-15-1869 (1-16-1869) [Ro]
Goury?, Thomas A. to E. C. Sams 12-14-1868 (12-15-1868) [Ro]
Gowins, William D. to Sarah E. Morris 3-18-1861 (3-20-1861) [Ro]
Grabner, Charles G. to Emily A. Knoblauch 2-13-1862 [Ro]
Graham, George to Martha M. Cloud 8-19-1871 (8-20-1871) [Ro]
Graham, Saml. to Martha Deatherage 8-13-1869 8-19-1869 [Ro]
Grammer, B. F. to Nancy J. Marney 12-22-1870 [Ro]
Grand, T. B. to Elizabeth Stuffels 8-13-1867 (8-15-1867) [Ro]
Grant, Isaac C. to Elizabeth Luttrell 12-21-1857 (12-24-1857) [Ro]
Graves, John E. to Mary Shackelford 11-8-1866 [Ro]
Gray, James to Callie Wilson 4-27-1872 (4-28-1872) [Ro]
Gray, John to Martha Solomon 6-13-1868 [Ro]
Gray, Wm. A. to Elizabeth N. Staley 6-21-1869 (7-18-1869) [Ro]
Green, C. C. to Letha A. Gillum 9-16-1871 (9-21-1871) [Ro]
Green, Drury D. to Lucinda Hicks 6-25-1860 [Ro]
Green, George W. to Mary E. Ford 8-5-1873 [Ro]
Green, Henry to Nancy Taliaferro no dates (with 1870) B [Ro]
Green, Joseph to Cordelia Morgan 11-28-1872 [Ro]
Green, Joseph S. to Mary McKinney 1-2-1868 [Ro]
Green, Thomas to Mary Wilson 5-5-1864 [Ro]
Greene, Amos C. to Amanda M. Moore 3-12-1864 [Ro]
Greene, Bluford Y. to Elizabeth Hester 10-1-1857 (10-9-1857) [Ro]
Greene, George W. to Jane Gray 7-22-1859 [Ro]
Greene, Henry P. to Mollie M. Barnett 9-7-1865 [Ro]
Greene, James to Nancy J. Scott 2-2-1867 (2-3-1867) [Ro]
Greene, James to Sarah Roberson 1-31-1861 [Ro]
Gregory, John to Amanda Gerron 9-25-1864 [Ro]
Grider, Sidney to Mary Jane Ashley 9-3-1864 [Ro]
Griffeth, William K. to Elizabeth Olliver 12-15-1858 [Ro]
Griffeths, Wm. to Eliza Carter 1-7-1861 (1-10-1861) [Ro]
Griffin, W. T. to Nancy C. Munday 10-27-1873 (10-30-1873) [Ro]
Griffis, John T. to Mary Wilhoit 4-6-1867 (4-7-1867) [Ro]
Griffith, Alfred M. to Charlotte C. Butler 9-24-1864 (10-5-1864) [Ro]
Griffith, N.? J. to Catherine Lockett 1-4-1864 (1-6?-1864) [Ro]
Grifith, Daniel to Alcey Hackler 2-8-1864 (not executed) [Ro]
Grifith, Daniel to Lottie Hicks 2-17-1864 [Ro]
Grigsby, James A. to Paulina E. Carter 8-14-1856 (8-21-1856) [Ro]
Grimes, William to Della M. Dennis 8-7-1868 (8-16-1868) [Ro]
Grimes, William to Mary J. Hickey 6-27-1873 [Ro]
Grimsley, John W. to Martha Johnson 12-12-1856 [Ro]
Gross, Wm. to Mary E. Odom 2-24-1869 (2-5?-1869) [Ro]

Roane County Grooms

Grubb, Franklin B. to Ruth Copeland 7-18-1865 (7-20-1865) [Ro]
Grubb, Jackson to Mary A. Russell 7-2-1860 (7-8-1860) [Ro]
Grubb, James M. to Margaret A. Cook 2-23-1867 (3-10-1867) [Ro]
Grubb, John F. to Nancy Seabert 4-10-1861 (4-11-1861) [Ro]
Grubb, King W. to Catharine J. Evans 9-12-1866 (9-13-1866) [Ro]
Guenther, G. A. to Sallie Martin 2-12-1874 [Ro]
Guffee, A. W. to Rebecca O. Hyatt 6-19-1871 (6-25-1871) [Ro]
Guffee, Ephraim to Elizabeth Walker 12-26-1862 [Ro]
Guffee, William C. to Lucinda Raby 9-18-1858 (9-19-1858) [Ro]
Guffey, William to Clementine Kincade 12-4-1860 (12-7-1860) [Ro]
Guffie, Albert C. to Nancy C. Deatherige 4-17-1866 (4-19-1866) [Ro]
Guinn, Lemuel to Eliza J. Taylor 12-28-1868 (12-31-1868) [Ro]
Guinn, Lemuel to Mary F. Wright 1-1-1866 (1-4-1866) [Ro]
Guy, George W. to Elizabeth J. Micael 1-2-1867 (1-3-1867) [Ro]
Guy, Wm. W. to Emiline Lovelass 9-23-1864 (9-27-1864) [Ro]
Hacker, Alfred to Sabrie Roberts 10-31-1864 [Ro]
Hacker, August B. to Elizabeth R. Goddard 3-29-1856 [Ro]
Hacker, Bernhard to Nancy Maberry 7-29-1861 [Ro]
Hacker, Geo. to Mary Nelson 3-9-1865 (3-12-1865) [Ro]
Hacker, Jesse to Mary F. Silvey 4-22-1874 (4-23-1874) [Ro]
Hacker, John to Elizabeth Roberts 9-4-1858 [Ro]
Hacker, Joseph to Eliza Jane Sylvey 3-31-1866 (4-1-1866) [Ro]
Hacker, Thomas to Catharine Roberts 4-30-1874 [Ro]
Hackney, Hugh J. to Margaret J. Phelps 3-11-1857 (3-15-1857) [Ro]
Haggard, H. C. to Callina Pottier 5-14-1864 [Ro]
Haggard, Henry to Rachel Potter 11-25-1869 11-23-1869? [Ro]
Haggard, John N. to Sarah J. Peters 2-2-1865 (2-9-1865) [Ro]
Hagler, B. T. to Elizabeth C. Burns 6-9-1870 6-29-1870 [Ro]
Hagler, Benjamin T. to Cyntha Ann Abbot 11-23-1861 [Ro]
Haire, James A. to Ann Bowers 2-14-1857 (2-17-1857) [Ro]
Halburt, Rufus J. to Mary G. Crass 4-7-1871 (4-9-1871) [Ro]
Halder, Richard to Margaret M. Martin 9-21-1870 9-23-1870 [Ro]
Halder, Thomas to Malinda Martin 12-3-1864 (12-5-1864) [Ro]
Haley, John C. to Mary Jane Montgomery 2-23-1866 (2-28-1866) [Ro]
Hall, Andrew J. to Mary E. Swicegood 1-11-1867 [Ro]
Hall, Felix H. to Elizabeth Hart 10-15-1857 [Ro]
Hall, Jesse to Margaret E. McAlister 7-18-1874 (7-19-1874) [Ro]
Hall, M. V. to Malissa D. Hall 3-2-1865 [Ro]
Hall, William M. to Mary Jane Neergard 12-20-1866 [Ro]
Hall, William M. to Susannah Dutton 12-9-1858 [Ro]
Halloway, Major to Malinda Treadaway 9-24-1872 (9-25-1872) [Ro]
Hambright, Right to Bashler McCaleb 9-15-1869 [Ro]
Hamby, J. E. to Mary E. Phifer 10-11-1865 [Ro]
Hamby, Jas. . to Amanda A. Narramore 12-14-1869 12-15-1869 [Ro]
Hamby, Lindsey L. to Nancy A. Martin 5-9-1861 (5-10-1861) [Ro]
Hamilton, Jas. to Susan Bevllin 12-13-1868 (12-15-1868) [Ro]
Hamilton, Jefferson to Mary Wheat 12-2-1860 (12-4-1860) [Ro]
Hamilton, Samuel to Emily Jane Ladd 11-3-1866 (11-4-1866) [Ro]
Hamilton, William J. to J. Evaline Elkins 11-24-1860 [Ro]
Hammonds, John C. to Elisabeth Smith 12-26-1874 (12-31-1874) [Ro]
Hammons, Isaac J. to Polly Ann Brackett 7-20-1865 [Ro]
Hammons, Jesse to Nancy Thrailkill 12-20-1860 [Ro]
Hampson, Samuel to Eliza Boling 9-21-1858 (9-23-1858) [Ro]

Roane County Grooms

Hampton, Jas. A. to Mary W. Watts 5-24-1870 5-25-1870 [Ro]
Hampton, Wm. D. to Elizabeth E. Calaham 12-3-1867 (12-8-1867) [Ro]
Haney, M. H. to A. E. Conner 10-21-1865 (10-22-1865) [Ro]
Haney, Richard to Margaret Wirick 8-8-1867 [Ro]
Haney, S. C. to Sarah L. Cofer 3-2-1871 (3-5-1871) [Ro]
Haney, Thomas J. to Eliza J. (Miss) Cook 4-5-1873 (4-6-1873) [Ro]
Haney, Wm. to Sarah E. Smith 12-18-1872 (12-19-1872) [Ro]
Hankin, R. H. to H. H. Jones 9-19-1868 (9-20-1868) [Ro]
Hardbarger, Rufus to Kittie Mathis 5-6-1864 [Ro]
Hardin, G. W. to Julia C. Winton 7-27-1861 [Ro]
Hardin, Geo. G. to Matilda C. Smith 12-16-1867 (12-19-1867) [Ro]
Harmon, Jas. A. to Tennessee J. Chapman 8-1-1867 [Ro]
Harmon, John to Velorie Beavers 2-6-1864 (2-7-1864) [Ro]
Harp, Alonzo to Mary Cables 1-16-1875 [Ro]
Harp, John to Margaret Carroll 11-30-1858 [Ro]
Harp, Leonidas to Elizabeth Hampton 8-17-1873 [Ro]
Harrison, J. J. to M. B. McCray 6-18-1870 6-23-1870 [Ro]
Harrison, James M. to Laura H. Mayo 12-26-1860 [Ro]
Harrison, Joseph J. to Lizzie W. Abbott 8-13-1864 [Ro]
Harrison, M. P. to Sarah E. Harrison 11-26-1864 [Ro]
Hart, Aaron to Elizabeth Boyd 12-26-1860 [Ro]
Hart, Aaron to Elizabeth Hornsby 9-8-1866 (9-13-1866) [Ro]
Hart, Amos to Mary Ann Staley 5-9-1866 (5-10-1866) [Ro]
Hart, R. M. to Sarah Wells 8-19-1869 [Ro]
Hart, Samuel to Surreloa Narramore 11-13-1869 11-14-1869 [Ro]
Hartley, Clingen to Margaret Shoate 9-11-1873 (9-12-1873) [Ro]
Hartley, James W. to Maggie E. Lowery 11-1-1871 [Ro]
Hartley, Wm. J. to Louise Elise Guenther 10-18-1866 (11-17-1866) [Ro]
Hartman, Archibald R. to Margaret A. Fender 11-27-1861 (12-1-1861) [Ro]
Hartsell, Joseph L. to Dianah E. Matthews 11-13-1867 (11-17-1867) [Ro]
Harvey, George to Margaret Hagler 12-20-1871 (12-21-1871) [Ro]
Harvey, J. F. to M. A. M. Ellis 10-24-1867 [Ro]
Harvey, J. W. to Amanda E. Eblen 4-5-1869 (4-8-1869) [Ro]
Harvey, Joshua B. to Martha K. Johnson 11-6-1860 (11-8-1860) [Ro]
Harvey, Robt. M. to Margaret Miller 2-22-1865 (2-24-1865) [Ro]
Harvey, Samuel E. to Elizabeth C. Matlock 2-18-1874 (2-19-1874) [Ro]
Harvey, Thomas S. to Martha W. Cofer 10-26-1865 [Ro]
Harvey, William W. to Mary Browder 10-7-1856 (10-8-1856) [Ro]
Harwell, W. M. R. to Susan Boyd 8-5-1867 [Ro]
Hashbarger, William to Mary J. Baldwin 12-26-1874 (12-27-1874) [Ro]
Hashbarger, William to Nancy E. Chrisp 11-14-1868 (11-15-1868) [Ro]
Haskins, B. A. to Levina Wallace 3-29-1864 [Ro]
Hatfield, George to Anna Long 5-3-1867 (5-8-1867) [Ro]
Hatfield, William G. to Sarah J. Grimsley 5-1-1861 (5-7-1861) [Ro]
Haun, Wm. S. to Martha J. MDyer 6-18-1864 [Ro]
Hawkins, Morgan B. to Mariah L. Tedder 10-20-1863 (10-30-1863) [Ro]
Hays, J. P.? to Kiziah Hartley 11-10-1862 (11-11-1862) [Ro]
Hayworth, Jonathan to Nancy J. Halcomb 12-19-1865 (12-21-1865) [Ro]
Headrick, Jos. S.? to Margaret E. Adams 1-26-1875 [Ro]
Heath, Elisha to Elizabeth Hall 9-10-1856 (10-20-1856) [Ro]
Heath, James to Sarah Allen 2-28-1857 (3-1-1857) [Ro]
Heaton, Robert to Rachel Myers 3-26-1867 (3-27-1867) [Ro]
Heder, Millard F. to Mariah Hacker 1-1-1874 [Ro]

Roane County Grooms

Hedgecock, John R. to Amanda Christian 7-25-1868 (7-26-1868)   [Ro]
Hedgecock, Thomas to Martha Ladd 1-28-1858 (2-4-1858)   [Ro]
Heins, Jacob to Lina Fauscher 3-11-1870 3-12-1870   [Ro]
Hellums, John J. to Martha M. Wright 1-14-1873 (1-16-1873)   [Ro]
Helms, George W. to Nancy S. K. Hagler 4-18-1857   [Ro]
Helton, Daniel to Jane Shell 12-18-1866   [Ro]
Helton, James H. to Martha Clark 1-6-1866 (1-7-1866)   [Ro]
Helton, Jason A. to Mary E. Wilson 12-23-1857 (12-27-1857)   [Ro]
Helton, Silas M. to Selina Francis 8-4-1860 (8-5-1860)   [Ro]
Hembree, Eli to Sarah C. Hart 6-27-1857 (6-28-1857)   [Ro]
Hembree, Elihu L. to Louisa J. Powell 11-16-1867 (11-17-1867)   [Ro]
Hembree, G. W. to Teresa P. Chrisenberry 7-7-1869   [Ro]
Hembree, Isaac N. to Manerva Carter 3-4-1858   [Ro]
Hembree, J. C. to S. J. Pickel 1-4-1875   [Ro]
Hembree, James to mary Kirkland 9-1-1860   [Ro]
Hembree, Joel D. to Delilah C. Staples 4-22-1868 (4-23-1868)   [Ro]
Hembree, Joseph J. to Ella A. Hanley 12-15-1874 (12-11?-1874)   [Ro]
Hembree, Wm. to Sarah E. Melton 11-9-1864   [Ro]
Hembree, Wm. R. to Elizabeth Lowery 3-7-1868 (3-8-1868)   [Ro]
Henderson, Caswell to Susan Dyke 12-17-1857   [Ro]
Henderson, James m. to Mary Robertson 9-7-1861 (9-10-1861)   [Ro]
Henderson, John to Elizabeth Bumpass 12-27-1869   [Ro]
Henderson, Thomas S. to Rebecca Robinson 11-6-1865 (11-7-1865)   [Ro]
Henderson, William P. to Mary Pursley 8-9-1856 (8-19-1856)   [Ro]
Hendrickson, Benj. L. to Martha J. McKinney 7-2-1860 (7-12-1860)   [Ro]
Hendrickson, Samuel J. to Amanda C. Delosier 4-17-1869 (4-18-1869)   [Ro]
Hendrix, Eli to Julia Green 6-15-1872 (6-16-1872)   [Ro]
Hendrix, John R. to Margaret Morrison 2-22-1868 (2-23-1868)   [Ro]
Henry, J. H. to Tennessee Loning? 12-31-1874   [Ro]
Hensley, Benjamin F. to Sarah Easter 8-22-1866 (8-31-1866)   [Ro]
Hensley, Marshall G. to Jenny Caroline Black 2-26-1856 (3-2-1856)   [Ro]
Hensley, Thomas J. to Mary Cooley 12-5-1872 (12-8-1872)   [Ro]
Hensly, B. to Sarah Montgomery 3-9-1860 (3-15-1860)   [Ro]
Henson, George W. to Sarah Qualls 6-21-1859   [Ro]
Henson, John to Eliza J. Allred 10-2-1874 (10-3-1874)   [Ro]
Herin, Ulrich to Susannah Stewart 3-14-1857 (3-15-1857)   [Ro]
Herold, William R. to Rachel E. Johnson 2-2-1860   [Ro]
Hester, Abner to Sarah Lively 3-21-1859 (3-24-1859)   [Ro]
Hester, Basil to Rebecca McKinney 5-14-1857   [Ro]
Hester, Churchwell to Mary Ann Brashers 1-2-1865 (1-3-1865)   [Ro]
Hester, G. W. to Margaret T. Robertson 11-5-1867 (11-14-1867)   [Ro]
Hester, Jackson to Rhona Lane 10-8-1873   [Ro]
Hester, Jackson to Sarah Wright 4-9-1874   [Ro]
Hester, Jacob to Nancy J. Hembree 4-9-1861 (4-11-1861)   [Ro]
Hester, Louis to Mary Ludick? 4-16-1869 (4-18-1869)   [Ro]
Hester, P. F. to Louisa Z.? Hacker 11-19-1874   [Ro]
Hickey, James to Eliza M. Bailey 1-28-1862   [Ro]
Hickey, James to Sarah Whitlock 2-10-1863 (2-11-1863)   [Ro]
Hickey, James P. to Rachel E. Harner 3-30-1859   [Ro]
Hicks, Albert to Caroline Kirkland 6-20-1872 (6-23-1872)   [Ro]
Hicks, Alvis V. to Nancy Perry 2-5-1859 (2-6-1859)   [Ro]
Hicks, Francis A. to Jane Roberts 7-21-1870   [Ro]
Hicks, Martin G. to Rebecca A. Hackler 12-28-1874 (12-29-1874)   [Ro]

Hicks, Martin M. to Sarah E. Sliger 9-9-1872 (9-12-1872) [Ro]
Hicks, William J. to Sarah Ann Roberts 12-7-1859 (12-8-1859) [Ro]
Hicks, Winfield to Elizabeth J. Morris 12-3-1866 (12-4-1866) [Ro]
Hilands, Charles to Louisa J. Gray 1-7-1869 (1-14-1869) [Ro]
Hill, Elijah to Mary Jane Elliot 11-15-1865 (11-16-1865) [Ro]
Hill, Isaac A. to Margaret A. Kindrick 11-8-1870 [Ro]
Hill, John to Mary A. England 6-11-1864 [Ro]
Hill, John N. to Mary D. Dixon 3-25-1871 (3-26-1871) [Ro]
Hill, Michael to Margaret C. Jiles 8-20-1870 8-21-1870 [Ro]
Hill, O. P. to Mary Carter 11-5-1867 (11-7-1867) [Ro]
Hill, William C. to Nancy S. Rector 10-30-1866 (10-31-1866) [Ro]
Hilton, Elkaney to Amanda A. Mee 7-6-1874 [Ro]
Hilton, Ransom P. to Susan Brown 3-24-1868 (3-29-1868) [Ro]
Hinds, Albert N. to Susan M. Harner 8-10-1866 (8-12-1866) [Ro]
Hinds, G. W. to Mary J. Percy 2-8-1871 (3-12-1871) [Ro]
Hinds, Henry to Selah Jordan 8-5-1870 8-11-1870 [Ro]
Hinds, J. C. to Rutha C. Bacon 11-21-1868 (11-26-1868) [Ro]
Hinds, James M. to Charlotte B. Russell 7-30-1861 (8-1-1861) [Ro]
Hinds, Joseph A. to Sarah A. Waller 12-8-1860 (12-10-1860) [Ro]
Hipps, Levi C. to Susanah Gibbs 3-19-1866 [Ro]
Hix, Martin M. to Celicia Tinker 8-10-1869 8-12-1869 [Ro]
Hodge, Charles Amos to Rachel Lavica Gammon 8-19-1858 (9-1-1858) [Ro]
Hodges, M. D. to Nancy J. Green 3-6-1874 (3-8-1874) [Ro]
Hogsett, J. Y. to Annie M. Long 11-20-1869 11-21-1869 [Ro]
Holder, John W. to Julia A. J. Minton 2-20-1865 (2-23-1865) [Ro]
Holder, William to Lorinda Keener 3-22-1861 (3-24-1861) [Ro]
Holder, Wm. B. to Minerva A. Blackwell 6-10-1869 [Ro]
Holland, Lorenzo F. to Queen V. Walker 10-1-1872 (10-3-1872) [Ro]
Holt, Jas. to Hannah Lewis 3-2-1869 (3-3-1869) [Ro]
Holt, John J. to Anna A. Pickel 10-4-1866 [Ro]
Honeycutt, John M. to Tabitha? Cuthbertson 7-13-1865 (7-19-1865) [Ro]
Hood, F. A. to M. J. Butler 4-9-1872 (4-11-1872) [Ro]
Hood, Haywood to Lucy Ann Begwell 10-26-1864 (10-27-1864) [Ro]
Hood, Rufus to Susan Hardbarger 10-6-1863 [Ro]
Hood, Rufus to Susannah Hardbarger 10-6-1863 [Ro]
Hood, Seborn to Martha Nicholson 2-6-1874 (2-7-1874) [Ro]
Hood, Seborn to Susan Nicholson 5-7-1870 5-8-1870 [Ro]
Hood, Thos. L. to Susan Hagler 4-11-1867 [Ro]
Hooker, R. L. to D. E. Gamble 4-6-1865 [Ro]
Hope, Hardin to Barthy Powers 2-12-1864 (2-14-1864) [Ro]
Hope, Samuel J. to Hannah C. Cook 4-20-1867 (4-21-1867) [Ro]
Hope, Wm. B. to Sarah C. Robinson 4-10-1862 [Ro]
Hormsley, Wm. B. to Sarah Jane Leffever 10-17-1867 [Ro]
Horne, Lenoindas to Matilda E. Moore 9-8-1870 [Ro]
Hornsby, Franklin to Ellen Kilpatrick 9-16-1874 (9-20-1874) [Ro]
Hornsby, W. J. to A. M. Estabrook 7-23-1868 [Ro]
Hornsby, William to Rebecca Johnson 11-6-1869 11-7-1869 [Ro]
Hoskins, Jasper M. to Malinda Seiber 8-30-1871 (9-1-1871) [Ro]
Houghton, F. E. to Rebecca Barnwell 9-25-1874 (9-26-1874) [Ro]
Houser, W. T. to Elizabeth M. Breaker 11-1-1873 (11-2-1873) [Ro]
Houston, R. F. to Eliza Bailey 5-27-1863 (5-29-1863) [Ro]
Hout, Wm. H. to Mary J. Edmonds 1-6-1865 [Ro]
Howard, Asa to Feriba Morgan 12-30-1858 [Ro]

Roane County Grooms

Howard, Lewis to Catharine Thompson 12-31-1872 [Ro]
Howard, William to Milly Russell 9-29-1860 (10-1-1860) [Ro]
Howard, Wm. J. to M. O.? Reeves 8-15-1870 8-16-1870 [Ro]
Howell, John J. to Hannah E. Hartsell 9-11-1869 [Ro]
Hudelston, Leroy R. to Adaline Tapp 9-15-1862 [Ro]
Hudgins, William to Sarah Getgood 7-5-1859 [Ro]
Hudgins, Wm. to Sophia Bacon 9-9-1872 (9-10-1872) [Ro]
Hudleson, Wm. to Manerva Tap 10-13-1865 (10-16-1865) [Ro]
Hudson, John W. to Jane N. Margile? 3-15-1865 (4-23-1865) [Ro]
Hudson, Rufus M. to Elizabeth J. S. Robinson 11-26-1864 (12-1-1864) [Ro]
Hudson, Ryland? to Elizabeth Hudson 3-25-1862 (3-26-1862) [Ro]
Hudson, Thomas to Josephine Hensley 12-27-1860 [Ro]
Huff, Jas. W. to Elizabeth Anderson 5-29-1867 (5-30-1867) [Ro]
Huffin, Charles F. to Sarah J. Breazeale 12-24-1873 (12-25-1873) [Ro]
Huffine, Benjamin to Amanda L. Bacon 11-4-1858 (11-11-1858) [Ro]
Huffine, Benjamin L. to Elizabeth E. Littleton 1-21-1871 (1-22-1871) [Ro]
Huffine, Daniel to Amanda J. Burris 7-5-1861 [Ro]
Huffine, Ephraim M. to Mary A. Littleton 7-26-1856 [Ro]
Huffine, James M. to Jane Smalley 8-4-1864 [Ro]
Huffine, Joseph to Emily McRea 1-19-1869 B [Ro]
Huffine, William H. to Amanda Smalley 10-6-1857 (10-8-1857) [Ro]
Huffine, Wm. H. to Nancy J. Brown 2-7-1873 (2-9-1873) [Ro]
Huffman, Douthet to Lucinda William 11-4-1857 (11-7-1857) [Ro]
Huffman, Elbert to Lotty Russell 1-26-1860 [Ro]
Huffman, Elbert to Mary Ann Pass 5-10-1873 [Ro]
Hufstettler, Philip to Elizabeth Jane Cagle 8-20-1857 [Ro]
Hughes, James to Margaret Jordan 8-5-1870 8-11-1870 [Ro]
Hughes, Josiah to Elizabeth Forrester 2-23-1863 [Ro]
Hughes, Philip to J. E. Rutherford 12-20-1873 (12-25-1873) [Ro]
Hughes, Samuel G. to Rebecca J. Mathis 7-17-1866 (7-18-1866) [Ro]
Hughes, Tho. W. to Amanda Eller 12-8-1869 12-9-1869 [Ro]
Hughs, Josiah to Matilda Matlock 5-1-1856 [Ro]
Hukey, John J. to Polly Ann Mynatt 8-26-1856 [Ro]
Hulen, Jonathan to Mary Jane Smith 4-30-1859 (5-1-1859) [Ro]
Huling, Johnson G.? to Margaret Turnbill 11-9-1867 (11-10-1867) [Ro]
Humphrey, J. L. to Amanda M. Sharp 8-25-1870 8-28-1870 [Ro]
Humphreys, Philip to Margaret Neil 9-1-1865 [Ro]
Hurley, John to Sarah Whitlock 9-20-1864 [Ro]
Hutchinson, A. P. to Nannie Hartsell 1-19-1869 [Ro]
Hutsell, George M. to Arballa F. Guthrie 4-18-1864 [Ro]
Hutsell, Samuel S. to Alice J. Stevenson 9-12-1872 [Ro]
Ingram, A. J. to Sarah Smith 1-22-1866 (1-25-1866) [Ro]
Ingram, David J. to Mary S. Smith 9-25-1865 [Ro]
Ingram, Elisha T. to Martha Caroline Smith 5-26-1857 [Ro]
Ingram, Moses to Amanda W. Breazeale 7-4-1859 [Ro]
Ingram, Sanford to Catherine Littleton 5-12-1857 [Ro]
Inman, John W. to Sarah F. Coleman 8-19-1864 [Ro]
Irons, Alvin J. to Ellen Fritts 3-7-1863 [Ro]
Isbel, John H. to Elizabeth P. Thomas 3-24-1868 [Ro]
Isham, Elijah to Mary J. Delosier 1-10-1871 (1-11-1871) [Ro]
Isham, Elijah to Rebecca Jane Eblen 10-6-1857 [Ro]
Isham, George to Mary Smicegood 4-10-1869 (4-11-1869) [Ro]
Isham, Henry to Margaret T. Gooram? 2-26-1867 [Ro]

Roane County Grooms

Isham, Joel H. to Francess Cofer 2-4-1858   [Ro]
Isham, John B. to Elizabeth Leffew 3-18-1872 (3-19-1872)   [Ro]
Isham, John L. to Josephine Thompson 9-14-1872 (9-15-1872)   [Ro]
Isham, Preston to Amanda Marney 4-1-1869   [Ro]
Isham, Preston to Susan H. Martin 6-11-1870 6-12-1870   [Ro]
Isham, Thomas to Josaphine M. Adkisson 7-9-1870 7-10-1870   [Ro]
Ivey, J. F. to Elizabeth Woody 7-1-1872 (7-25-1872)   [Ro]
Jackson, Leland to Mary J. Littleton 10-8-1858   [Ro]
Jackson, Wm. to Hannah Bowling 3-28-1865 (6-4-1865)   [Ro]
James, Caleb to Elizabeth Wood 5-3-1870 5-5-1870   [Ro]
James, Henry to Susan Burnett 4-7-1864   [Ro]
James, W. F. to Mary Henry 3-25-1871 (3-26-1871)   [Ro]
Jeffers, Jacob to Hannah Reed 12-18-1872   [Ro]
Jeffries, William to Elizabeth W. Hackney 3-20-1856 (4-10-1856)   [Ro]
Jenkins, Charley to Margaret Keeling 9-10-1869 9-11-1869   [Ro]
Jenkins, Jacob to Fanny Jenkins 6-17-1867 (6-20-1867)   [Ro]
Jenkins, L. M. to Emily Jane Crouch 2-12-1862   [Ro]
Jenkins, L. T. to Elizabeth C. Brayshear 3-20-1871   [Ro]
Jewell, S. H. to China Green 11-21-1874   [Ro]
Jinkins, David to Fanny Shubert 4-11-1859   [Ro]
Johnson, A. B. to H. N. (Mrs.) Hankins 8-23-1869 8-30-1869   [Ro]
Johnson, A. M. to Sallie Boyd 12-24-1868 (12-23?-1868)   [Ro]
Johnson, Berry H. to D. C. Munsey 11-16-1865 (11-23-1865)   [Ro]
Johnson, Chas. to Malinda Fritts 4-20-1867 (4-23-1867)   [Ro]
Johnson, David R. to Sarah A. Gambol 1-19-1865   [Ro]
Johnson, F. L. B. to Elizabeth McPherson 4-2-1866 (4-3-1866)   [Ro]
Johnson, George W. to Nancy Jane Cooley 8-23-1859 (8-25-1859)   [Ro]
Johnson, J. Lafayett to Mary J. Blair 2-14-1857 (2-12?-1857)   [Ro]
Johnson, James E. to Mary Peters 7-2-1866 (7-5-1866)   [Ro]
Johnson, Jas. M. to Mary E. C. Ambrose 12-26-1865 (12-28-1865)   [Ro]
Johnson, Jesse to Elizabeth Patty 10-13-1863   [Ro]
Johnson, John H. to Mary J. Jackson 6-2-1860   [Ro]
Johnson, Joseph C. to Mary Elizabeth Clowers 3-29-1864 (4-9-1864)   [Ro]
Johnson, L. L. to H. A. Mathis 12-21-1867 (1-2-1868)   [Ro]
Johnson, Nicholas to Barsheban M. Bowman 10-23-1862   [Ro]
Johnson, Peter to Mary Jane Harvey 12-29-1863   [Ro]
Johnson, Robt. W. to Susan J. Harvey 2-28-1865   [Ro]
Johnson, S. H. to M. J. Wilson 8-7-1869   [Ro]
Johnson, S. J. T. to Eliza M. Coldwell 10-13-1856 (10-14-1856)   [Ro]
Johnson, Samuel H. to Mary Davis 2-7-1872 (2-8-1872)   [Ro]
Johnson, Thomas to Rachel A. Dizney 10-3-1860   [Ro]
Johnson, Thos. to Martha J. Littleton 12-19-1868 (12-20-1868)   [Ro]
Johnson, W. D. to Call E. Blair 8-23-1869 9-14-1869   [Ro]
Johnson, james H. to Mary Smith 2-10-1866 (2-15-1866)   [Ro]
Johnston, Francis M. to Mary A. Henderson 10-4-1856   [Ro]
Johnston, James H. to Adeline Philips 2-12-1856   [Ro]
Johnston, Jas. H. to Mary A. Kline 10-9-1866 (10-18-1866)   [Ro]
Johnston, John to Sarah C. Goldston 1-31-1872 (1?-1-1872)   [Ro]
Jolley, William to Sallie East 4-9-1870 4-10-1870   [Ro]
Jones, Henry B. to Mary A. Hudson 3-5-1860 (3-22-1860)   [Ro]
Jones, J. L. to Clementine Grasen 12-30-1864 (1-2-1865)   [Ro]
Jones, James to Charity Smalley 1-2-1873   [Ro]
Jones, James to Elizabeth J. Pope 2-11-1868   [Ro]

Roane County Grooms

Jones, James M. to Emily J. Pickel 8-28-1867   [Ro]
Jones, John to Selia Ann Love 12-20-1867 (12-21-1867)   [Ro]
Jones, John C. to Sarah K. Waller 8-6-1859   [Ro]
Jones, John S. to Ruth E. Sharp 12-16-1873   [Ro]
Jones, John W. to Eliza C. W. Vann 12-16-1869 12-19-1869   [Ro]
Jones, Joseph to Adeline Vaughn 8-1-1866 (8-2-1866)   [Ro]
Jones, S. H. to Nancy C. Rankins 8-18-1866 (8-21-1866)   [Ro]
Jones, W. N. B. to Martha E. Blair 11-24-1868 (11-26-1868)   [Ro]
Jones, Wm. J. to Savannah M. Waller 9-17-1869   [Ro]
Jones, john to Orpa Lowe 12-20-1862 (12-22-1862)   [Ro]
Jordan, James T. to Louisa Hinds 9-11-1872 (9-12-1872)   [Ro]
Jordan, Jesse F. to Lucinda Eblen 11-20-1857   [Ro]
Jordan, John V. to Martha Eblen 10-21-1857 (10-22-1857)   [Ro]
Jordon, Benjamin to Eliza J. Owings 1-7-1870 1-16-1870   [Ro]
Kagley, Lewis Y. to Sarah C. Bullen 7-22-1861 (7-23-1861)   [Ro]
Kain, Andrew to Elizabeth Lestner? 12-28-1859 (12-29-1859)   [Ro]
Keagan, Duke to Savanah Mathis 9-19-1860   [Ro]
Kearsey, Wiley to Eliza Dinkins 12-19-1866 (12-20-1866)   [Ro]
Keelin, Alexander to Elis. A. Renfroe 11-17-1874 (11-19-1874)   [Ro]
Keelin, James H. to Rhoda A. Fuller 8-7-1872 (8-8-1872)   [Ro]
Keelin, Jehu to Nancy Anderson 1-14-1865 (1-15-1865)   [Ro]
Keelin, Wm. J. to Elizabeth E. Hope 9-27-1867   [Ro]
Keeling, Thomas to Harriet L. Renfro 5-4-1869 (5-6-1869)   [Ro]
Keener, Thomas C. to Pheba J. Howard 7-23-1870   [Ro]
Keeton, Frank to Line Motney 12-5-1874 (12-7-1874)   [Ro]
Keith, J. L. to Mary Jane Corbin 7-16-1870 7-17-1870   [Ro]
Keith, James P. to Harriet S. Barger 1-17-1874 (1-18-1874)   [Ro]
Kelam, Asbery to Martha Ivis 2-14-1864   [Ro]
Kelley, James B. to Barbara P. Robertson 8-31-1874 (9-2-1874)   [Ro]
Kelly, Robt. M. to Lucinda G. Wilson 11-7-1865 (11-9-1865)   [Ro]
Kelsay, John to Sarah Ann Lewis 9-24-1860 (9-27-1860)   [Ro]
Kelsay, Joseph M. to Nancy J. Pope 12-17-1867 (12-19-1867)   [Ro]
Kelsay, W. D. to Martha M. Delosier 12-22-170 12-22-1870   [Ro]
Kelsay, William F. to Martha C. Dean 6-30-1874 (7-1-1874)   [Ro]
Kelsey, David C. to Delila Woody 3-26-1858 (3-28-1858)   [Ro]
Kendrick, Enoch J. to Eliza C. Owings 1-1-1862 (1-2-1862)   [Ro]
Kendrick, Rufus F. to Elanor W. Cunningham 8-25-1860   [Ro]
Kenner, Benj. F. to Elizabeth Copeland 12-22-1860   [Ro]
Kenney, James M. to Margaret A. Lockett 6-14-1872 (6-16-1872)   [Ro]
Kenney, R. E. to L. E. Baily 9-16-1864 (9-22-1864)   [Ro]
Kerr, Samuel L. to Fanny A. Winton 12-19-1859 (12-22-1859)   [Ro]
Ketchum, James C. to Lorinda Stevens 8-12-1874 (8-4?-1874)   [Ro]
Key, David M. to Lizzie J. Lenoir 6-25-1857 (7-1-1857)   [Ro]
Keylon, J. S. to Sarah E. East 8-26-1874 (8-27-1874)   [Ro]
Kezziah, James to Sarah Hardbarger 10-14-1874 (10-15-1874)   [Ro]
Kibble, Elias to Martha A. Cate 5-21-1862   [Ro]
Kiker, Uriah to Clara Johnson 1-24-1862   [Ro]
Kile, Wm. F. to Sarah J. Cooley 7-27-1870 7-28-1870   [Ro]
Kimbrough, Rufus M. to Catharine Brown 3-8-1865   [Ro]
Kimbrough, William to Rebecca C. Ellis 8-16-1856   [Ro]
Kindrich, R. S. to Alice Wester 1-1-1870   [Ro]
King, Allen L. to Lydia (Mrs.) Carroll 8-2-1870 8-4-1870   [Ro]
King, Barney B. to Margaret Green 10-7-1861 (10-8-1861)   [Ro]

Roane County Grooms

King, G. W. to Mary A. Hamby 5-5-1873 (5-15-1873) [Ro]
King, J. B. to Sallie T. Haley 11-10-1873 (11-13-1873) [Ro]
King, Joseph to Minerva Watson 5-8-1857 [Ro]
King, Leroy to Sarah Ann Choat 10-21-1864 (10-22-1864) [Ro]
King, Robert to Kizziah T. Perkins 2-16-1857 [Ro]
King, S. L. to M. J. Donlap 7-22-1868 (7-25-1868) [Ro]
King, W. H. to Mary Ann Taylor 9-12-1870 [Ro]
King, William H. to Cynthia T. Fryar 11-26-1867 (11-28-1867) [Ro]
King, Wm. to Nancy Hurst 10-11-1865 [Ro]
King, Wm. C. to Sarah E. Day 7-13-1865 (7-20-1865) [Ro]
Kings, John H. to Nancy A. Cooly 7-21-1860 [Ro]
Kinney, John M. to Sarah Adkisson 1-12-1857 (1-13-1857) [Ro]
Kinnick, Joseph J. to Sarah Riley 8-11-1868 (8-13-1868) [Ro]
Kirkland, Adam to Martha J. Mallsiore? 7-29-1872 (7-30-1872) [Ro]
Kirkland, Jefferson W. to Malinda J. Branaham 6-3-1867 (6-6-1867) [Ro]
Kirksey, Elija to Mary Ann Ables 12-8-1864 [Ro]
Kitchner, James C. to Sarah A. Newcomb 9-9-1869 9-12-1869 [Ro]
Kitrell, F. M. to Sarah J. Gideon 5-8-1865 (5-11-1865) [Ro]
Kittrell, Wiley to Abby Jane Hartley 5-26-1858 (5-27-1858) [Ro]
Kizer, John to Mahaley Nelson 3-7-1859 (3-8-1859) [Ro]
Knapp, D. A. to Sarah Haney 7-24-1873 [Ro]
Knight, Jesse to Mary Collins 7-25-1867 [Ro]
Knox, Jas. C. to Lavina T. Reed 5-25-1869 (5-20?-1869) [Ro]
Knox, Wm. L. to Sarah G. Mitchell 2-2-1869 (2-3-1869) [Ro]
Kollick, Joseph to Martha E. Duff 10-6-1863 [Ro]
Kreis, Deaderick to Margaret Breashers 12-24-1870 12-25-1870 [Ro]
Kries, Deaderick to Almeda S. Patterson 9-10-1874 [Ro]
Kyle, G. W. to Sarah Russell 4-6-1874 (4-17-1874) [Ro]
Kyle, George to Ann Sams 9-11-1860 (9-13-1860) [Ro]
Lacey, Abraham to Maria Norman 11-18-1867 (11-22-1867) [Ro]
Lackey, Andrew J. to Elizabeth Welcker 8-13-1867 (8-15-1867) [Ro]
Lackey, Hugh to Mary A. Henston 9-5-1864 (not executed) [Ro]
Lackey, Hugh to Nancy A. Houston 12-3-1864 (12-4-1864) [Ro]
Lackey, William to Margaret Smith 11-5-1867 [Ro]
Lacy, John to Polly Hornsby 11-30-1857 (12-3-1857) [Ro]
Lacy, Ruben to Mahaily Deathrage 11-3-1868 (11-4-1868) [Ro]
Ladd, Evan to Campbell Williams 11-8-1873 [Ro]
Ladd, Frank to Dora Kries 12-24-1873 (1-1-1874) [Ro]
Ladd, John W. to Celena A. Langen 6-24-1862 (6-29-1862) [Ro]
Ladd, Robert M. to Sophia S. Johnston 7-2-1859 [Ro]
Ladd, William J. to Margaret K. Johnson 2-18-1858 [Ro]
Lane, Albert to Orlena Sharp 4-6-1865 (4-16-1865) [Ro]
Lane, John to Elizabeth Hall 12-9-1859 (12-11-1859) [Ro]
Lane, Thos. J. to Caroline Anderson 10-4-1873 (10-5-1873) [Ro]
Langen, John to P. Melinda Smith 6-14-1862 (7-3-1862) [Ro]
Langley, Ephraim to Susan E. De Armand 11-7-1866 (11-8-1866) [Ro]
Langley, Miles to Sarah E. Morris 9-21-1869 9-26-1869 [Ro]
Lankford, J. W. to Caroline Morris 1-15-1873 (1-19-1873) [Ro]
Largin, A. W. to Martha Ladd 11-7-1861 [Ro]
Lasey, Wm. to Lydia Shubart 9-8-1860 (9-9-1860) [Ro]
Lauderdale, John F. to Laura Hotchkiss 10-9-1865 [Ro]
Lauller, Thomas to Lizzie McEwen 12-12-1863 [Ro]
Lavender, Livingston to Margaret Nichol 12-18-1866 [Ro]

Roane County Grooms

Lawson, David to Frances Carter 4-27-1869 (4-28-1869) [Ro]
Lawson, Edmond to Pearsy M. Hogue 7-31-1865 (8-2-1865) [Ro]
Lawson, John F. to Mary A. R. West 10-12-1872 [Ro]
Lawson, John R. to Sarah Cain 1-6-1858 [Ro]
Lea, George H. to Amy Daniel 2-4-1860 [Ro]
Lea, George H. to Amy Daniel 2-4-1860 (2-1?-1860) [Ro]
Lea, Jas. W. to Eliza Pyatt 4-22-1867 [Ro]
Lea, Wm. to Maria D'Armond 5-23-1868 B [Ro]
Leach, Enoch to Rebeca Jane Kyle 4-16-1862 (4-24-1862) [Ro]
Ledford, B. M. to Sarah Blair 7-29-1863 [Ro]
Ledford, Marion to Nancy Vaughn 9-15-1866 (9-16-1866) [Ro]
Leffew, Albert P. to H. T. Selvige 9-16-1871 (9-17-1871) [Ro]
Leffew, John to Kizziah McDuffie 12-30-1857 [Ro]
Leffew, John H. to Martha J. Swicegood? 8-22-1867 [Ro]
Leffew, Joseph to Sarah A. Henson 8-7-1873 [Ro]
Leffew, Pleasant to Mary Floyd 6-9-1856 (6-10-1856) [Ro]
Leffew, William to Elizabeth Cook 8-19-1861 (8-22-1861) [Ro]
Leffew, Wm. J. to Mary J. Lasley 9-26-1871 (9-27-1871) [Ro]
Leftgo?, Samul to Elizabeth Dalton 9-16-1868 (9-17-1869?) [Ro]
Lemus?, Calvin to Mary Cain 11-20-1860 [Ro]
Lenard, John H. to Ellen Johnson 11-17-1859 [Ro]
Letner, William to Rutha Crisp 5-12-1858 [Ro]
Letsinger, William F. to Delila Bailey 7-21-1857 (8-6-1857) [Ro]
Letsinger, William H. to Rutha E. Crews 8-28-1858 (8-31-1858) [Ro]
Lewis, James to Lotta Looney 4-15-1856 (4-21-1856) [Ro]
Lewis, John L. to Rebecca A. Thompson 2-23-1867 (2-24-1867) [Ro]
Lewis, Thomas L. to Sarah E. Snow 12-5-1866 (12-6-1866) [Ro]
Lewis, Thos. J. to Mary A. Porter 2-1-1869 [Ro]
Lewis, Wm. A. to Minerva Hodge 9-4-1874 (9-6-1874) [Ro]
Libby, C. O. to Mary O. Robinson 2-24-1871 (3-5-1871) [Ro]
Liggett, Henry jr. to Anna C. Lloyd 10-22-1859 (10-23-1859) [Ro]
Liles, Abner C. to Martha A. Hacker 11-9-1867 (11-10-1867) [Ro]
Liles, Calvin M. to Providence B. Dixon 1-8-1866 (1-9-1866) [Ro]
Liles, James to Amanda D. Cox 8-5-1861 [Ro]
Liles, Joseph to Mary E. Nelson 5-19-1866 (5-24-1866) [Ro]
Liles, Lenzey to Nancy Ann Davis 8-16-1858 (8-26-1858) [Ro]
Liles, William H. to Betheny Leith 12-24-1866 (12-25-1866) [Ro]
Lillard, A. J. to Samantha C. Taliaferro 11-9-1866 (1-29-1867) [Ro]
Limbo, Hans to Margaret E. Allen 10-17-1867 [Ro]
Limbo, John H. to Ann E. Ladd 9-9-1868 (9-10-1868) [Ro]
Lindsey, S. W. to Martha J. Belew 7-11-1867 (7-12-1867) [Ro]
Ling, William F. to Mary E. Harris 4-19-1870 [Ro]
Linsey, J. F. to M. J. Copland 11-5-1875 [Ro]
Littleton, D. R. to Mary J. Farmer 12-22-1872 (12-26-1872) [Ro]
Littleton, G. M. to Eliza F. Taylor 1-28-1875 [Ro]
Littleton, George P. to Mary A. Huffine 1-2-1869 (1-3-1869) [Ro]
Littleton, George W. to Telitha J. Hall 9-22-1856 (9-23-1856) [Ro]
Littleton, J. H. to Catharine Bowers 11-19-1874 (11-22-1874) [Ro]
Littleton, James H. to Stacey E. Littleton 9-12-1863 [Ro]
Littleton, Pleasant G. to Elizabeth A. Ingram 9-13-1867 [Ro]
Littleton, Samuel H. to Elizabeth Crow 12-5-1871 (12-7-1871) [Ro]
Littleton, Sanford N. to Mary P. Pickel 10-6-1873 (11-2-1873) [Ro]
Littleton, William R. to Rachel F. A. Cormany 5-2-1857 (8-9-1857) [Ro]

Littleton, Wm. to Mary Matlock 5-15-1864   [Ro]
Littleton, Wm. F. to Nancy J. Eblen 1-23-1873 (1-26-1873)   [Ro]
Littleton, Wm. S. to Nancy A. Harvey 12-4-1865 (12-7-1865)   [Ro]
Lloyd, Wm. G. to Mary A. McNutt 4-9-1867   [Ro]
Locke, B. M. to Margaret L. Sliger 2-18-1871 (2-26-1871)   [Ro]
Lockett, Wm. to Nancy Richmond 5-24-1866   [Ro]
Lollis, William to Fanny Rainey 9-1-1858   [Ro]
Lollis, Wm. to Elizabeth Ann Russell 4-7-1865 (4-9-1865)   [Ro]
Long, William to Jerome? Clower 8-14-1868 (8-16-1868)   [Ro]
Longbottom, S. F. to Rachel E. Huffine 12-30-1874 (12-31-1874)   [Ro]
Love, J. R. to M. L. Hotchkiss 3-6-1867 (3-7-1867)   [Ro]
Love, Joseph N. to Christiana Wilson 4-24-1872 (4-25-1872)   [Ro]
Love?, Joseph N. to Mary Jane Isham 9-9-1856 (9-11-1856)   [Ro]
Lowery, G. W. to M. E. Ray 3-1-1867 (3-3-1867)   [Ro]
Lowery, John A. to C. J. Shouse 9-2-1868 (9-3-1868)   [Ro]
Lowery, R. S. to Sarah J. Lovelace 9-25-1872 (9-26-1872)   [Ro]
Lowery, Richard S. to Martha Ambrose 12-26-1865 (12-28-1865)   [Ro]
Lowrey, Wm. T. to Elizabeth S. Young 10-26-1865   [Ro]
Luffman, Benj. to Elizabeth Dullon 2-1-1864   [Ro]
Luffman, Isaac M. to Bettie J. Williams 7-27-1869 7-29-1869   [Ro]
Luffman, Robert to Nancy E. Dridman? 8-14-1865 (8-19-1865)   [Ro]
Luffman, W. F. to Catharine Miller 12-14-1872 (12-19-1872)   [Ro]
Luttrell, Jacob to Sarah E. Burk? 9-15-1863 (9-17-1863)   [Ro]
Lynch, M. L. to Lillie F. Ebbens 11-18-1873   [Ro]
Lynn, Elijah D. to Emily Branham 10-25-1856 (10-26-1856)   [Ro]
Lynn, Thos. J. to M. J. Hammontree 4-2-1867 (4-4-1867)   [Ro]
Lyon, James A. to Martha J. Hicks 2-7-1874 (2-8-1874)   [Ro]
Magill, A. M. to Margaret E. Duncan 2-21-1857 (2-22-1857)   [Ro]
Magill, James M. to Nancy E. Daniel 3-1-1872 (3-5-1872)   [Ro]
Magill, Robert to Mary Magill 12-5-1874 (11?-6-1874)   [Ro]
Magill, Robert M. to Margaret Ward 5-21-1870 5-22-1870   [Ro]
Magill, Wm. to Martha J. Philips 12-21-1864 (12-22-1864)   [Ro]
Maham, A. Mack to Elizabeth A. Turpin 7-9-1874 (7-10-1874)   [Ro]
Mahoney, John T. to Jennie E. Greene 9-6-1870   [Ro]
Mahoney, M. to M. Clouce 3-19-1870 3-20-1870   [Ro]
Majors, Geo. W. to Annaliza Hickey 10-8-1866 (9?-10-1866)   [Ro]
Majors, James to Susan Johnson 10-25-1869 10-28-1869   [Ro]
Majors, John to Catharine Hews 7-23-1870 7-24-1870   [Ro]
Majors, John to Mary Bear 7-28-1868   [Ro]
Malone, J. W. to Melviny Wilky 7-27-1865   [Ro]
Mamey, Samuel to Margaret S. Walker 1-6-1872 (1-11-1872)   [Ro]
Mann, John W. to Arrabella J. Winton 7-24-1861 (8-1-1861)   [Ro]
Mannon, John to Sarh E. Whaley 12-22-1868 (12-24-1868)   [Ro]
Maples, Wilson to Jane Underwood 6-1-1865 (6-4-1865)   [Ro]
Margrave, J. M. to C. E. Margrave 8-6-1868   [Ro]
Margrave, John to Emma Mayberry 10-7-1869   [Ro]
Markis?, Houston A. to Talitha C. Miller 2-7-1872 (2-8-1872)   [Ro]
Marlin, John to Rachel Lewis 5-30-1873   [Ro]
Marney, Amos to Sarah C. Wright 2-20-1867 (2-21-1867)   [Ro]
Marney, John to Allice Edwards 8-19-1869   [Ro]
Marney, John to Sarah Dalton 11-21-1867   [Ro]
Marney, Samuel to Matilda Y. Taylor 2-9-1858 (2-14-1858)   [Ro]
Martin, Daniel to Eliza Eskridge 7-30-1870 B [Ro]

Roane County Grooms

Martin, James to Susan J. McPhearson 7-26-1859   [Ro]
Martin, Jas. T. to Sarah C. Wormsley 1-10-1872 (1-11-1872)   [Ro]
Martin, John C. to Susan E. Delcyris? 10-1-1868 (10-4-1868)   [Ro]
Martin, R. C. to Louisa Hacker 1-8-1868 (1-9-1868)   [Ro]
Martin, Robert to Caroline Selvidge 3-4-1857 (not endorsed)   [Ro]
Martin, Robert N. to Patsy Derruitt? 2-12-1857   [Ro]
Martin, Samuel to Caroline Brown 9-17-1869   [Ro]
Martin, Samuel to Mariah Seiber 12-27-1869 12-28-1869   [Ro]
Martin, Wm. to Alice Shackelford 4-26-1865   [Ro]
Martin, Wm. P. to Eliza Jane Brown 10-8-1856   [Ro]
Massey, John to Mary Ann Stout 3-3-1868   [Ro]
Matheny, Samuel R. S. to Nancy E. Bowman 8-3-1857 (8-6-1857)   [Ro]
Mathews, T. J. to Permelia Norman 8-6-1864 (8-7-1864)   [Ro]
Mathis, Arthur S. to Eliza J. Small 3-2-1858   [Ro]
Mathis, Asa to Alsey J. Johnson 11-20-1856 (11-23-1856)   [Ro]
Mathis, John to Eda P. Russell 9-14-1872 (9-19-1872)   [Ro]
Mathis, Lindsey to Vesta Clavey 6-11-1859 (6-12-1859)   [Ro]
Mathis, Nelson to Sarah E. Heston 3-19-1869 (3-21-1869)   [Ro]
Mathis, Obediah to Anne Wilson 2-11-1864   [Ro]
Mathis, Stephen C. to Malvina C. Millican 3-22-1856 (3-23-1856)   [Ro]
Matlock, James to Elizabeth Hudson 4-30-1859 (5-3-1859)   [Ro]
Matlock, John C. to Mary Jane Oliphant 11-15-1858 (11-18-1858)   [Ro]
Matz, Martin to Martha J. Hendrichson 8-8-1873 (8-10-1873)   [Ro]
Maupin, John to Virginia Hutsell 6-10-1864   [Ro]
May, Abraham to Sallie J. Wilson 7-22-1871 (7-27-1871)   [Ro]
May, Eli to Elizabeth A.(N.?) Edwards 10-30-1872   [Ro]
May, Eli to Jane Webster 4-29-1861   [Ro]
May, J. A. to Cornelia A. Edwards 6-30-1860 (7-2-1860)   [Ro]
May, Michael A. to Malinda D. Silvey 9-26-1872   [Ro]
Mayes, J. P. to Sarah J. Julian 10-2-1858 (10-5-1858)   [Ro]
Mayfield, William to Laura Jane Grooms 4-12-1856   [Ro]
Mays, Levi V. to Eliza Pickel 3-29-1865 (4-3-1865)   [Ro]
Mayton, J. T. to Mollie E. Bagwell 8-19-1868 (8-20-1868)   [Ro]
Mayton, Jackson to Mary A. Mooton 7-11-1868 (7-12-1868)   [Ro]
Mayton, Jacob to Mary J. Delany 12-24-1873 (12-31-1873)   [Ro]
Mayton, John W. to Angenira Howard 5-23-1868 (not executed) *   [Ro]
Mayton, Wm. H. H. to Matilda Miller 8-15-1857 (8-16-1857)   [Ro]
McAllen, A. J. to Mary Dail 12-7-1872 (12-8-1872)   [Ro]
McAllister, Thos. to Mary Chesser 12-20-1864 (12-22-1864)   [Ro]
McAnally, Jasper N. to Lucretia Cook 2-5-1859 (2-14-1859)   [Ro]
McBride, Jas. to Amanda Britt 2-4-1865 (2-5-1865)   [Ro]
McCaleb, Andrew to Eliza Slack 4-3-1856   [Ro]
McCall, Enoch to Martha Watt 11-26-1873 (11-27-1873)   [Ro]
McCall, Saml. to Mary Clemens 12-15-1863   [Ro]
McCamish, James to Eliza Cook 12-25-1864   [Ro]
McCamy, James to Mary J. Davis 2-21-1874 (2-22-1874)   [Ro]
McCarroll, Albert to Elizabeth J. Lewis 3-5-1856 (3-6-1856)   [Ro]
McCarroll, Columbus to Leathy E. Watts 2-6-1860   [Ro]
McCarroll, James P. to Lydia E. White 1-4-1858 (1-6-1858)   [Ro]
McCarroll, John to Julinda E. Rucker 6-16-1860 (6-17-1860)   [Ro]
McCarroll, William to Linda Brown 5-27-1863   [Ro]
McCarroll, Wm. to Sarah Burnett 5-4-1871 (5-7-1871)   [Ro]
McCarroll, Wm. G. to Susan Boyd 9-1-1868 (9-6-1868)   [Ro]

Roane County Grooms

McCelland, G. L. D. to M. F. Martin 11-28-1868 (12-3-1868) [Ro]
McClane, T. L. C. to E. C. Carter 1-13-1866 (1-14-1866) [Ro]
McClellan, Andrew to Margaret Jiles 9-3-1870 9-10-1870 [Ro]
McClellan, J. C. to Eliza J. Casteel no dates (with 1870) [Ro]
McClendon, Sanders to Tolly Ann Pelt? 6-4-1858 [Ro]
McClure, Rufus A. to Nancy J. Wintin 2-5-1856 [Ro]
McClure, Wm. L. to Sarah Ann Hartley 7-3-1868 (7-5-1868) [Ro]
McCollum, Saml. to Alzy French 8-7-1869 8-10-1869 [Ro]
McCollum, Wm. M. to Susan H. Kile 7-28-1860 (8-2-1860) [Ro]
McCoy, John N. to Martha C. Delosier 9-4-1867 (9-5-1867) [Ro]
McCoy, William to Mary A. Enochs 3-19-1863 [Ro]
McCrary, James to Rebecca Roberts 3-9-1865 [Ro]
McCristian, James T. to M. P. Phillips 5-10-1864 (5-12-1864) [Ro]
McCroskey, P. T. to Mary M. Gallaher 12-22-1858 (12-23-1858) [Ro]
McCulley, F. P. to S. R. Haney 9-17-1870 9-18-1870 [Ro]
McCulley, W. H. H. to Emiline Hinds 9-28-1866 (9-30-1866) [Ro]
McCulley, Wallace to Amanda Bowles 8-21-1873 (8-24-1873) [Ro]
McDaniel, Thomas F. to Mary Snow 8-22-1860 (?-3-1860) [Ro]
McDermond, W. H. to Malinda C. Fritts 7-3-1864 (8-4-1864) [Ro]
McDonald, T. J. to Mary J. Edes 10-18-1867 (10-19-1867) [Ro]
McDonough, J. S. to M. L. Lenoir 3-7-1867 (3-13-1867) [Ro]
McDuffe, Benj. H. to Luisa Leffers 3-27-1868 (3-29-1868) [Ro]
McDuffee, D. R. to Mary Nichols 9-29-1869 9-30-1869 [Ro]
McDuffie, James M. to Malinda C. Delezier 5-4-1860 [Ro]
McElhancey, James to Mary E. Malone 6-22-1858 (6-24-1858) [Ro]
McElroy, Andrew to Georgiana Scarbrough 7-25-1872 [Ro]
McElwee, Wm. E. to Martha R. Brown 12-11-1867 (12-12-1867) [Ro]
McEwen, _____ to _____ Carling? 11-28-1864 (12-1-1864) [Ro]
McGee, William H. to Nancy Jane Hagler 5-13-1858 [Ro]
McGoins, Robert to Mary M. Hensley 4-25-1873 [Ro]
McInally, Tho. to Nancy Roberts 9-1-1870 [Ro]
McIver, Daniel J. to Eliza J. Narramore 3-30-1867 (4-4-1867) [Ro]
McKenzie, John A. to Serena Wilhoit 3-30-1867 (3-31-1867) [Ro]
McKinney, Ananias to Pheabe Seiber 12-18-1865 (12-24-1865) [Ro]
McKinney, Caswell W. to Margaret C. Hacker 3-27-1861 (3-28-1861) [Ro]
McKinney, H. H. to Martha J. Harvey 10-15-1864 (10-20-1864) [Ro]
McKinney, Isaac N. to Amanda M. Jones 10-25-1871 (10-29-1871) [Ro]
McKinney, J. L. to Ada Sellars 11-21-1874 (11-22-1874) [Ro]
McKinney, Jas. M. to Margaret1859) [Ro]
McKinney, Jesse S. to Adaline A. Wright 3-24-1869 (3-25-1869) [Ro]
McKinney, Joseph to Susan E. Evans 2-15-1859 [Ro]
McKinney, Lewis B. to Matilda Fields 11-27-1865 (12-12?-1865) [Ro]
McKinney, Nathaniel to Julia A. Phillips 10-23-1866 [Ro]
McKinzie, P. A. to Sarah J. Blair 12-8-1856 (12-17-1856) [Ro]
McLean, C. O. to Ruth S. Edes 11-12-1866 (11-15-1866) [Ro]
McLendin?, James to Mary E. Burnett 2-13-1869 (2-14-1869) [Ro]
McMahan, Joseph F. to Josephine Edwards 2-6-1858 (2-7-1858) [Ro]
McMillen, George to Sarah Lewis 11-18-1872 [Ro]
McMillen, Saml. to Martha Ervin 9-13-1873 (9-14-1873) [Ro]
McMillon, Samuel to Darcus Ann Duker 5-29-1858 (5-30-1858) [Ro]
McMinnas?, Wm. J. to Mariah E. Watson 1-14-1870 1-19-1870 [Ro]
McMullin, Marion to Sarah Ann Buller 2-27-1864 [Ro]
McNutt, Jas. W. to Sarah M. Roberts 8-8-1865 [Ro]

Roane County Grooms

Mead, Jas. H. to Martha E. Alderson 4-21-1861   [Ro]
Medford, John F. to Virginia Davis 3-23-1864 (3-4?-1864)   [Ro]
Mee, Luke to Sarah Acuff 11-12-1870 11-15-1870   [Ro]
Mee, R. A. to Mary Margrave 2-24-1866 (2-25-1866)   [Ro]
Melton, Absalom to Sarah A. J. Rausin 12-13-1870 12-15-1870   [Ro]
Melton, D. A. to Sarah Mathis 11-24-1869 11-25-1869   [Ro]
Melton, George W. to Elisebeth H. Ruggles 12-3-1864 (12-4-1864)   [Ro]
Melton, George W. to Nancy C. Thompson 10-7-1873 (10-9-1873)   [Ro]
Melton, Joseph E. to Elizabeth J. Daniels 4-19-1866 (4-21?-1866)   [Ro]
Meroney, William to Caroline Yarber 12-3-1862   [Ro]
Mifflin, Wm. B. to Eliza Perry 3-8-1873 (3-9-1873)   [Ro]
Miles, Henry to Catharine Hensley 10-6-1866 (10-21-1866)   [Ro]
Miles, Jas. H. to Margaret J. Lack 4-23-1869 (4-24-1869)   [Ro]
Miles, John to Julia A. Gallamore 3-18-1871 B [Ro]
Miles, Saml. to Elizabeth Adamson 12-23-1863   [Ro]
Miller, A. J. M. to Maryann Culveyhouse 3-24-1864   [Ro]
Miller, Casper to Edney Enochs 11-21-1874 (11-22-1874)   [Ro]
Miller, F.? R. to Nancy Brown 12-23-1874 (12-24-1874)   [Ro]
Miller, Hezikah to Nancy Thompson 9-4-1868 (9-6-1868)   [Ro]
Miller, James D. to Elizabeth A. Robinson 10-22-1867 (10-24-1867)   [Ro]
Miller, James L. to Minerva Babb 3-15-1866 (3-18-1866)   [Ro]
Miller, Jas. T. to Nancy J. Hall 2-13-1875   [Ro]
Miller, Jason to Martha C. Pierce 5-28-1870 5-29-1870   [Ro]
Miller, John J. to Eliza Jane Tinel 12-27-1865 (12-28-1865)   [Ro]
Miller, John T. to Matilda C. Clark 10-6-1864   [Ro]
Miller, Jos. K. to Margaret L. Whaley 9-18-1867 (9-26-1867)   [Ro]
Miller, M. S. to M. C. Holmes 6-16-1868 (6-17-1868)   [Ro]
Miller, M. W. to Rhoda S. Nipper 10-6-1856 (10-8-1856)   [Ro]
Miller, Mark S. to Mary Galyon 10-12-1859   [Ro]
Miller, Mark S. to Tempy J. Parker 10-12-1859   [Ro]
Miller, Newal W. to Rachel M. Kyle 10-3-1865 (10-5-1865)   [Ro]
Miller, Newton S. to Cynthia J. Dennis 4-29-1868 (5-7-1868)   [Ro]
Miller, T. L. to Edda Campbell 9-9-1867 (9-10-1867)   [Ro]
Miller, Tho. J. to Mary E. Parker 1-16-1860?   [Ro]
Miller, Thomas J. to Martha A. Bailey 4-30-1861   [Ro]
Miller, Thos. J. to Mary E. Parker 1-11-1860 (1-17-1860)   [Ro]
Miller, Wiley P. to Elizabeth Mongen 6-29-1867 (6-30-1867)   [Ro]
Miller, William to Jane Smith 12-17-1866 (12-20-1866)   [Ro]
Miller, William F. to Margaret E. Goodman 4-11-1856 (4-12-1856)   [Ro]
Millican, John H. to Susan Abels 9-24-1859 (9-29-1859)   [Ro]
Millican, Moses F. to Sarah C. Delosier 10-25-1866   [Ro]
Mills, Henry C. to Catharine A. Wester 9-1-1865   [Ro]
Milsaps, Mark to Mary M. Johnson 6-25-1873   [Ro]
Milsaps, Thomas to Nancy A. Fleming 9-26-1873 (9-27-1873)   [Ro]
Mincey, David to Margaret Byram 7-20-1865   [Ro]
Monday, Malchi to Rebecca Ann Hays 8-14-1865 (8-17-1865)   [Ro]
Monday, Skelvin? to Lydia Cates 11-5-1857   [Ro]
Monger, Isaac L. to Mary L. Haun 12-8-1866 (12-9-1866)   [Ro]
Monger, John M. to Martha E. Jones 2-12-1868 (2-13-1868)   [Ro]
Monger, W. M. to M. L. Breazeale 1-23-1874 (1-25-1874)   [Ro]
Monroe, Elisha to Amanda Brewster 7-24-1860 (7-25-1860)   [Ro]
Montgomery, Emanuel to Julia Suddeth 5-1-1872 B [Ro]
Montgomery, Francis M. to Hannah F.? Johnson 10-29-1866 (11-1-1866)   [Ro]

Roane County Grooms

Montgomery, John to Elizabeth Kindrick 4-2-1870 5-19-1870   [Ro]
Montgomery, John A. to Nancy Hinds 6-28-1873 (6-29-1873)   [Ro]
Montgomery, John M. to Mary J. Wilkerson 11-25-1867 (11-29-1867)   [Ro]
Moore, Chas. to Jane Newman 4-21-1865 (4-27-1865)   [Ro]
Moore, George W. to Malinda Jackson 11-4-1873   [Ro]
Moore, James W. to Martha M. Smith 9-14-1866 (9-20-1866)   [Ro]
Moore, John to Nancy Linn 7-15-1861 (7-20-1861)   [Ro]
Moore, John N. A. to Arminta A. Delaney 11-9-1869 11-10-1869   [Ro]
Moore, M. L. to A. W. Smith 4-25-1874 (4-26-1874)   [Ro]
Moore, Marshall to Isabel D. Ladd 5-29-1857   [Ro]
Moore, Robert to Vianna McClure 9-9-1868 (9-10-1868)   [Ro]
Moore, Robert L. to Mary J. Delaney 7-28-1870 7-31-1870   [Ro]
Moore, W. J. to Jennie Lloyd 10-29-1873 (10-30-1873)   [Ro]
Moore, Wm. J. to Sarah A. Grimes 5-7-1870 5-8-1870   [Ro]
Moreland, William to Mary M. Warren 12-15-1860   [Ro]
Morgan, John T. to Margaret J. Hackney 8-30-1866   [Ro]
Morris, John to Mary Snow 12-25-1858 (12-30-1858)   [Ro]
Morrison, Geo. W. to Lucinda Branham 11-2-1867 (11-3-1867)   [Ro]
Morrison, Gideon P. to Martha J. Edgmond 11-14-170 11-15-1870   [Ro]
Morrison, John E. to Malinda J. Clark 9-20-1862 (9-24-1862)   [Ro]
Morrone?, John B. to Tabitha J. Narramore 12-6-1865 (12-7-1865)   [Ro]
Morrow, George to Calafornia Cummings 1-23-1871   [Ro]
Morten, William to Martha Fortner 5-2-1862 (5-8-1862)   [Ro]
Morton, William B. to Martha W. Locket 2-9-1872 (2-15-1872)   [Ro]
Moser, Samuel J. to Sarah C. Martin 8-1-1857 (8-2-1857)   [Ro]
Mosier, James M. to Hannah Robinson 11-6-1858 (11-7-1858)   [Ro]
Moss, Edmond to Rebecca Yarber 8-11-1865 (8-12-1865)   [Ro]
Moss, Jackson to Sarah Shoat 2-27-1866 (3-1-18660   [Ro]
Moss, James to Eliza Ponder 5-23-1863   [Ro]
Moss, T. J. to Josee M. Clark 12-17-1872 (12-19-1872)   [Ro]
Moss, Thos. G. to Rheoda A. Winton 9-24-1868   [Ro]
Mounger, Henry to Mary E. Byrd 9-11-1856   [Ro]
Mounger, James to Nancy J. Richardson 3-4-1874 (3-5-1874)   [Ro]
Mounger, John to Caroline M. Delany 11-11-1874 (11-12-1874)   [Ro]
Muecke, Joseph A. to Henrietta A. Neorgrard? 12-12-1872   [Ro]
Mulinix, Wm. O. to Elizabeth Sharp 2-25-1873   [Ro]
Mullings, J. L. to Grizzelle White 3-16-1861 (3-17-1861)   [Ro]
Mullins, John to Mary E. Edwards 1-28-1860 (1-29-1860)   [Ro]
Mullins, M. B. to Fanny A. Price 1-26-1871   [Ro]
Mullins, W. R. to Anna Keelin 12-21-1866 (12-23-1866)   [Ro]
Murphey, Jesse W. to Lucinda J. Campbell 10-19-1863 (10-20-1863)   [Ro]
Murphey, John to Susan P. Clark 10-11-1865 (10-12-1865)   [Ro]
Murphy, John to Susan P. Clark 10-12-1865 (10-13-1865)   [Ro]
Murray, Stephen to Huldah Jane Hitch? 9-22-1856   [Ro]
Murry, F. M. to A. E. Hood 12-19-1865 (12-20-1865)   [Ro]
Myers, Albert to Frances C. Beard 1-2-1867 (1-3-1867)   [Ro]
Mynatt, Lynville to Jemima A. Hinds 12-30-1857   [Ro]
Myres, Allen to Lucy M. Ramsay 2-14-1868   [Ro]
Myres, Fritts to Cyntha Smart 8-12-1868 (8-13-1868)   [Ro]
Myres, James C. to Christenia Bowers 12-26-1874 (12-27-1874)   [Ro]
Nalley, Jessee A. to Elizabeth E. McClure 10-2-1867 (10-6-1867)   [Ro]
Naramore, Jas. to Serena Hinds 8-12-1869 8-15-1869   [Ro]
Narimore, John H. to Serulda Morris 9-1-1857 (9-3-1857)   [Ro]

Roane County Grooms

Narramore, D. H. to Martha J. Moore 3-3-1874 (3-8-1874) [Ro]
Narrimore, Wm. L. to Maryakette Vann 2-9-1864 (2-10-1864) [Ro]
Nave, Presley W. to Elizabeth J. Mitchell 6-26-1861 (6-27-1861) [Ro]
Neal, John R. to Mary E. Brown 11-13-1862 [Ro]
Neal, Newton O. to Esther M. Wright 1-8-1862 [Ro]
Neill, James L. to Margaret C. Parker 8-22-1860 (8-23-1860) [Ro]
Nelon, John to Nancy J. McKinney 11-12-1872 (11-14-1872) [Ro]
Nelson, James to Lucinda Couch 10-10-1864 (10-12-1864) [Ro]
Nelson, John C. to Louisa D. Weneter 2-25-1859 (2-6-1859) [Ro]
Nelson, John H. to Nancy E. Jiles 1-29-1866 [Ro]
Nelson, Richard to Rachel Rowe 1-1-1861 (1-4-1861) [Ro]
Nelson, Wm. P. to Martha J. Easter 10-20-1866 (10-23-1866) [Ro]
Nelson, Zachrich T. to Caroline May 12-24-1866 (12-25-1866) [Ro]
Netherland, George to Matilda H. McEwen 12-26-1865 [Ro]
Newcomb, Levi to Mary J. Crabtree 5-21-1873 (5-22-1873) [Ro]
Newcome, Wm. P. to Elizabeth Wray 12-24-1868 (12-27-1868) [Ro]
Newman, George W. to Malinda Beals 7-26-1870 [Ro]
Newman, John to Sarah Reins 2-13-1865 [Ro]
Newman, Ricahrd to Susan Rayborn 7-19-1856 (7-21-1856) [Ro]
Newton, J. A. to C. A. Guenther 6-19-1873 [Ro]
Niceley, John to Jane Crisp 3-13-1861 [Ro]
Nichol, John to Addie(Abbey) Kilgore 12-14-1866 (12-19-1866) [Ro]
Nichol, John J. to Sarah J. Wright 11-24-1864 [Ro]
Nichols, Henry C. to Mary M. Palmer 1-29-1866 (1-30-1866) [Ro]
Nichols, Wm. B. to Mahala D'Armand 7-28-1866 (7-29-1866) [Ro]
Nipper, R. B. V. to Laura J. Bowman 9-6-1863 (9-7-1865?) [Ro]
Nipper, Thomas to Vianna Green 2-1-1856 (2-3-1856) [Ro]
Nipper, Wm. P. to Martha Easter 8-22-1866 (8-25-1866) [Ro]
Nodes, George to Selah Ann Roday 8-6-1864 (8-7-1864) [Ro]
Norman, Gideon P. to Margaret E. Clark 10-15-1860 [Ro]
Nothern?, Nelson to Sarah Schooler 4-22-1862 [Ro]
Nunn, John H. to Nancy E. Cardwell 2-27-1858 (2-29-1858) [Ro]
Odem, T. C. to Margaret Brown 8-15-1874 (8-16-1874) [Ro]
Odum, D. W. to Catharine Haynes 2-29-1856 (4-1-1856) [Ro]
Oliver, Richard to Margaret A. Smith 4-26-1862 (4-29-1862) [Ro]
Ollis, George to Tabitha Wright 3-16-1860 [Ro]
Ollis, Thomas to Sarah Lawson 2-14-1856 [Ro]
Ortin, James to Margaret Thomas 9-16-1856 [Ro]
Overton, John J. to Elizabeth Narramore 2-1-1860 [Ro]
Overton, John J. to Sarrah Jane McLey 3-3-1863? (3-2?-1863) [Ro]
Overton, Robert to Lucy Hale Farmer 9-19-1860 [Ro]
Owens, Wm. to Nancy J. Forester 6-28-1873 [Ro]
Owings, Albert M. to Mary E. Hill 7-7-1866 (7-8-1866) [Ro]
Owings, Elihu R. to Eliza J. Work 2-11-1859 (2-20-1859) [Ro]
Owings, Jas. C. to Matilda Acuff 11-28-1866 [Ro]
Pair, Saml. A. to Elizabeth M. Johnson 10-11-1865 (10-12-1865) [Ro]
Parker, James to Martha L. Simpson 7-29-1873 (7-30-1873) [Ro]
Parker, Joseph to Margaret Whelock 8-15-1863 [Ro]
Parks, George to Rachel E. Qualls 2-17-1874 (2-20-1874) [Ro]
Parks, James to Nancy Ann Weese 6-20-1856 (6-21-1856) [Ro]
Parks, John to Eliza J. Patterson 9-19-1872 [Ro]
Parson, John E. to Sarah J. Cook 5-22-1872 (5-26-1872) [Ro]
Pass, Arch to Lucretia Dean 4-8-1874 (4-9-1874) [Ro]

Roane County Grooms

Pass, Jesse to Mary Sperling 12-22-170   [Ro]
Passe?, Wm. E. to V. L. Galyon 11-12-1867 (11-14-1867)   [Ro]
Patterson, James D.? to Nancy E. Matheny 9-19-1866 (9-20-1866)   [Ro]
Patterson, John F. to Margaret Ladd 12-26-1857 (12-28-1857)   [Ro]
Patton, Wm. W. to Adelia Martin 10-13-1870   [Ro]
Patty, Jesse J. to Lutitia Wilson 6-1-1858 (6-4-1858)   [Ro]
Patty, Jesse J. to Sarah Smalley 2-18-1856 (2-21-1856)   [Ro]
Patty, Thomas to Elizabeth Brown 10-23-1856   [Ro]
Paul, W. B. to Mary Ann Robinson 3-2-1870 4-3-1870   [Ro]
Peak, C. S. to Margaret J. Doss 6-25-1863   [Ro]
Peak, Luke to Nancy Bellew 3-31-1869   [Ro]
Pearson, Jas.? P. to Parthena McPhearson 3-1-1861 (3-5-1861)   [Ro]
PeckASSSSf, N. O. to Henrietta Barnett 1-22-1861   [Ro]
Peirce, Otter to Betsey J. Ollison 7-3-1869 (7-4-1869)   [Ro]
Pelfry, John to Eliza J. Mathis 5-5-1864 (5-6-1864)   [Ro]
Perkins, James to Nancy Jones 3-5-1866 (3-11-1866)   [Ro]
Perry, Marshall C. to Sarah C. Lynn 8-20-1856   [Ro]
Perry, Rufus to Vina Ambrose 12-2-1861 (12-23-1861)   [Ro]
Persinger, George to Harriet Alderson 11-7-1865 (11-8-1865)   [Ro]
Peterman, John B. to Martha A. Rose 3-3-1866 (3-4-1866)   [Ro]
Peters, James to Martha Ann Martin 9-1-1868 (9-3-1868)   [Ro]
Peters, James W. to Nancy E. Dail 8-2-1865   [Ro]
Petty, Wm. to Martha J. Foster 7-29-1867   [Ro]
Philips, Allen to Amanda Poland 6-12-1872   [Ro]
Philips, Allen to Sarah Poland 1-2-1874 (1-4-1874)   [Ro]
Philips, Geo. W. to Eliza N. Jones 1-21-1865 (1-26-1865)   [Ro]
Philips, Isaih to Mary Jones 4-1874? (not executed)   [Ro]
Philips, John to Mary Jane Ivey 2-22-1860   [Ro]
Philips, Thomas to Charlotte Hicks 3-10-1871   [Ro]
Phillips, Edmond to Mary Wright 9-26-1859 (9-27-1859)   [Ro]
Phillips, George to Martha Selvey? 4-27-1864   [Ro]
Phillips, Isaih to Mahala Henderson 8-4-1874   [Ro]
Phillips, John T. to Mary E. Ellis 11-19-1866 (11-20-1866)   [Ro]
Phillips, Lewis J. to Clara Andrews 10-24-1859   [Ro]
Phillips, William to Elizabeth Walls 9-22-1859 (9-26-1859)   [Ro]
Phillips, Wm. to Louisa Branson 8-15-1866 (8-16-1866)   [Ro]
Philpot, Irvin L. to Sarah E. Underwood 10-17-1866 (10-18-1866)   [Ro]
Pickel, Bird to Lucy A. Smith 10-8-1867 (10-17-1867)   [Ro]
Pickel, W. J. to Ann Harvey 1-5-1875   [Ro]
Pickel, Wm. M. to Sarilda B. Morgan 8-7-1865 (8-16-1865)   [Ro]
Pickelsammers, Geo. to Mary H. Floyd 12-28-1865 (11?-30-1865)   [Ro]
Pickins, James B. to Phebe E. Felts 10-10-1856 (10-12-1856)   [Ro]
Pickle, John M. to Mary Winton 5-18-1869 (5-25-1869)   [Ro]
Pierce, R. L. to Columbia A. Richerson 4-20-1865   [Ro]
Pierce, Walker to Martha C. Dillinger 11-11-1873   [Ro]
Pierce, Zadock to Sarah Jane Isham 9-26-1867   [Ro]
Pinyan, Albert to Truthena Owings 5-21-1867 (5-26-1867)   [Ro]
Pitman, Jasper to Isabella Wright 10-7-1859   [Ro]
Pitman, Robert L. to Caroline McCarrol 1-29-1861 (1-31-1861)   [Ro]
Pittman, Granville to Sally Ann Wright 12-18-1859   [Ro]
Pitts, Moses to Sarah Nealy 10-9-1871 (10-12-1871)   [Ro]
Pleming, C. N. to Caroline Thompson 6-7-1873 (6-16-1873)   [Ro]
Plumadore, J. E. to Cora? Gardner? 10-15-1862 (10-16-1862)   [Ro]

Roane County Grooms

Pogue, Cary J. to Nancy L. Marcus 7-31-1865   [Ro]
Poland, James to Rebecca Enox 10-25-1865   [Ro]
Pollard, John O. to Catherine Deatherage 1-12-1859   [Ro]
Ponder, Volentine to Nancy Potter 3-9-1858 (3-10-1858)   [Ro]
Pool, J. H. to S. A. Thompson 7-19-1873 (7-20-1873)   [Ro]
Pope, Byrd to Harritt Roddie 3-21-1868   B [Ro]
Pope, James C. to Matilda C. Mathis 9-5-1864 (5-17-1865)   [Ro]
Pope, John D. to Elizabeth J. Deatherige 1-17-1867 (1-20-1867)   [Ro]
Pope, John M. to Jane Clark 3-2-1874 (3-5-1874)   [Ro]
Pope, Smith? to Nancy I. Sharp 11-4-1870 11-10-1870   [Ro]
Pope, Wm. H. to Margaret E. Kelsay 11-4-1870 11-6-1870   [Ro]
Porter, James R. to Elizabeth Miller 3-7-1868 (3-8-1868)   [Ro]
Porter, John R. to Mary S. Kincade 9-23-1856   [Ro]
Porter, Wm. A. to Nancy J. Clark 11-15-1866 (11-18-1866)   [Ro]
Potter, Elihu to Caroline Hughs? 5-4-1860   [Ro]
Prater, James to Eliza N. Gill 12-30-1863   [Ro]
Preston, Robert to Mary Narramon 8-23-1856 (8-25-1856)   [Ro]
Price, Calvin to Hilah M. Tankersly 7-26-1871   [Ro]
Price, M. T. to K. M. Morris 7-24-1873   [Ro]
Priddy, Martin to Elizabeth C. Clark 4-11-1860   [Ro]
Priddy, William to Martha J. Solomon 10-3-1859 (10-4-1859)   [Ro]
Proffett, Wm. P. to Mary Johnson 10-17-1857 (10-18-1857)   [Ro]
Proffitt, G. E. to Sarah E. Jolly 12-19-1865 (12-25-1865)   [Ro]
Proffitt, Wm. P. to Malinda Dykes 8-30-1866   [Ro]
Props, James A. to Abigail Ruggles 4-9-1856 (4-10-1856)   [Ro]
Pyatt, J. H. to R. E. Hughs 10-21-1874 (10-14?-1874)   [Ro]
Qualls, George to Charlotte Sylvey 12-2-1870 12-4-1870   [Ro]
Qualls, John N. to Mahala J. Pelfry 10-4-1872 (10-5-1872)   [Ro]
Quartermous, Warren to Susanah Davis 2-7-1857 (2-8-1857)   [Ro]
Raehl?, Franklin to Rebbecca A. Gillam 3-4-1874 (3-5-1874)   [Ro]
Ragan, W. P. to E. J. Brown 11-9-1872 (11-10-1872)   [Ro]
Ralston, George to Calie Davis 4-9-1869   [Ro]
Ramsey, William L. to Louisa V. McCampbell 6-19-1858 (6-23-1858)   [Ro]
Randolph, James L. to Elizabeth B. Garland 2-26-1869 (2-27-1869)   [Ro]
Randolph, William to Sarah May Cora W. Scott 4-25-1868   [Ro]
Raney, G. W. to Nancy A. Solomon 9-8-1866 (9-9-1866)   [Ro]
Rasin, Edward to Parthena Duncan 1-28-1858   [Ro]
Rather, Wm. C. to Paralee Gardenhire 5-4-1874 (5-10-1874)   [Ro]
Ray, William to Celia J. Thacker 9-2-1872 (9-8-1872)   [Ro]
Rayborn, Jno. to Minerva C. Wheat 11-13-1869 11-14-1869   [Ro]
Rayborn, William to Sarah M. Capps 5-30-1857 (5-31-1857)   [Ro]
Raybourne, Esau to Sarah Wester 8-1-1862 (8-3-1862)   [Ro]
Rayburn, Wm. M. to Martha C. Waller 5-13-1868 (5-14-1868)   [Ro]
Rayby, Elija to Malinda Brown 8-16-1865   [Ro]
Rayby, John to Lucinda Dines? 10-20-1866 (10-21-1866)   [Ro]
Re____, Jacob B. to Nancy Ann Magill? 12-19-1859   [Ro]
Reaves, M. to Matilda Hicks 8-15-1870 8-16-1870   [Ro]
Rector, Absalom K. to Sarah Ann Hinds 12-11-1867 (12-12-1867)   [Ro]
Rector, John to Martha J. Hanson 10-2-1858   [Ro]
Rector, Richard to Sarah Taylor 7-3-1871 (7-4-1871)   [Ro]
Redferren, Charles to Clarissa Rosier 8-14-1856 (not endorsed)   [Ro]
Redman, John G. to Amanda J. Odem 10-10-1866 (10-11-1866)   [Ro]
Redman, Nelson C. to Martha A. Cade 6-11-1861 (6-16-1861)   [Ro]

Roane County Grooms

Redman, Nelson C. to Mary B. Porter 10-20-1860   [Ro]
Reed, George R. to Elizabeth Guffie 3-24-1866   [Ro]
Reed, James to Sarah (Mrs.) Morris 12-1-1870   [Ro]
Reed, Raymond to Nancy McAmy? 10-12-1874 (10-13-1874)   [Ro]
Reed, Thomas Y. to Amey Lundie 10-22-1857 (10-24-1857)   [Ro]
Reed, William R. to Hester A. V. Haynes 6-2-1856 (6-11-1856)   [Ro]
Reese, Samuel to Sallie E. Huff 12-21-1866 (12-23-1866)   [Ro]
Reeves, John D. to Permelia Fritts 1-3-1866 (1-4-1866)   [Ro]
Renfro, J. P. to M. J. Baley 4-24-1869 (4-25-1869)   [Ro]
Renfro, W. F. to Mary A. Jackson 5-23-1871 (5-24-1871)   [Ro]
Renfro, William M. to Nancy E. Wyrick 1-24-1872 (1-25-1872)   [Ro]
Retherford, Wm. to Sarah Ellis 5-13-1865 (5-14-1865)   [Ro]
Reynolds, A. B. to M. E. Allen 10-17-1874 (10-18-1874)   [Ro]
Reynolds, Austin to Margaret E. Miller 3-18-1856 (3-20-1856)   [Ro]
Reynolds, James H. to Martha Jane Browder 11-18-1857   [Ro]
Reynolds, John B. to Margaret Brewer 7-11-1864 (7-21-1864)   [Ro]
Reynolds, T. P. to Elizabeth Campbell 10-29-1866 (11-4-1866)   [Ro]
Rhea, Joseph G. to Mary E. Bill 7-4-1865 (7-15-1865)   [Ro]
Rice, C. L. to A. A. Medlin 7-16-1870 7-17-1870   [Ro]
Rice, James H. to Mary E. Hodge 5-24-1860   [Ro]
Rice, Joseph M. to E. C. Sams 1-25-1865 (1-26-1865)   [Ro]
Rice, William to Emeline Bumpass 9-24-1867 (9-26-1867)   [Ro]
Rice, William T. to Nancy L. Suddath 9-1-1857   [Ro]
Rich, Robert to Frances E. Johnson 9-14-1868 (9-15-1868)   [Ro]
Rich, Wm. J. to Catharine Littleton 11-14-1866 (11-16-1866)   [Ro]
Richards, G. W. to Margaret E. MSagill 9-13-1864   [Ro]
Richardson, John to Margaret C. Horne 5-3-1866 (5-11-1866)   [Ro]
Richardson, Saml. D. to Nancy Ann Eblen 9-22-1857 (9-23-1857)   [Ro]
Richison, Stephen to Catharine Evans 8-19-1865 (8-20-1865)   [Ro]
Richmond, E. to Amanda Ezell 2-28-1865 (3-1-1865)   [Ro]
Richmond, Wiley H. to Mary M. Stinecipher 3-1-1869 (3-4-1869)   [Ro]
Riddle, James P. to Martha Lynn 1-29-1866 (1-30-1866)   [Ro]
Riggs, Joseph to Martha M. Hacker 1-18-1866 (1-31-1866)   [Ro]
Right, Samuel to Mary M. Gammon 1-14-1857 (1-15-1857)   [Ro]
Right, William to Mary M. Gammon 12-8-1856   [Ro]
Riley, Wm. to Sarrah L. Brown 3-7-1864 (3-11-1864)   [Ro]
Roach, Benj. to Elizabeth Watenbarger 1-29-1861   [Ro]
Roach, Berry to Sarah White 11-4-1865 (11-9-1865)   [Ro]
Roach, Samuel to M. D. Billings 10-22-1874 (11-1-1874)   [Ro]
Robbs, Edward W. to Louisa Abels 2-21-1860   [Ro]
Robbs, J. S. to Mary Short 10-17-1874 (10-18-1874)   [Ro]
Roberts, B. F. to Caroline Gardnierr 8-12-1871 (8-13-1871)   [Ro]
Roberts, Bazel to Margaret Hester 4-3-1858   [Ro]
Roberts, Chas. W. to Mary E. Amos 1-16-1867 (1-17-1867)   [Ro]
Roberts, Edwd. C. to Harriet Coffee 3-13-1860 (3-18-1860)   [Ro]
Roberts, George W. to Elizabeth Hacker 9-22-1870   [Ro]
Roberts, Isaac S. T. to CAroline M. Ladd 5-10-1860   [Ro]
Roberts, James to Margaret Cannon 8-17-1859   [Ro]
Roberts, James D. to Emma Wilshire 5-20-1872 (5-23-1872)   [Ro]
Roberts, James? to Elizabeth Cook 4-17-1860   [Ro]
Roberts, Jas. to Sarah West 1-27-1865 (1-28-1865)   [Ro]
Roberts, Joseph to Dicy Smith 10-17-1860 (10-18-1860)   [Ro]
Roberts, Lewis to Deanah Short 3-17-1866 (3-18-1866)   [Ro]

Roane County Grooms

Roberts, Robert S. to Louisa Hester 11-22-1856 (11-23-1856)   [Ro]
Roberts, Robert Z. to Saraphina Burnett 4-19-1859   [Ro]
Roberts, Samul H. to Mary Edwards 10-22-1868   [Ro]
Roberts, Thomas to Louisa Horn 7-8-1874 (7-10-1874)   [Ro]
Roberts, Thomas L. to Mary Jane Adkisson 6-17-1857 (6-18-1857)   [Ro]
Roberts, W. F. to Eliza G. Jones 12-23-1874 (12-24-1874)   [Ro]
Roberts, W. M. to Nancy G. Silvey 5-6-1865   [Ro]
Robinson, Charles J. to Matilda J. Cross 10-23-1867 (10-24-1867)   [Ro]
Robinson, James W. to Margaret Crow 12-17-1873 (12-18-1873)   [Ro]
Robinson, Samuel P. to Rosannah Culvyhouse 6-26-1858 (6-27-1858)   [Ro]
Robinson, W. M. to E. C. Cassady 11-10-1874   [Ro]
Roda, P. D. to Deannah E. Mathis 6-29-1861   [Ro]
Roddy, W. S. to Mattie Kimbrough 6-16-1871 (6-22-1871)   [Ro]
Rodgers, Jonathan N. to Martha J. Patterson 1-17-1859 (1-27-1859)   [Ro]
Rodgers, S. A. to M. C. Byerley 10-22-1867 (10-30-1867)   [Ro]
Rodgers, Samuel A. to Sarah E. Rhea 5-7-1863 (5-10-1863)   [Ro]
Rodgers, Thomas L. to Louisa E. Alexander 12-8-1860 (12-9-1860)   [Ro]
Rodgers, Wm. M. to mary Ann McAnally 8-2-1860 (8-10-1860)   [Ro]
Roe, J. L. to Martha A. Niece 8-5-1870 8-7-1870 [Ro]
Rose, Alexander to Elizabeth Truet 8-25-1869 8-26-1869 [Ro]
Rose, Elisha to Nancy Ann Wallace 2-20-1867   [Ro]
Rose, James E. to Malinda Smalley 8-22-1865   [Ro]
Rose, John to Amanda Roehl? 4-8-1874   [Ro]
Rose, Joseph W. to Rachel Miller 4-2-1864 (4-3-1864)   [Ro]
Rose, Mitchell V. to Sarah Price 1-27-1859 (2-2-1859)   [Ro]
Rose, Washington B. to Emma E. Tolleferro 12-3-1867 (12-5-1867)   [Ro]
Rose, Wilson to Elizabeth J. Smalley 9-15-1858 (9-16-1858)   [Ro]
Rothwell, A. J. to Margaret Haggard 9-19-1866 (9-20-1866)   [Ro]
Row, James to E. Waldrip 8-9-1866 (8-10-1866)   [Ro]
Rowden, J. N. to Margarett E. Fuller 9-1-1868 (9-3-1868)   [Ro]
Rowden, John H. to Rachel S. Wasson 12-9-1864 (12-15-1864)   [Ro]
Rowden, Thomas M. to Caroline Bacon 7-14-1860   [Ro]
Rucker, Thomas N. to Nancy A. Keelin 9-7-1871   [Ro]
Rudder, B. R. to Nancy J. Wyatt 7-27-1874 (8-6-1874)   [Ro]
Rudder, J. B. to T. L. Philips 8-12-1873 (8-13-1873)   [Ro]
Ruggles, Thomas C. to Margaret Davis 10-31-1867   [Ro]
Ruoff, Chas. A. to Marie E. Loyd 5-3-1865 (5-4-1865)   [Ro]
Ruoff, James Frederick to Amanda Underwood 4-19-1859   [Ro]
Russell, A. L. to Sarah E. Hays 4-29-1859 (5-1-1859)   [Ro]
Russell, Aaron to Barbara Miller 8-17-1865   [Ro]
Russell, Ambrose to Elizabeth Foster 12-24-1872 (12-25-1872)   [Ro]
Russell, Frank A. to Nancy J. Bowers? 10-27-1873 (10-28-1873)   [Ro]
Russell, George W. to Betsy Jane Robertson 6-15-1858 (6-17-1858)   [Ro]
Russell, J. P. to Margaret A. Talent 8-8-1864   [Ro]
Russell, Jas. to Ann Eliza Ketchum 1-19-1865   [Ro]
Russell, Jas. W. to Catharine Forrister 12-15-1874   [Ro]
Russell, John to Elizabeth Brannom 6-20-1871 (6-21-1871)   [Ro]
Russell, John M. to Mary R. Taylor 7-16-1866 (7-19-1866)   [Ro]
Russell, John S. to Rhoda Easter 10-4-1860 (10-7-1860)   [Ro]
Russell, Joseph to Jane Lawson 10-25-1860   [Ro]
Russell, Levi to Martha Marthis 3-13-1868 (3-15-1868)   [Ro]
Russell, Tho. J. to Maggie Gallaher 5-20-1874 (5-21-1874)   [Ro]
Rutherford, Frank to Susannah Ambrose 8-27-1857   [Ro]

Roane County Grooms

Sante, Nicholas to Mary Ann Morrison 8-5-1856 (8-7-1856) [Ro]
Saunders, Thos. to Martha J. Woods 12-6-1864 (12-8-1864) [Ro]
Scapehart, Hugh H. to Margaret N. Wiggins 1-10-1856 [Ro]
Scarborough, James M. to Martha J. Cook 9-2-1867 (9-5-1867) [Ro]
Scarborough, John to Catharine Rogers 12-30-1865 (1-4-1866) [Ro]
Scarborough, John R. to Mary E. Loveless 4-23-1859 (4-24-1859) [Ro]
Scarborough, Jonathan M. to Mary J. Johnston 6-7-1872 (6-9-1872) [Ro]
Scarborough, William to Sarah Woody 12-27-1866 [Ro]
Scarbrough, George to Mary M. Hamilton 3-6-1874 (2?-7-1874) [Ro]
Scarbrough, James to P. C. Taylor 3-10-1868 (3-15-1868) [Ro]
Scarbrough, Jas. A. to Louisa E. Vann 12-14-1874 (12-20-1874) [Ro]
Scarbrough, John to Melinda C. Jones 1-25-1861 (1-31-1861) [Ro]
Scarbrough, Jonathan to Mary A. Potter 8-11-1871 (8-13-1871) [Ro]
Scarbrough, Robert M. to Elender McClendon 10-29-1858 [Ro]
Scarbrough, Thomas P. to Mary McClenden 11-2-1858 [Ro]
Scarbrough, Wm. H. to Amanda E. M. Bullin 11-5-1865 (11-8-1865) [Ro]
Scarbrough, Wm. M. to Keziah C. Waller 9-1-1871 [Ro]
Schrimpsher, Greenberry to Sarah Ann Parker 12-24-1868 (12-25-1868) [Ro]
Scott, George to Louisa E. Scott 8-27-1868 (8-30-1868) [Ro]
Scott, Harvey to Margaret Rowe 1-30-1858 (1-31-1858) [Ro]
Scott, William to Frances A. Ward 9-20-1867 (9-21-1867) [Ro]
Scrimpsher, James to Emiline Hays 5-25-1866 (5-26-1866) [Ro]
Scroggins, Thomas to Margaret Majors 10-25-1869 10-26-1869 [Ro]
Seber, Frederick to Nancy Burns 8-9-1862 [Ro]
Seiber, Calvin to Elizabeth Sylvey 12-15-1865 [Ro]
Seiber, Frederick to Eliza Yancy 9-14-1866 (10-30-1866) [Ro]
Seiber, Stephen to Mahala Swaner 12-5-1867 [Ro]
Seinknecht, Therson to Ailan? M. Wensch? 12-23-1869 [Ro]
Sellers, Newton M. to Mary A. Philips 2-11-1856 (2-12-1856) [Ro]
Selvage, John to Elizabeth Ambrose 10-5-1860 (10-7-1860) [Ro]
Selvage, John to Mary A. Shackelford 8-2-1864 [Ro]
Selvidge, William H. to Sarah Brackett 11-26-1856 (11-30-1856) [Ro]
Selvige, Jeremiah to Matilda Easter 10-10-1874 [Ro]
Selvy, Samuel sr. to Cealea Ann Wright 1-5-1863 [Ro]
Shackelford, Geo. W. to Cloaan F. Williams 6-28-1867 (7-4-1867) [Ro]
Shackelford, Joseph to Mary Ann Huckaby 8-12-1865 (8-27-1865) [Ro]
Shackelford, William to Polly Brackett 4-30-1857 [Ro]
Shackelford, Wm. J. to Julia Seiber 7-20-1872 (7-21-1872) [Ro]
Shackelford, Z. to Eliza Sharp 2-24-1870 [Ro]
Shadden, Joseph A. to Sarah A. Tedder 6-20-1867 (6-21-1867) [Ro]
Shahan, Daniel to America J. E. Luttrell 8-21-1867 (8-22-1867) [Ro]
Sharp, Caloway to Bashaba Bowman 6-5-1858 (6-13-1858) [Ro]
Sharp, Columbus to Mary Jane Whaley 9-24-1867 (8?-26-1867) [Ro]
Sharp, Gideon M. to Elizabeth M. Million 9-24-1858 (9-26-1858) [Ro]
Sharp, J. P. to N. E. Brown 9-30-1873 (10-5-1873) [Ro]
Sharp, J. W. to Harriett Childs 3-2-1869 [Ro]
Sharp, James to Eliza Rose 7-26-1873 (8-26-1873) [Ro]
Sharp, Meredith jr. to Margaret E. Crocket 8-29-1862 (8-30-1862) [Ro]
Sharp, Newton C. to Eveline Tuton 11-8-1867 (11-10-1867) [Ro]
Sharp, Pleasant to Mary Bryant 4-25-1864 (5-1-1864) [Ro]
Sharp, Samuel to Malinda E. Johnson 10-23-1865 [Ro]
Sharp, Samuel jr. to Nancy Bowman 10-24-1860 [Ro]
Sharp, Wm. to Elizabeth Lane 3-25-1869 [Ro]

Roane County Grooms

Shearwood, Edward C. to Mary A. Haggard 6-6-1857 (6-9-1857)   [Ro]
Sheets, Mathew to Mary Munday 5-19-1874 (5-23-1874)   [Ro]
Shelton, A. J. to Mary R. Woody 4-10-1866 (4-14-1866)   [Ro]
Shelton, James T. to Lorinda Carter 7-5-1866 (7-19-1866)   [Ro]
Shelton, Wm. A. to Minerva A. Amos 5-26-1868 (5-28-1868)   [Ro]
Shelton, Wm. B. to Sarah E. Fryar 12-1-1865 (12-7-1865)   [Ro]
Shelton?, J. F. to Flora A. Fryar 8-21-1869   [Ro]
Sherwood, David? to _____ A. Walton 7-20-1864 (7-28-1864)   [Ro]
Sherwood, Edward C. to Margaret L. Lyles 2-27-1866   [Ro]
Sherwood, Robert to Mary Simpson 6-28-1861   [Ro]
Sherwood, Wm. E. to Lurena J. Milsaps 9-5-1871 (9-7-1871)   [Ro]
Shewbart, Harrison H. to Eliza Lacy 8-24-1860 (12-14-1860)   [Ro]
Shields, John J. to Elizabeth J. Wirick 8-18-1870 8-18-1870   [Ro]
Shinpaugh, H. H. to Margaret E. Duff 7-25-1866 (7-26-1866)   [Ro]
Shinpaugh, Hugh L. to Eliza P. Duncan 12-10-1866 (12-13-1866)   [Ro]
Shipley, J. T. to Sallie A. Tally 2-18-1871 (2-19-1871)   [Ro]
Shipley, John H. to H. R. H. Guffee 1-17-1866 (1-18-1866)   [Ro]
Shipley, Wm. S. to Malinda J. Bain 12-20-1872 (12-22-1872)   [Ro]
Shoat, James to Jane? Mullins 8-4-1864   [Ro]
Shoat, John to Martha Martin 1-4-1868 (1-5-1868)   [Ro]
Shoebert, William to Sarah Everton 5-6-1869 (5-7-1869)   [Ro]
Short, D. C. to Nancy Hinds 6-12-1873   [Ro]
Short, E. B. to Sarah A. Stencil 1-11-1869   [Ro]
Short, George G. to Olla Query 5-16-1874 (5-17-1874)   [Ro]
Short, Joseph A. to Caroline Underwood 11-11-1871   [Ro]
Shote, Samuel to Betsey Shote 3-25-1873   [Ro]
Shubart, James C. J. to Sarah C. Harris 4-10-1871 (4-13-1871)   [Ro]
Shubart, Wm. to Nancy Davis 1-25-1873 (1-26-1873)   [Ro]
Shubird, Henry M. to Moin Ann McReynold 8-24-1857 (8-25-1857)   [Ro]
Shurits, James W. to Lusettie J----on 10-3-1867 (10-20-1867)   [Ro]
Sigman, L. W. to M. J. Miligan 6-14-1864   [Ro]
Siler, David W. to Martha J. Osborne 5-30-1862 (6-4-1862)   [Ro]
Silvey, Samel to Cynthia A. Williamson 11-9-1872   [Ro]
Silvey, W. R. to Mary C. May 8-2-1859 (8-7-1859)   [Ro]
Silvy, John W. to Malinda McCamy 8-19-1874 (8-20-1874)   [Ro]
Simpson, Adam M. to Mary D. Branson 5-29-1873 (6-5-1873)   [Ro]
Simpson, Anthony to Margaret A. Babb 10-13-1866 (10-18-1866)   [Ro]
Simpson, Jacob to Martha C. Underwood 5-7-1867   [Ro]
Simpson, William A. to Mary A. Burnett 9-15-1857 (9-20-1857)   [Ro]
Slagle, Peter H. to Rhoda E. English 10-27-1868 (10-29-1868)   [Ro]
Sliger, Thomas F. to Harriet L. Odom 12-21-1860   [Ro]
Sliger, Wm. to Emily E. Odem 6-4-1866 (6-6-1866)   [Ro]
Smicegood, George A. to Rebecca Jane Blackwell 10-6-1865 (10-8-1865)   [Ro]
Smith, A. J. to Mary C. Taylor 9-10-1868 (9-11-1868)   [Ro]
Smith, Allen to Elizabeth Crase 7-19-1873 (7-20-1873)   [Ro]
Smith, Anthony to Lucinda Pearson 12-28-1870 (12-29-1870)   [Ro]
Smith, Benjam to Elizabeth Moore 9-8-1868 (9-13-1868)   [Ro]
Smith, Benjamin F. to Susan Harwell 8-2-1866   [Ro]
Smith, Chas. D. to Eliza N. Wyatt 11-5-1870 11-9-1870   [Ro]
Smith, Daniel to Eliza Hall 12-3-1856 (12-7-1856)   [Ro]
Smith, Geo. to Elizabeth Eaton 8-19-1863   [Ro]
Smith, J. B. to S. A. Summers 7-6-1869 (7-7-1869)   [Ro]
Smith, J. H. to Martha A. Pain 3-15-1870 3-16-1870   [Ro]

Roane County Grooms

Smith, Jackson W. to Sarah A. Phifer 2-20-1865 (2-21-1865)   [Ro]
Smith, James to Mary Selvege 5-7-1864 (5-6?-1864)   [Ro]
Smith, James A. to Mary J. E. Miller 8-12-1865 (8-13-1865)   [Ro]
Smith, James D. to Matilda Bowers 10-29-1873 (10-13?-1873)   [Ro]
Smith, James G. to Lucinda Davis 1-14-1870 2-14-1870   [Ro]
Smith, Jas. to Amanda Philips 1-19-1865 (1-21-1865)   [Ro]
Smith, John to Elizabeth Howe 7-2-1862 (5-5-1862?)   [Ro]
Smith, John to Margaret F. Rector 1-12-1871 (1-22-1871)   [Ro]
Smith, John F. to Mary J. Toilett 4-8-1858   [Ro]
Smith, John S. to Easter F. Butler 3-9-1872 (3-10-1872)   [Ro]
Smith, Joseph to Jane Griffiths 3-16-1861   [Ro]
Smith, Joseph to Mariah Allison 4-10-1856   [Ro]
Smith, Josiah to Martha Thompson 8-24-1867 (11-25-1867)   [Ro]
Smith, M. E. to Mary A. Thomas 4-9-1870 4-10-1870   [Ro]
Smith, Nathaniel J. to Sarah M. Helton 10-3-1864   [Ro]
Smith, R. E. to M. E. Hawkins 10-5-1874   [Ro]
Smith, Thomas to Sallie Sellars 9-10-1873 (9-11-1873)   [Ro]
Smith, Wm. to Susan(Miss) Davis 1-6-1872 (1-17-1872)   [Ro]
Snow, A. J. to Sarah E. Bowman 7-2-1866 (7-4-1866)   [Ro]
Snow, Abner to Sarrah E. Carden 4-19-1864 (4-23-1864)   [Ro]
Snow, John A. to Martha McDaniel 2-23-1858 (2-25-1858)   [Ro]
Soard, Saml. to Sarah J. Fink 3-3-1873   [Ro]
Solomon, Andrew to Margaret J. Evans 1-10-1870 1-11-1870   [Ro]
Solomon, James to Mary Reiney 10-28-1867 (10-29-1867)   [Ro]
Sopsher, Winfield to Elizabeth Cooley 7-25-1867 (7-28-1867)   [Ro]
Soward, Henry W. to Sarah A. Hamilton 9-15-1866 (9-16-1866)   [Ro]
Soward, John H. to Sarah E. Cowan 9-14-1866 (9-16-1866)   [Ro]
Soward, Robert W. to Charlotta Carter 7-26-1856 (7-27-1856)   [Ro]
Soward, William B. to M. A. Bowman 12-30-1863 (12-31-1863)   [Ro]
Sparks, D. C. to Arminda A. Wilson 3-23-1870 3-24-1870   [Ro]
St. John, G. W. to Martha A. Blair 4-20-1866 (5-10-1866)   [Ro]
St. John, Napoleon to Eliza Nipper 2-11-1864   [Ro]
Stafford, Frank to Sarah Wiggins 10-18-1870   [Ro]
Stamper, Haskew to Mary Ann Page 2-29-1860   [Ro]
Stamper, Leander to Rutha E. Campbell 12-24-1872 (12-26-1872)   [Ro]
Stanfield, George M. to Evaline Suddath 11-25-1858 (11-30-1858)   [Ro]
Stansbury, H. R. to Louisa C. Taylor 9-17-1873   [Ro]
Stansbury, John to Elizabeth C. Shinpaugh 11-4-1861   [Ro]
Stansbury, M. H. to Matilda Tauscher 8-6-1873 (8-7-1873)   [Ro]
Staples, M. A. to Elizabeth C. Goodman 2-2-1872 (2-5-1872)   [Ro]
Staples, Thos. J. to Elizabeth Davis 5-21-1870 5-22-1870   [Ro]
Staples, Wm. to Elizabeth Bradley 10-10-1865 (10-15-1865)   [Ro]
Steed, James to Lizzie Cardwell 5-18-1867 (5-19-1867)   [Ro]
Stephens, Jessee to Eliza Adams 12-11-1867 (12-12-1867)   [Ro]
Stephens, Wm. H. to Talitha Price 4-7-1866   [Ro]
Stewart, Jacob to Eliza Kirkland 2-1-1873 (2-2-1873)   [Ro]
Stewart, Jacob to Sarah Ann Reed 1-16-1874   [Ro]
Stewart, Moses N. to Louis West 5-2-1874 (5-3-1874)   [Ro]
Stewart, T. J. to Ann Fagan 11-1-1870 11-2-1870   [Ro]
Stgall?, John P. to Joshua A. Williams 7-23-1866   [Ro]
Stinecipher, Ezra R. to Rebecca Byrd 9-3-1866 (9-6-1866)   [Ro]
Stinett, Geo. W. to Nancy A. Rogers 8-17-1865 (8-19-1865)   [Ro]
Stockton, James W. to Nancy A. Redfearn 9-9-1857 (9-12-1857)   [Ro]

Roane County Grooms

Stone, Daniel C. to Melissa A. McDuffie 9-25-1856   [Ro]
Stone, James to Marinda Roberts 7-6-1865   [Ro]
Stone, Stephen H. to Matilda C. Pasty 10-14-1865 (10-19-1865)   [Ro]
Stout, Isaac A. to Rebekah Letsinger 4-14-1864   [Ro]
Stout, Wm. to Teda? Lesley 5-9-1874   [Ro]
Stow, Martin V. to Lucinda J. Ingram 9-22-1859   [Ro]
Stratford, Frank to Emiline Mamey 8-24-1867 (8-25-1867)   [Ro]
Stricklen, James L. to Mary Childress 6-18-1863   [Ro]
Stringer, Jordan to Elizabeth Ollis 2-14-1856   [Ro]
Stringfield, James to Amanda Erwin 1-2-1867   [Ro]
Strutton, Thomas to Margaret Branom 5-19-1871 (5-20-1871)   [Ro]
Stubbs, Jackson to Malinda Davis 11-1-1858   [Ro]
Stubbs, James H. to Jane Taylor 6-18-1873 (7-6-1873)   [Ro]
Sturges, John E. to Susan Moore 10-30-1872 (10-31-1872)   [Ro]
Sturges, Thomas H. to Sarah J. Ellis 11-28-1866 (11-29-1866)   [Ro]
Sturgess, James M. to Rachel L. Wester 3-26-1859 (4-10-1859)   [Ro]
Suddath, Francis K. to Mary E. Hassler 2-20-1868   [Ro]
Suddath, M. M. to Susan E. Graves 11-5-1857   [Ro]
Suddath, S. B. to Sarah E. Maberry 9-3-1868   [Ro]
Suddeth, Thomas K. to Margaret E. Haley 11-22-1865   [Ro]
Sullins, Josiah to Nancy Jane Williams 4-5-1866 (4-8-1866)   [Ro]
Sullivan, John O. to Frances A. Ingalls 1-14-1859 (1-25-1859)   [Ro]
Suttle, Noah to Rebeca Brooks 4-4-1868 (4-5-1868)   [Ro]
Sutton, Andrew J. to Louisa Roberts 7-19-1858 (7-19-1858)   [Ro]
Swicegood, A. M. to M. A. Wilson 12-27-1871 (12-28-1871)   [Ro]
Sword?, Benj. to Catharine Farriss 5-26-1864 (5-27-1864)   [Ro]
Syler?, John A. to Martha A. Tuterow 1-10-1871 (1-12-1871)   [Ro]
Sylvey, James M. to Elizabeth Davis 12-14-1864 (12-29-1864)   [Ro]
Sylvey, Saml. to Mary J. Bird 1-4-1865 (1-6-1865)   [Ro]
Tacker, William C. to Polly Ann Bearden 1-21-1856   [Ro]
Taliaferro, Chas. P. to Fanny Ann Ballard 8-30-1866 (9-11-1866)   [Ro]
Taliaferro, Samuel L. to Eliza Waller 9-14-1871   [Ro]
Tallent, Aron P. to Martha A. Phifer 11-30-1857 (12-3-1857)   [Ro]
Tankless, John A. to H. M. Stephens 9-4-1862   [Ro]
Tarwater, Jas. F. to Rebecca A. Kindrick 7-31-1871 (8-2-1871)   [Ro]
Tarwater, W. H. to Sarah C. Robbs 12-31-1872 (1-1-1873)   [Ro]
Tate, William P.? to Sarah E. Rose 10-6-1871 (10-8-1871)   [Ro]
Tate, Wm. M. to Margaret Ann Rose 8-31-1860 (SB 1864?)   [Ro]
Tate, Wm.? M. to Margaret Ann Rose 8-31-1864 (9-1-1864)   [Ro]
Taylor, Albert H. to Hannah E. Yokely 2-12-1869 (2-1?-1869)   [Ro]
Taylor, Chas. W. to Malinda Seiber 2-4-1867 (2-8-1867)   [Ro]
Taylor, F. W. to Eliza L. Galyon 11-5-1867 (11-14-1867)   [Ro]
Taylor, G. to M. E. Fleming 5-23-1871 (5-23-1871)   [Ro]
Taylor, J. H. to Mary E. Mee 1-28-1874 (1-29-1874)   [Ro]
Taylor, James to Caroline Gallimore 2-14-1862 (2-23-1862)   [Ro]
Taylor, James K. to Emiline Cook 5-22-1865 (5-23-1865)   [Ro]
Taylor, John to Martha Narramore 1-10-1859   [Ro]
Taylor, Jos. H. to Jane Liles 10-6-1874 (10-7-1874)   [Ro]
Tedder, Jas. D. to Susan C. Cofer 10-3-1857 (10-6-1857)   [Ro]
Temple, John to Cynthia J. McCulley 7-16-1869 7-19-1869   [Ro]
Terry, Jesse to Ellen Irons 4-17-1869 (4-18-1869)   [Ro]
Thacker, Gilbert to Elly Heniger Johnson 11-15-1856 (11-16-1856)   [Ro]
Thacker, Umphrey to Mary Hogwood 9-15-1873 (9-18-1873)   [Ro]

Roane County Grooms

Thomas, Griffin to Elvira Shuburt 5-12-1871 (5-18-1871) [Ro]
Thomas, Henry H. to Evaline Hamilton 6-1-1867 (6-2-1867) [Ro]
Thomas, John to Mary Wycuff 2-16-1869 [Ro]
Thomas, Wm. to Caroline Chapman 1-15-1870 1-16-1870 [Ro]
Thombrough, Allen W. to Mary E. Basket 6-23-1859 [Ro]
Thompson, A. M. to Margaret Campbell 7-18-1873 (7-20-1873) [Ro]
Thompson, A. P. to Caroline Hines 5-17-1865 (5-18-1865) [Ro]
Thompson, Benjamin to Elizabeth Herontree? 2-13-1869 (2-18-1869) [Ro]
Thompson, Daniel G. to Margaret S. Cates 4-30-1873 (5-1-1873) [Ro]
Thompson, Danl. to Louisa Hand Morris 7-2-1860 [Ro]
Thompson, James to Emma Shahan 2-3-1875 [Ro]
Thompson, John L. to Mary Grammer 11-1-1871 (11-2-1871) [Ro]
Thompson, Joseph to Mary Breadle 10-9-1867 [Ro]
Thompson, Oscar L. to Louisa C. Hamer 4-5-1868 (4-12-1868) [Ro]
Thompson, Verlian H. to Margaret H. R. E. Everett 8-18-1856 [Ro]
Thompson, William L. to Nancy J. Fifer 10-5-1859 (10-6-1859) [Ro]
Thornton, Emanuel to Nancy Row 8-7-1858 [Ro]
Thrower, Henry to Tennessee Chapman 10-4-1862 [Ro]
Tibbs, Jacob A. to Lavinia S. Russell 6-15-1858 (6-14?-1858) [Ro]
Tindle, Jessee to Dorcas Overton 4-3-1868 (4-5-1868) [Ro]
Tinel, Jackson to Sarah S. Hunt? 4-21-1856 (4-24-1856) [Ro]
Tinel, Jesse to Mary Parks 3-29-1873 [Ro]
Tinel, John M. to Sarah Clark 10-3-1874 (7?-11-1874) [Ro]
Tinel, William to Sarah Jackson 8-2-1858 (8-5-1858) [Ro]
Tinnell, R. A. to Sarah E. Miller 1-7-1870 1-9-1870 [Ro]
Tipton, John Y. to Mary J. Womble 11-14-1871 [Ro]
Tomey, John to S. A. C. Carter 8-12-1868 (8-13-1868) [Ro]
Tootle, Robt to Amanda C. Campbell 3-11-1868 (3-12-1868) [Ro]
Toucher, M. G. to Amelia Hitshen 11-1-1873 (11-2-1873) [Ro]
Tow, Shade to Marylin Sharp 10-26-1866 (11-1-1866) [Ro]
Treadway, Joseph to Susan M. Britt 9-13-1865 [Ro]
Tuck, Alexander to Mary Crumbless 10-6-1858 (10-7-1858) [Ro]
Tucker, John to Fanny Henderson 9-12-1865 (5-13-1865) [Ro]
Tucker, William to Sarah Brogling 12-8-1864 [Ro]
Tudor, Elijah G. to Saraette Adamson 1-20-1858 (1-21-1858) [Ro]
Tudor, William B. to Margaret C. Wheat 2-22-1860 [Ro]
Turk, C. L. to Dotty? Gottard 7-26-1864 (7-28-1864) [Ro]
Turnbill, John to Susan Luttrell 1-24-1865 [Ro]
Turnbill, Richard to Mary E. Crumpley 5-13-1859 (5-19-1859) [Ro]
Turner, Joseph D. to Mary E. Roberts 8-7-1858 (8-12-1858) [Ro]
Turpen, William to Louis Isabella Cristenbury 2-29-1864 (2-25?-1864) [Ro
Turpin, Columbus to Mollie Kirby 9-23-1874 (9-24-1874) [Ro]
Turpin, G. W. to Nancy J. Currier? 7-24-1867 (7-25-1867) [Ro]
Turpin, Isaac to Kate C. Sherwood 6-7-1865 (6-8-1865) [Ro]
Turpin, Joseph to Eliza N. Powell 6-27-1871 (7-6-1871) [Ro]
Turpin, Thomas to Ruth Thacker 7-29-1874 [Ro]
Tusler?, Adison J. to Susan E. Arnett 9-22-1858 (9-23-1858) [Ro]
Tuten, Joseph to Catharine Brogden 3-5-1859 (3-6-1859) [Ro]
Tuterow, Wm. P. to Mary Jane Shinpaugh 7-25-1866 (8-2-1866) [Ro]
Tuterrow, Dalmon A. to Sarah E. Roberts 3-13-1872 [Ro]
Tutterow, Balser to Elendor Andrew 11-18-1874 [Ro]
Tutterow, Wiley to Mary E. Coley 8-28-1874 (8-30-1874) [Ro]
Tyler, John to Amanda Yost 2-24-1869 B [Ro]

Roane County Grooms

Underwood, Benjamin F. to Lucy A. Russell 8-31-1861 (9-4-1861)   [Ro]
Underwood, James to Mahala Hamby 10-4-1867 (10-6-1867)   [Ro]
Underwood, James to Sophronia Nelon 8-5-1874 (8-6-1874)   [Ro]
Underwood, W. B. to M. C. Crow 10-24-1871   [Ro]
Underwood, Wm. H. to Margaret Davis 10-24-1872   [Ro]
Upton, Thos. N. to Sarah E. Dodson 9-4-1874 (9-6-1874)   [Ro]
Utley, Monroe to Ves Ward 12-21-1869 12-22-1869   [Ro]
Vaine?, Isaac to Mary A. Maupins 8-9-1871 (8-18-1871)   [Ro]
Van, Washington to Elizabeth Phillipie 4-2-1869   [Ro]
Vance, Pleasant to Charlotte Nicholson 11-30-1873 (12-1-1873)   [Ro]
Vann, Andrew J. to Mary Hall 2-4-1863   [Ro]
Vann, Jasper to Elizabeth Powell 2-8-1859 (2-9-1859)   [Ro]
Vann, Martin V. to Jane Z. Dawson 8-1-1865 (8-3-1865)   [Ro]
Vann, Wm. H. to Eliza A. Jones 11-9-1872 (11-14-1872)   [Ro]
Varner?, Robert to Jane Wells 6-8-1861 (6-9-1861)   [Ro]
Venzant, William H. to A. M. Doughty 6-23-1874   [Ro]
Vials, Ransom to Martha J. Moore 6-9-1860 (6-10-1860)   [Ro]
Viar, John to Mollie Hartsell 10-13-1870 10-12-1870?   [Ro]
Viar, Robert to B. J. Couvy? 8-20-1866 (not executed)   [Ro]
Vier, Robert to Elizabeth Aikin 9-20-1866 (9-21-1866)   [Ro]
Voiles, James C. to Mary A. McInally 3-23-1865 (3-26-1865)   [Ro]
Voiles, Philip to Charity M. Hulen 7-2-1858 (7-4-1858)   [Ro]
Waddle, B. F. to Mary Burns 1-12-1865 (1-15-1865)   [Ro]
Wade, Andrew J. to Sarah Edgmon 9-10-1862 (9-13-1862)   [Ro]
Walker, C. C. to Prescilla Burns 7-14-1870   [Ro]
Walker, Charles to Nancy Ann Clark 10-4-1859 (10-8-1859)   [Ro]
Walker, Elias to Nancy J. Clower 3-17-1874 (3-19-1874)   [Ro]
Walker, James W. to Telitha Reagan 9-20-1856 (9-21-1856)   [Ro]
Walker, John to Elizabeth Miller 5-3-1862   [Ro]
Walker, John T. to Sarah A. Kelsay 10-13-1869 10-17-1869   [Ro]
Walker, R. A. to Susanna Burns 4-1-1860   [Ro]
Walker, Samuel H. to Mary Edgmon 9-16-1873 (9-18-1873)   [Ro]
Wallace, Isaac to Martha J. Huffine 7-5-1856 (7-6-1856)   [Ro]
Wallace, John to Francess H. Lewis 8-2-1858 (8-10-1858)   [Ro]
Wallace, William to Jane Blankenbicker 8-13-1867 (8-15-1867)   [Ro]
Wallace, William to Sarah Couston 10-27-1868 (11-2-1868)   [Ro]
Waller, C. M. to Ann Monger 12-31-1866   [Ro]
Waller, George P. to Margaret Waller 2-15-1867 (2-17-1867)   [Ro]
Waller, Henry A. to Sophronia C. Dickey 11-12-1866 (11-15-1866)   [Ro]
Waller, John P. to Sarah White 1-25-1868 (1-26-1868)   [Ro]
Waller, John W. to Mary A. Montgomery 5-10-1860   [Ro]
Waller, Robert to Matilda (Mrs.) Sellars 11-8-1873 (11-9-1873)   [Ro]
Wallice, J. W. to Margaret E. Latten 7-25-1867 (7-27-1867)   [Ro]
Ward, Henry to Rebecca A. Green 4-30-1872 (5-2-1872)   [Ro]
Ward, John to Louisa Rector 12-14-1869 12-15-1869   [Ro]
Ward, Martin F. to Mary E. Parks 7-12-1872 (7-13-1872)   [Ro]
Ward, Sterling to Rebecca F. Liles 8-23-1873 (8-26-1874?)   [Ro]
Ward, Wm. G. to Giszeal? Mullins 1-1-1872 (1-2-1872)   [Ro]
Warren, B. L. to N. E. Gilbert 2-7-1865   [Ro]
Washam, George to MaryC. Rutherford 3-27-1864   [Ro]
Washam, William to Catherine M. Wiggins 5-3-1857 (5-7-1857)   [Ro]
Washington, Geo. to NSancy Wells 5-14-1864 (5-16-1864)   [Ro]
Watkins, Henry to Martha Davis 6-25-1870   [Ro]

Roane County Grooms

Watson, Alfred G. to Thursey Ann Cooper 2-4-1867 (2-7-1867)   [Ro]
Watson, James W. to Artalissa McKinney 1-18-1859   [Ro]
Watson, Wm. J. to Mary E. McKinney 1-29-1865   [Ro]
Watt, Jacob to Susannah Freeh 11-22-1856 (11-23-1856)   [Ro]
Watts, John to Elizabeth Martin 9-11-1866 (9-13-1866)   [Ro]
Watts, John to Lucinda Carrol? 1-27-1858 (1-28-1858)   [Ro]
Watts, P. H. to Sarah L. Burns 2-12-1873 (3-30-1873)   [Ro]
Weatherford, James T. to Rachel Davis 12-21-1869 12-26-1869   [Ro]
Weatherford, T. W. to Sarah C. Crow 2-2-1874 (2-4-1874)   [Ro]
Webb, D. S. to Mahala Sanders 11-3-1869 11-4-1869   [Ro]
Webb, John M. to Sarah J. Clower 6-5-1862 (6-8-1862)   [Ro]
Webb, Reuben A. to Sarah J. Redman 9-20-1873 (9-21-1873)   [Ro]
Webb, William to Susan Dean 11-26-1862   [Ro]
Webb, William R. to Sarah Ollis 6-26-1856 (6-29-1858)   [Ro]
Webster, D. B. to Mary L. Minton 9-27-1869 9-29-1869   [Ro]
Webster, Gooden to Sarah Phillips 4-19-1865 (4-21-1865)   [Ro]
Webster, J. S. to L. L. Wilson 11-15-1873 (11-16-1873)   [Ro]
Webster, John H. to CLythia D. Russell 2-2-1872 (2-4-1872)   [Ro]
Webster, Robert to Jemmima C. Sharp 12-18-1871 (12-21-1871)   [Ro]
Webster, W. R. to Taupa Howard 2-22-1867 (2-24-1867)   [Ro]
Weese, John J. to Margaret E. Tate 10-12-1870 10-13-1870   [Ro]
Weese, Stewart to Orfin Soward 3-6-1860 (3-8-1860)   [Ro]
Weese, Wm. J. to Nancy J. Mullins 11-2-1865 (11-5-1865)   [Ro]
Wegner, Ferdinand to Katrina Limburgh 11-13-1872 (11-14-1872)   [Ro]
Wells, George W. to Mary King 10-3-1865 (10-5-1865)   [Ro]
Wells, J. C. to Mary Branson 4-9-1868   [Ro]
Wells, James to Teresa A. Tuterow 11-29-1864 (11-30-1864)   [Ro]
Wells, John A. to Margaret E. Blackburn 9-2-1868 (9-6-1868)   [Ro]
Wells, Stephen to Maranthas J. Felts 9-7-1860   [Ro]
Wells, W. M. to E. J. Jenkins 2-14-1874 (2-15-1874)   [Ro]
Wells, William J. to Nancy King 9-18-1866 (9-20-1866)   [Ro]
West, Eli to Delilah Barnes 9-5-1870   [Ro]
West, J. A. to Polly E. Stewart 5-2-1874 (5-3-1874)   [Ro]
West, John to Mary E. Gammon 3-25-1859 (3-31-1859)   [Ro]
West, Noah N. to Sarah E. Johnson 10-1-1870 10-2-1870   [Ro]
West, Wm. R. to Betsy Kollie 11-7-1868 (11-8-1868)   [Ro]
Wester, Albert G. to Penina C. Boyd ;5-12-1860   [Ro]
Wester, Henry C. to Elizabeth Ellis 9-15-1869 9-19-1869   [Ro]
Wester, John M. to josephine M. Wester 2-20-1867 (2-25-1867)   [Ro]
Whaley, Isaac T. to Mary S. Campbell 8-7-1866 (8-16-1866)   [Ro]
Whaley, John to Patsy Day 7-28-1858 (8-5-1858)   [Ro]
Whaley, John W. to Malissa Brackell 10-7-1865 (10-8-1865)   [Ro]
Whaley, Wm. B. to Eliza Shuburt 7-25-1866 (8-5-1866)   [Ro]
Wheat, George W. to Elizabeth J. Lyle 6-4-1859 (6-9-1859)   [Ro]
Wheat, Houston to E. W. Moore 1-5-1857   [Ro]
Wheat, Wiley Houston to Eliza Eblen 10-16-1857 (10-18-1857)   [Ro]
Whelock, George to M. J. Robertson 8-10-1863   [Ro]
Whisenhunt, Absolem to Susan Brown 8-17-1859   [Ro]
Whisenhunt, Henry to Margaret Philips 6-16-1857   [Ro]
White, Alson to S. L. McCullin 10-25-1865 (10-26-1865)   [Ro]
White, Amasa H. to Nancy C. Kitzay 10-21-1873 (10-23-1873)   [Ro]
White, D. C. to Sarafina Watt 5-2-1872 (5-31-1872)   [Ro]
White, Franklin to Letha A. Cooper 3-7-1867 (3-12-1867)   [Ro]

Roane County Grooms

White, George to Joanna B. Litsinger 3-1-1858 (3-4-1858) [Ro]
White, Joel to Martha Butler 12-3-1873 (12-9-1873) [Ro]
White, John to Margaret Wilson 7-21-1863 [Ro]
White, John to Margaret Wilson 7-22-1863 [Ro]
White, John L. to Sarah Robinson 10-16-1867 (10-17-1867) [Ro]
White, Richard to Sarah Sturgess 1-18-1858 [Ro]
White, S. B. to Margaret E. Kile 2-10-1866 (2-15-1866) [Ro]
White, Wm. P. to Catharine Edwards 9-15-1869 not solemnized [Ro]
Whitlock, N.W. to Mary C. Sams 1-27-1864 (2-11-1864) [Ro]
Whitlock, Sherwood to Dicy Cook 4-10-1859 (4-21-1859) [Ro]
Whitlock, T. J. to Eliza J. Burnett 11-8-1865 (11-9-1865) [Ro]
Whitlock, Thos. C. to Mary A. Lane 5-6-1865 (5-11-1865) [Ro]
Whitlock, Thos. S. to Caroline Johnson 1-4-1869 (6?-6-1869) [Ro]
Whitlock, W. P. to L. C. Boyd 6-6-1874 (6-14-1874) [Ro]
Whitlock, William to Mary J. Minsey 6-10-1858 [Ro]
Whitlock, William to Msary C. Bowman 12-19-1857 (12-24-1857) [Ro]
Whitlock, Wm. to Parthena Ellis 5-2-1874 (5-3-1874) [Ro]
Whitson, Isaac to Sarah C. Cooper 5-16-1865 (5-18-1865) [Ro]
Whittenbury, Nathan to Sarah J. Underwood 2-9-1857 (2-10-1857) [Ro]
Whittier, M. V. to Mary J. Huddleston 9-1-1870 [Ro]
Wiggins, Benjamin F. to Julia Ann Watts 9-4-1858 [Ro]
Wiggins, Leonidas F. to Mary Elizabeth Watts 1-31-1866 (2-1-1866) [Ro]
Wilder, H. M. to Maggie C. Somerville 5-29-1871 (5-30-1871) [Ro]
Wilkerson, George to Martha Shaham 7-17-1857 (7-19-1857) [Ro]
Wilkerson, Henry C. to Mariah Shahan 8-1-1863 [Ro]
Wilkerson, John to Polly Ann Branham 12-31-1857 (1-3-1858) [Ro]
Wilkerson, Major W. to Sarah A. Wilson 8-26-1858 [Ro]
Wilkerson, W. J. to Sarah J. Selvage 4-24-1865 (4-31?-1865) [Ro]
Wilkey, C. C. to E. T. Tilley 9-17-1874 [Ro]
Wilkey, C. C. to Malinda J. Morrison 8-16-1865 (8-17-1865) [Ro]
Wilkey, C. V. to Elvira Underwood 10-14-1865 [Ro]
Wilkie, Campbell to Emaline Roberts 2-16-1864 [Ro]
Wilkison, Robert to Mary Eblen 2-27-1869 (3-4-1869) [Ro]
William, Samuel P. to Sarah A. Hudson 10-27-1868 (10-29-1868) [Ro]
Williams, A. M. to Nancy Isabel Hall 9-16-1858 (9-23-1858) [Ro]
Williams, Alexander to Malinda Talent 7-20-1870 7-23-1870 [Ro]
Williams, Charles J. to Selina Davis 9-27-1873 (10-12-1873) [Ro]
Williams, Jacob to Mary Huffman 1-27-1869 (1-28-1869) [Ro]
Williams, James M. to Mary A. E. Williams 10-24-1856 [Ro]
Williams, John A. to Mary E. Shields 3-1-1867 (2?-5-1867) [Ro]
Williams, John F. to Emeline H. Baily 4-22-1857 (4-23-1857) [Ro]
Williams, John F. to Sophia Phillips 5-30-1860 [Ro]
Williams, Lewis to Mary Ann Thomas 6-17-1872 (6-22-1872) [Ro]
Williams, Mathias to Frances K. Hudson 9-23-1857 [Ro]
Williams, R. M. to Frances B. Hudson 5-3-1873 (5-8-1873) [Ro]
Williams, Richard S. to Margaret A. (Mrs.) Barnard? 9-9-1873 [Ro]
Williams, Samuel H. to Sarah A. Deatherage 9-12-1867 [Ro]
Williamson, C. W. to Cornelia Robinson 5-2-1871 [Ro]
Wilson, Andrew to Henrietta Simpson 4-13-1865 [Ro]
Wilson, G. T. to Sarah C. Cassady 6-4-1867 (6-6-1867) [Ro]
Wilson, George T. to Martha Jane Montgomery 8-17-1861 (8-19-1861) [Ro]
Wilson, J. W. C. to Elizabeth Haley 7-22-1868 [Ro]
Wilson, JSames L. to Mary J. Ballard 9-13-1862 [Ro]

Roane County Grooms

Wilson, John to Lucinda Bogart 1-17-1856   [Ro]
Wilson, Philip to Nancy J. McGee 12-20-1866 (12-21-1866)   [Ro]
Wilson, Pleasant to Mary Wilkey 11-26-1868   [Ro]
Wilson, Rufus to Sarah J. Eldridge 2-19-1859   [Ro]
Wilson, Saml. M. to Mary E. Wright 8-20-1874   [Ro]
Wilson, Squire to Jane Smith 7-16-1870 7-17-1870   [Ro]
Wilson, W. T. to Missouri Adkins 7-30-1867   [Ro]
Wilson, Wiley to Mary Bogart 1-7-1868 (1-9-1868)   [Ro]
Wilson, William to Emily C. Littleton 1-1-1857   [Ro]
Wilson, Wm. to Lillie L. Harp 1-16-1875   [Ro]
Wilson, Wm. M. to Amanda M. (Miss) Brown 10-26-1871   [Ro]
Winchester, James to Sarah Goodman 4-29-1868 (5-3-1868)   [Ro]
Winters, M. W. to Margaret Baurs 10-4-1873 (10-5-1873)   [Ro]
Wirick, George W. to Sarah Ambrose 7-4-1856   [Ro]
Wirick, James H. to Sarah C. Russell 9-25-1873 (9-28-1873)   [Ro]
Wirick, Jas. L. to Nancy L. Clower 12-9-1869 12-23-1869   [Ro]
Wirick, Rufus M. to Betsey Jane Galyon 1-17-1860   [Ro]
Wirick, Wm. L. to Hannah Brown 9-17-1867 (9-18-1867)   [Ro]
Wirrick, James A. to Mary A. Brackett 10-27-1859   [Ro]
Witt, Isaac B. to Mary M. Hickey 11-10-1871 (11-12-1871)   [Ro]
Witt, J. M. to Sarah J. Hickey 11-2-1872 (11-3-1872)   [Ro]
Woodey, Hesekiah to Martha Ann Smith 4-10-1866 (4-12-1866)   [Ro]
Woodruff, James E. to Frances Lowery 9-20-1860 (9-25-1860)   [Ro]
Woods, James W. to Mary S. Porter 6-6-1862 (6-8-1862)   [Ro]
Woody, Henry B. to Caroline M. Erwin 11-23-1864 (11-24-1864)   [Ro]
Woody, James to Phinnette J. Ward 2-7-1868 (2-9-1868)   [Ro]
Woody, Robert to Elender Smith 12-13-1857   [Ro]
Woody, Wm. M to Mary J. Matney 3-14-1868 (3-15-1868)   [Ro]
Woolsey, Fithrus? to Margaret Hornsby 6-18-1856 (6-19-1856)   [Ro]
Woolsey, John to Alice Godard 3-27-1873   [Ro]
Word, William A. to Lottie J. Hagler 4-12-1870 4-17-1870   [Ro]
Work, W. A. to Polly A. Stokes 4-7-1874 (4-9-1874)   [Ro]
Worsham, J. L. to Eliza Allison 9-30-1871 (10-1-1871)   [Ro]
Worsham, J. W. to Mary E. Underwood 6-26-1869 (6-27-1869)   [Ro]
Worsham, Wm. to Isabel Vann 5-9-1874 (crossed out) B? [Ro]
Worsham, Wm. T. to Emma C. Wright 10-20-1867   [Ro]
Wright, Brownlow to Julia Ann Cagle 8-23-1858 (8-24-1858)   [Ro]
Wright, Calvin to Mary Jane Hammons 8-12-1871 (8-14-1871)   [Ro]
Wright, Geo. D. to Sarah Turner 9-25-1856 (10-2-1856)   [Ro]
Wright, George W. to Sarah Qualls 6-7-1865   [Ro]
Wright, Isreal E. to Elizabeth Laughton 2-25-1865 (2-26-1865)   [Ro]
Wright, James to Mary Biggs 4-29-1864 (4-30-1864)   [Ro]
Wright, John to Eliza Wright 10-14-1865   [Ro]
Wright, John to Nancy Howard 9-2-1856   [Ro]
Wright, John H. to Maggie J. Wester 3-19-1874   [Ro]
Wright, John H. to S. A. Rayborn 12-13-1866 (12-14-1866)   [Ro]
Wright, Samuel E. to Eliza Young 7-12-1859 (7-13-1859)   [Ro]
Wright, T. C. to Martha Wilkey 12-27-1871   [Ro]
Wright, T. J. to M. J. Hamilton 1-20-1872 (1-25-1872)   [Ro]
Wright, William to Mary Roberts 1-1-1864 (1-5-1864)   [Ro]
Wright, William A. to Rebecca C. Wilson 2-23-1866 (2-27-1866)   [Ro]
Wright, Wm. J. to Emiline Berry 1-11-1866   [Ro]
Wycuff, James to Caroline Brewer 11-2-1867   [Ro]

Roane County Grooms

```
Wycuff, William to Sarah Dumar? 4-5-1870  4-6-1870   [Ro]
Wylie, F. M. to G. J. D'Armond 6-25-1861 (6-26-1861)   [Ro]
Wyrick, E. N. to Milberry Carpenter 8-17-1871 (8-20-1871)   [Ro]
Wyrick, Robt. M. to Margaret J. Easter 7-11-1872 (7-14-1872)   [Ro]
Yarber, Jasper to Caroline Rogers 10-24-1865    [Ro]
Yarber, Jasper to Jane Martin 1-1-1863    [Ro]
Yates, James K. P. to Mary M. Kelsey 7-19-1861 (7-21-1861)   [Ro]
Yost, E. A. to Nancy J. Center 11-10-1857    [Ro]
Young, Henry G. to Elizabeth J. Jones 1-31-1866 (2-1-1866)   [Ro]
Young, Isham to Margaret C. Adkisson 12-20-1858 (12-21-1858)   [Ro]
Young, John W. to Adaline Miles 8-6-1860    [Ro]
Zenn, J. H. to Julia A. Atwood 3-2-1863 (3-3-1863)   [Ro]
Zwicker, Gustave to Sarah C. Penex 2-7-1874 (2-8-1874)   [Ro]
Zwickes, A. F. to W. F. Martin 4-6-1861 (4-7-1861)   [Ro]
_____, James F. to Naomi J. Whitlock 1-5-1860 (1-8-1860)   [Ro]
____is, John? to Emilin Harrison? 3-19-1868 (3-22-1868)   [Ro]
```

Roane County Brides

Abbot, Cyntha Ann to Benjamin T. Hagler 11-23-1861
Abbott, Elzena to Riley Cook 3-13-1862
Abbott, Lizzie W. to Joseph J. Harrison 8-13-1864
Abbott, M. A. to S. W. Farmer 10-4-1873 (10-5-1873)
Abbott, Sarah L. to James S. T. Baird 8-17-1857 (8-19-1857)
Abels, Louisa to Edward W. Robbs 2-21-1860
Abels, Susan to John H. Millican 9-24-1859 (9-29-1859)
Ables, Mary Ann to Elija Kirksey 12-8-1864
Absten, Mary Elizabeth to James M. Dupre 4-24-1858 (4-25-1858)
Acuff, Matilda to Jas. C. Owings 11-28-1866
Acuff, Sarah to Luke Mee 11-12-1870 11-15-1870
Adams, Eliza to Jessee Stephens 12-11-1867 (12-12-1867)
Adams, Margaret E. to Jos. S.? Headrick 1-26-1875
Adamson, Elizabeth to Saml. Miles 12-23-1863
Adamson, Ellen to Wm. Dunn 11-6-1865 (11-9-1865)
Adamson, Saraette to Elijah G. Tudor 1-20-1858 (1-21-1858)
Adkins, Missouri to W. T. Wilson 7-30-1867
Adkisson, Josaphine M. to Thomas Isham 7-9-1870 7-10-1870
Adkisson, Margaret C. to Isham Young 12-20-1858 (12-21-1858)
Adkisson, Mary C. to James A. Daniel 2-7-1860
Adkisson, Mary Jane to Thomas L. Roberts 6-17-1857 (6-18-1857)
Adkisson, Sarah to John M. Kinney 1-12-1857 (1-13-1857)
Ahart, Mahaley to Joseph Brackett 4-13-1857
Ahart, Sarah E. to J. H. Cook 12-22-1871 (12-4?-1871)
Aikin, Elizabeth to Robert Vier 9-20-1866 (9-21-1866)
Alderson, Harriet to George Persinger 11-7-1865 (11-8-1865)
Alderson, Martha E. to Jas. H. Mead 4-21-1861
Alexander, Louisa E. to Thomas L. Rodgers 12-8-1860 (12-9-1860)
Alexander, Margaret D. to Elijah Goins 10-25-1865 (10-26-1865)
Aline?, Hannah to William Fry 3-24-1874 (3-26-1874)
Allen, M. E. to A. B. Reynolds 10-17-1874 (10-18-1874)
Allen, Margaret E. to Hans Limbo 10-17-1867
Allen, Sarah to James Heath 2-28-1857 (3-1-1857)
Allen, Sophia to E. G. Comly 2-4-1864
Allis, Rebecca J. to Samuel V. Bowers 12-4-1869 12-5-1869
Allison, Eliza to J. L. Worsham 9-30-1871 (10-1-1871)
Allison, Margaret E. to John C. Clark 2-21-1860
Allison, Mariah to Joseph Smith 4-10-1856
Allred, Eliza J. to John Henson 10-2-1874 (10-3-1874)
Ambrose, Elizabeth to Lea M. Galyon 1-19-1859 (1-20-1859)
Ambrose, Elizabeth to John Selvage 10-5-1860 (10-7-1860)
Ambrose, Eveline to William Bagwell 9-17-1856 (9-19-1856)
Ambrose, Jane to James Ambrose 7-8-1864 (7-10-1864)
Ambrose, Martha to Richard S. Lowery 12-26-1865 (12-28-1865)
Ambrose, Mary E. C. to Jas. M. Johnson 12-26-1865 (12-28-1865)
Ambrose, Nancy to John Collier 12-27-1863 (12-28-1863)
Ambrose, Sarah to George W. Wirick 7-4-1856
Ambrose, Susannah to Frank Rutherford 8-27-1857
Ambrose, Vina to Rufus Perry 12-2-1861 (12-23-1861)
Amos, M. J. to John H. Crabtree 2-13-1872 (2-15-1872)
Amos, Martha Jane to Moses Brooks 11-4-1861 (11-10-1861)
Amos, Mary E. to Chas. W. Roberts 1-16-1867 (1-17-1867)
Amos, Minerva A. to Wm. A. Shelton 5-26-1868 (5-28-1868)

Roane County Brides

Anderson, Caroline to Thos. J. Lane 10-4-1873 (10-5-1873)
Anderson, Elizabeth to Jas. W. Huff 5-29-1867 (5-30-1867)
Anderson, Nancy to Jehu Keelin 1-14-1865 (1-15-1865)
Anderson, Rachel A. to J. E. Crowder 4-6-1867 (4-7-1867)
Andes, Ann to William H. Ball 1-18-1858 (1-19-1858)
Andes, Emaline to D. H. Frank 11-5-1856
Andrew, Elendor to Balser Tutterow 11-18-1874
Andrews, Clara to Lewis J. Phillips 10-24-1859
Apperson, Eliza A. to Josiah N. Gamble 11-30-1864 (12-1-1864)
Arnett, Susan E. to Adison J. Tusler? 9-22-1858 (9-23-1858)
Ashley, Mary Jane to Sidney Grider 9-3-1864
Atwood, Julia A. to J. H. Zenn 3-2-1863 (3-3-1863)
Babb, Margaret A. to Anthony Simpson 10-13-1866 (10-18-1866)
Babb, Margarett to Harvey N. Dail 1-11-1859
Babb, Minerva to James L. Miller 3-15-1866 (3-18-1866)
Bacon, Amanda L. to Benjamin Huffine 11-4-1858 (11-11-1858)
Bacon, Caroline to Thomas M. Rowden 7-14-1860
Bacon, Mary J. to David F. Asbury 2-13-1860 (2-23-1860)
Bacon, Nancy to Wm. F. Bowling 3-9-1865 (3-23-1865)
Bacon, Rutha C. to J. C. Hinds 11-21-1868 (11-26-1868)
Bacon, Sophia to Wm. Hudgins 9-9-1872 (9-10-1872)
Bagwell, Mollie E. to J. T. Mayton 8-19-1868 (8-20-1868)
Bailey, Delila to William F. Letsinger 7-21-1857 (8-6-1857)
Bailey, Eliza to R. F. Houston 5-27-1863 (5-29-1863)
Bailey, Eliza M. to James Hickey 1-28-1862
Bailey, Martha A. to Thomas J. Miller 4-30-1861
Bailey, Milly to John W. Fritts 7-6-1858 (7-8-1858)
Baily, Emeline H. to John F. Williams 4-22-1857 (4-23-1857)
Baily, L. E. to R. E. Kenney 9-16-1864 (9-22-1864)
Bain, Malinda J. to Wm. S. Shipley 12-20-1872 (12-22-1872)
Baker, Lou E. to Mordicai S. Benton 10-6-1856 (10-7-1856)
Baker, Mary J. to Calaway H. Felts 12-2-1868 (12-3-1868)
Baldwin, Linda to Thomas Brackett 7-23-1856 (7-25-1856)
Baldwin, Mary J. to William Hashbarger 12-26-1874 (12-27-1874)
Baldwin, Melissa to John Brackett 1-14-1857 (1-15-1857)
Bales, Martha A. to M. M. Easter 2-4-1874 (2-5-1874)
Bales, Mary C. to M. M. Easter 5-8-1868 (5-10-1868)
Baley, M. J. to J. P. Renfro 4-24-1869 (4-25-1869)
Ballard, Fanny Ann to Chas. P. Taliaferro 8-30-1866 (9-11-1866)
Ballard, Mary A. to John H. Byrd 12-21-1867 (12-26-1867)
Ballard, Mary J. to JSames L. Wilson 9-13-1862
Barger, Harriet S. to James P. Keith 1-17-1874 (1-18-1874)
Barnard, Sarah F. to Arthur C. C. Erving 3-22-1858 (3-25-1858)
Barnard?, Margaret A. (Mrs.) to Richard S. Williams 9-9-1873
Barnes, Delilah to Eli West 9-5-1870
Barnett, Emaline to John Galyon 1-2-1860
Barnett, Henrietta to N. O. PeckASSSSf 1-22-1861
Barnett, Mollie M. to Henry P. Greene 9-7-1865
Barnwell, Rebecca to F. E. Houghton 9-25-1874 (9-26-1874)
Basket, Mary E. to Allen W. Thombrough 6-23-1859
Bates, Elizabeth F. to J. H. Derossett 10-23-1869 10-25-1869
Baurs, Margaret to M. W. Winters 10-4-1873 (10-5-1873)
Bazel, Nancy to Samuel Dunn 6-26-1874
Bazel, Susan to Tandy Gallamore 4-18-1864 (4-25-1864)

Roane County Brides

Beals, Malinda to George W. Newman 7-26-1870
Bear, Mary to John Majors 7-28-1868
Beard, Frances C. to Albert Myers 1-2-1867 (1-3-1867)
Bearden, Polly Ann to William C. Tacker 1-21-1856
Beaver, Dolly V. to Silas Fritts 5-29-1869
Beavers, Velorie to John Harmon 2-6-1864 (2-7-1864)
Been, Sarah A. E. to Henry Fritts 10-29-1856 (10-30-1856)
Begwell, Lucy Ann to Haywood Hood 10-26-1864 (10-27-1864)
Belew, Cyntha to Andrew Carter 7-3?-1862 (7-6-1862)
Belew, Martha J. to S. W. Lindsey 7-11-1867 (7-12-1867)
Belew, Mary E. to James P. Belew 10-22-1867
Belew, Surrelda J. to Thos. Bowling 5-2-1868 (5-3-1868)
Bell, Eliza J. to George Bell 6-18-1870
Bell, M. C. to J. N. Fritts 9-26-1868 (9-27-1868)
Bellew, Nancy to Luke Peak 3-31-1869
Benfield, Louisa to William Denham 9-29-1873
Bennett, Margaret to James Fentral 5-4-1870 5-5-1870
Berry, Emiline to Wm. J. Wright 1-11-1866
Bevens, Sarah to William Carroll 1-30-1858 (1-31-1858)
Bever, Nancy to Ezera J. Alger 3-24-1857
Bevllin, Susan to Jas. Hamilton 12-13-1868 (12-15-1868)
Bice, Malinda Jane to Samuel Carr 8-15-1865 (8-17-1865)
Biggs, Mary to James Wright 4-29-1864 (4-30-1864)
Bill, Mary E. to Joseph G. Rhea 7-4-1865 (7-15-1865)
Billings, M. D. to Samuel Roach 10-22-1874 (11-1-1874)
Billingsley, Mary E. to Samul W. Carter 9-29-1868 (10-1-1868)
Billingsley, Mary J. to John D. Gooden 1-2-1861
Billingsly, Eliza to John Fritts 4-23-1864
Billingsly, Elizabeth A. to Alexander Freels 10-30-1867 (10-31-1867)
Birchfield, Fanny to Lewis H. Fanscher 1-17-1872 (1-18-1872)
Bird, Mary J. to Saml. Sylvey 1-4-1865 (1-6-1865)
Black, Jenny Caroline to Marshall G. Hensley 2-26-1856 (3-2-1856)
Blackburn, Margaret E. to John A. Wells 9-2-1868 (9-6-1868)
Blackwell, Minerva A. to Wm. B. Holder 6-10-1869
Blackwell, Rebecca Jane to George A. Smicegood 10-6-1865 (10-8-1865)
Blair, Call E. to W. D. Johnson 8-23-1869 9-14-1869
Blair, Martha A. to G. W. St. John 4-20-1866 (5-10-1866)
Blair, Martha E. to W. N. B. Jones 11-24-1868 (11-26-1868)
Blair, Mary J. to J. Lafayett Johnson 2-14-1857 (2-12?-1857)
Blair, Sarah to B. M. Ledford 7-29-1863
Blair, Sarah J. to P. A. McKinzie 12-8-1856 (12-17-1856)
Blankenbicker, Clementine to Frank Burchfield 5-9-1874 (5-10-1874)
Blankenbicker, Jane to William Wallace 8-13-1867 (8-15-1867)
Blount, Hester V. to James S. Brown 6-27-1870 6-28-1870
Bogart, Lucinda to John Wilson 1-17-1856
Bogart, Margaret to R. B. Eldridge 3-15-1869 (3-18-1869)
Bogart, Mary to Wiley Wilson 1-7-1868 (1-9-1868)
Boling, Eliza to Samuel Hampson 9-21-1858 (9-23-1858)
Borum, Eleanor to William C. Bullen 1-2-1858 (1-3-1858)
Bouling, Linda to John Cates 9-19-1868 (9-20-1868)
Bowers, Ann to James A. Haire 2-14-1857 (2-17-1857)
Bowers, Caladonia to John D'Armond 10-28-1863 (10-29-1863)
Bowers, Catharine to J. H. Littleton 11-19-1874 (11-22-1874)
Bowers, Christenia to James C. Myres 12-26-1874 (12-27-1874)

Roane County Brides

Bowers, Mary E. to Patrick W. Evans 10-3-1866 (10-4-1866)
Bowers, Matilda to James D. Smith 10-29-1873 (10-13?-1873)
Bowers, Sarah C. to A. C. Dalton 9-18-1856
Bowers?, Nancy J. to Frank A. Russell 10-27-1873 (10-28-1873)
Bowles, Amanda to Wallace McCulley 8-21-1873 (8-24-1873)
Bowling, Hannah to Wm. Jackson 3-28-1865 (6-4-1865)
Bowman, Barsheban M. to Nicholas Johnson 10-23-1862
Bowman, Bashaba to Caloway Sharp 6-5-1858 (6-13-1858)
Bowman, Laura J. to R. B. V. Nipper 9-6-1863 (9-7-1865?)
Bowman, M. A. to William B. Soward 12-30-1863 (12-31-1863)
Bowman, Msary C. to William Whitlock 12-19-1857 (12-24-1857)
Bowman, Nancy to Samuel jr. Sharp 10-24-1860
Bowman, Nancy E. to Samuel R. S. Matheny 8-3-1857 (8-6-1857)
Bowman, Sarah E. to A. J. Snow 7-2-1866 (7-4-1866)
Bowman, Susan to W. M. Cox 2-25-1873
Boyd, Elizabeth to Aaron Hart 12-26-1860
Boyd, L. C. to W. P. Whitlock 6-6-1874 (6-14-1874)
Boyd, Maria P. to Wm. H. Dyke 12-16-1867 (12-19-1867)
Boyd, Mary M. to John W. Bacon 4-12-1871
Boyd, Mildred J. to John C. Gorin 8-19-1864
Boyd, Penina C. to Albert G. Wester ;5-12-1860
Boyd, Sallie to A. M. Johnson 12-24-1868 (12-23?-1868)
Boyd, Susan to W. M. R. Harwell 8-5-1867
Boyd, Susan to Wm. G. McCarroll 9-1-1868 (9-6-1868)
Boyle, Elizabeth to George Gallamore 7-23-1864 (2-24-1864)
Brackell, Malissa to John W. Whaley 10-7-1865 (10-8-1865)
Bracket, Mary E. to Francis Cook 1-8-1868 (1-9-1868)
Brackett, E. F. to T. F. Bailey 9-2-1870 9-4-1870
Brackett, Eliza to Stephen Brackett 6-13-1867 (6-16-1867)
Brackett, Mary A. to James A. Wirrick 10-27-1859
Brackett, Polly to William Shackelford 4-30-1857
Brackett, Polly Ann to Isaac J. Hammons 7-20-1865
Brackett, Sarah to William H. Selvidge 11-26-1856 (11-30-1856)
Bradley, Catharine to S.? W. Dail 10-24-1865
Bradley, Elizabeth to Wm. Staples 10-10-1865 (10-15-1865)
Bradley, Margaret A. to Jas. M. McKinney 8-16-1859 (8-17-1859)
Branaham, Malinda J. to Jefferson W. Kirkland 6-3-1867 (6-6-1867)
Branham, Emily to Elijah D. Lynn 10-25-1856 (10-26-1856)
Branham, Lucinda to Geo. W. Morrison 11-2-1867 (11-3-1867)
Branham, Martha Jane to James Burnett 6-5-1858
Branhom, Polly Ann to John Wilkerson 12-31-1857 (1-3-1858)
Brannom, Elizabeth to John Russell 6-20-1871 (6-21-1871)
Branom, Margaret to Thomas Strutton 5-19-1871 (5-20-1871)
Branson, Louisa to Wm. Phillips 8-15-1866 (8-16-1866)
Branson, Mary to J. C. Wells 4-9-1868
Branson, Mary D. to Adam M. Simpson 5-29-1873 (6-5-1873)
Branson, Polly to Ivy? Edwards 9-24-1856 (9-25-1856)
Brashears, Elizabeth C. to Absalom Cooper 9-30-1868 (10-1-1868)
Brashers, Mary Ann to Churchwell Hester 1-2-1865 (1-3-1865)
Brayshear, Elizabeth C. to L. T. Jenkins 3-20-1871
Breadle, Mary to Joseph Thompson 10-9-1867
Breaker, Elizabeth M. to W. T. Houser 11-1-1873 (11-2-1873)
Breashears, Rebecca E. to Wm. P. Byrd 10-1-1873 (10-2-1873)
Breashers, Margaret to Deaderick Kreis 12-24-1870 12-25-1870

Roane County Brides

Breazeale, Adaline to Columbus M. Duncan 10-19-1859
Breazeale, Amanda W. to Moses Ingram 7-4-1859
Breazeale, Elizabeth E. to William H. Brazeale 11-12-1858 (11-14-1858)
Breazeale, Isabella to James M. Bolt 2-12-1856
Breazeale, M. L. to W. M. Monger 1-23-1874 (1-25-1874)
Breazeale, Margaret to Andrew Cameron 11-13-1856 (11-23-1856)
Breazeale, Sarah J. to Charles F. Huffin 12-24-1873 (12-25-1873)
Breeden, Hannah J. to John H. Bacon 11-19-1867
Breeden, Lucinda to J. H. Bacon 4-27-1874
Brewer, Caroline to James Wycuff 11-2-1867
Brewer, Margaret to John B. Reynolds 7-11-1864 (7-21-1864)
Brewster, Amanda to Elisha Monroe 7-24-1860 (7-25-1860)
Britt, Amanda to Jas. McBride 2-4-1865 (2-5-1865)
Britt, Susan M. to Joseph Treadway 9-13-1865
Brogden, Catharine to Joseph Tuten 3-5-1859 (3-6-1859)
Brogden, Mary to James Campbell 2-7-1863 (2-8-1863)
Brogling, Sarah to William Tucker 12-8-1864
Brooks, Nancy A. to J. S. Fields 11-12-1867 (11-13-1867)
Brooks, Rebeca to Noah Suttle 4-4-1868 (4-5-1868)
Browder, Ella C. to W. T. Gallaher 10-16-1869 10-21-1869
Browder, Martha Jane to James H. Reynolds 11-18-1857
Browder, Mary to William W. Harvey 10-7-1856 (10-8-1856)
Brown, Amanda M. (Miss) to Wm. M. Wilson 10-26-1871
Brown, Caroline to Charels L. Downer 3-10-1864
Brown, Caroline to Samuel Martin 9-17-1869
Brown, Catharine to Rufus M. Kimbrough 3-8-1865
Brown, E. J. to W. P. Ragan 11-9-1872 (11-10-1872)
Brown, Eliza Jane to Wm. P. Martin 10-8-1856
Brown, Elizabeth to Thomas Patty 10-23-1856
Brown, Hannah to Wm. L. Wirick 9-17-1867 (9-18-1867)
Brown, Linda to William McCarroll 5-27-1863
Brown, Lucinda V. to Geo. L. Gillespie 8-12-1863 (8-13-1863)
Brown, Malinda to Elija Rayby 8-16-1865
Brown, Margaret to T. C. Odem 8-15-1874 (8-16-1874)
Brown, Martha R. to Wm. E. McElwee 12-11-1867 (12-12-1867)
Brown, Mary A. to John H. Cardwell 11-11-1871 (11-12-1871)
Brown, Mary E. to John R. Neal 11-13-1862
Brown, N. E. to J. P. Sharp 9-30-1873 (10-5-1873)
Brown, Nancy to F.? R. Miller 12-23-1874 (12-24-1874)
Brown, Nancy J. to Wm. H. Huffine 2-7-1873 (2-9-1873)
Brown, Rachel to John H. Coleman 5-5-1856 (5-6-1856)
Brown, Sarrah L. to Wm. Riley 3-7-1864 (3-11-1864)
Brown, Susan to Ransom P. Hilton 3-24-1868 (3-29-1868)
Brown, Susan to Absolem Whisenhunt 8-17-1859
Bruister, Adaline to Benjamin B. Burns 2-27-1866 (3-1-1866)
Bryant, Mary to Pleasant Sharp 4-25-1864 (5-1-1864)
Bullen, Lucinda to John R. Briggs 10-14-1868 (10-15-1868)
Bullen, Sarah C. to Lewis Y. Kagley 7-22-1861 (7-23-1861)
Buller, Sarah Ann to Marion McMullin 2-27-1864
Bullin, Amanda E. M. to Wm. H. Scarbrough 11-5-1865 (11-8-1865)
Bumpass, Elizabeth to John Henderson 12-27-1869
Bumpass, Emeline to William Rice 9-24-1867 (9-26-1867)
Bunn, F. J. to M. J. Fritts 11-6-1863
Burdine, Elizabeth to Jasper Clower 2-16-1856 (2-17-1856)

Roane County Brides

Burk?, Sarah E. to Jacob Luttrell 9-15-1863 (9-17-1863)
Burke, Eliza to James Burke 2-20-1873
Burke, Mary E. to F. H. Ferguson 11-8-1871 (11-9-1871)
Burnett, Clarissa J. to M. J. Burnett 6-8-1872 (6-10-1872)
Burnett, Eliza J. to T. J. Whitlock 11-8-1865 (11-9-1865)
Burnett, Mary A. to William A. Simpson 9-15-1857 (9-20-1857)
Burnett, Mary E. to Uriah S. Allison 3-5?-1864 (3-7-1864)
Burnett, Mary E. to James McLendin? 2-13-1869 (2-14-1869)
Burnett, Sarah to Wm. McCarroll 5-4-1871 (5-7-1871)
Burnett, Sarah E. to Houston Brown 11-4-1861 (11-12-1861)
Burnett, Saraphina to Robert Z. Roberts 4-19-1859
Burnett, Susan to Henry James 4-7-1864
Burns, Elizabeth C. to B. T. Hagler 6-9-1870 6-29-1870
Burns, Mary to B. F. Waddle 1-12-1865 (1-15-1865)
Burns, Nancy to Frederick Seber 8-9-1862
Burns, Prescilla to C. C. Walker 7-14-1870
Burns, Sarah L. to P. H. Watts 2-12-1873 (3-30-1873)
Burns, Susanna to R. A. Walker 4-1-1860
Burnum, Missouri C. to Wm. H. Davis 9-22-1869 9-26-1869
Burris, Amanda J. to Daniel Huffine 7-5-1861
Buse, Sarah J . to Thomas R. Gibbs 6-25-1870
Butler, Charlotte C. to Alfred M. Griffith 9-24-1864 (10-5-1864)
Butler, Cyntha C. to James M. Baker 2-10-1862 (2-13-1862)
Butler, Easter F. to John S. Smith 3-9-1872 (3-10-1872)
Butler, M. J. to F. A. Hood 4-9-1872 (4-11-1872)
Butler, Martha to Joel White 12-3-1873 (12-9-1873)
Butram, Margaret to Tho. T. Erwin 3-10-1870
Byerley, M. C. to S. A. Rodgers 10-22-1867 (10-30-1867)
Byerly, Sarah B. to Thos. J. Early 10-20-1856 (10-23-1856)
Byram, Margaret to David Mincey 7-20-1865
Byrd, Mary E. to Henry Mounger 9-11-1856
Byrd, Rebecca to Ezra R. Stinecipher 9-3-1866 (9-6-1866)
Byrd, Sarah R. to John H. Billingsley 1-16-1869 (1-17-1869)
Cables, Mary to Alonzo Harp 1-16-1875
Cade, M. L. to C. C. Crabtree 10-1-1873 (10-5-1873)
Cade, Martha A. to Nelson C. Redman 6-11-1861 (6-16-1861)
Cagle, Elizabeth Jane to Philip Hufstettler 8-20-1857
Cagle, Julia Ann to Brownlow Wright 8-23-1858 (8-24-1858)
Cagley, Christena J. to Frank George 8-4-1871
Cain, Mary to Calvin Lemus? 11-20-1860
Cain, Sarah to John R. Lawson 1-6-1858
Calaham, Elizabeth E. to Wm. D. Hampton 12-3-1867 (12-8-1867)
Campbell, Amanda C. to Robt Tootle 3-11-1868 (3-12-1868)
Campbell, Caroline to Robt. Clark 6-14-1864 (7-12-1864)
Campbell, Edda to T. L. Miller 9-9-1867 (9-10-1867)
Campbell, Elizabeth to T. P. Reynolds 10-29-1866 (11-4-1866)
Campbell, Lucinda J. to Jesse W. Murphey 10-19-1863 (10-20-1863)
Campbell, Margaret to A. M. Thompson 7-18-1873 (7-20-1873)
Campbell, Martha to Simeon Eaton 2-16-1871 (2-17-1871)
Campbell, Mary Jane to James M. Easter 8-31-1865 (9-3-1865)
Campbell, Mary S. to Isaac T. Whaley 8-7-1866 (8-16-1866)
Campbell, Rhoda E. to R. T. Baldwin 5-16-1873
Campbell, Rutha E. to Leander Stamper 12-24-1872 (12-26-1872)
Cannon, Margaret to James Roberts 8-17-1859

Roane County Brides

Capps, Sarah M. to William Rayborn 5-30-1857 (5-31-1857)
Carden, Sarrah E. to Abner Snow 4-19-1864 (4-23-1864)
Cardwell, Lizzie to James Steed 5-18-1867 (5-19-1867)
Cardwell, Nancy A. to Wm. W. Bogart 2-10-1870
Cardwell, Nancy E. to John H. Nunn 2-27-1858 (2-29-1858)
Carling?, _____ to _____ McEwen 11-28-1864 (12-1-1864)
Carol, Elizabeth to John Collins 6-10-1869 (6-13-1869)
Carpenter, Milberry to E. N. Wyrick 8-17-1871 (8-20-1871)
Carrimore, Sarah to Alfred Cook 8-5-1859
Carrol?, Lucinda to John Watts 1-27-1858 (1-28-1858)
Carroll, Amanda C. to James Brogdon 3-23-1858 (3-16-1858)
Carroll, Julinda to R. E. D. Clark 12-23-1872
Carroll, Lydia (Mrs.) to Allen L. King 8-2-1870 8-4-1870
Carroll, Margaret to John Harp 11-30-1858
Carroll, Mary to William Clark 8-5-1872 (8-8-1872)
Carroll, Parthena M. to John Ewell 8-6-1873 (8-7-1873)
Carroll, Sarah to Barton Dodson 2-19-1875
Carter, Adaline to Jackson Ervin 12-27-1869 12-28-1869
Carter, Ann E. to Ephraim H. Brown 8-30-1865
Carter, Caroline to Silvester F. Cormany 5-18-1857 (6-9-1857)
Carter, Charlotta to Robert W. Soward 7-26-1856 (7-27-1856)
Carter, E. C. to T. L. C. McClane 1-13-1866 (1-14-1866)
Carter, Eliza to Wm. Griffeths 1-7-1861 (1-10-1861)
Carter, Frances to David Lawson 4-27-1869 (4-28-1869)
Carter, Jane to John Baily 11-28-1865 (11-29-1865)
Carter, Lorinda to James T. Shelton 7-5-1866 (7-19-1866)
Carter, Manerva to Isaac N. Hembree 3-4-1858
Carter, Mary to O. P. Hill 11-5-1867 (11-7-1867)
Carter, Paulina E. to James A. Grigsby 8-14-1856 (8-21-1856)
Carter, S. A. C. to John Tomey 8-12-1868 (8-13-1868)
Carter, Sarah M. to Saml. J. Croswood 6-3-1869 (6-5-1869)
Carter, Sarena E. to Anthony W. Cardwell 5-18-1857 (5-20-1857)
Cassady, E. C. to W. M. Robinson 11-10-1874
Cassady, Sarah C. to G. T. Wilson 6-4-1867 (6-6-1867)
Cassady, Sarah J. to Gains R. Cox 3-5-1856 (3-8-1856)
Casteel, Eliza J. to J. C. McClellan no dates (with 1870)
Cate, Martha A. to Elias Kibble 5-21-1862
Cates, Lydia to Skelvin? Monday 11-5-1857
Cates, Margaret S. to Daniel G. Thompson 4-30-1873 (5-1-1873)
Cates, Nancy J. to Hugh Collins 12-6-1866 (12-13-1866)
Center, Nancy J. to E. A. Yost 11-10-1857
Chapman, Caroline to Wm. Thomas 1-15-1870 1-16-1870
Chapman, Tennessee to Henry Thrower 10-4-1862
Chapman, Tennessee J. to Jas. A. Harmon 8-1-1867
Chesser, Mary to Thos. McAllister 12-20-1864 (12-22-1864)
Childres, Mary G. to John B. Childress 10-27-1870
Childress, Martha to Abraham Cox 12-22-1864
Childress, Mary to James L. Stricklen 6-18-1863
Childress, Sarah L. to Walter B. Dalton 10-13-1863
Childs, Harriett to J. W. Sharp 3-2-1869
Choat, Sarah Ann to Leroy King 10-21-1864 (10-22-1864)
Chrisenberry, Teresa P. to G. W. Hembree 7-7-1869
Chrisp, Emelin to John Dixon 10-17-1868 (10-18-1868)
Chrisp, Nancy E. to William Hashbarger 11-14-1868 (11-15-1868)

Roane County Brides

Christenbury, Jane to William Dunlston? 8-25-1857
Christian, Amanda to John R. Hedgecock 7-25-1868 (7-26-1868)
Chumley, Elizabeth to T. M. Debary 9-16-1865 (9-17-1865)
Chumley, Elizabeth to T. M. Devoux 9-16-1866
Claibourn, Margaret A. to John T. Ambrose 6-1-1857
Clark, Catherine to James Allen 3-5-1864 (3-6-1864)
Clark, Elizabeth to N. W. Gersland 2-25-1868
Clark, Elizabeth C. to Martin Priddy 4-11-1860
Clark, Jane to William Abston 8-5-1873 (8-7-1873)
Clark, Jane to John M. Pope 3-2-1874 (3-5-1874)
Clark, Josee M. to T. J. Moss 12-17-1872 (12-19-1872)
Clark, Malinda J. to John E. Morrison 9-20-1862 (9-24-1862)
Clark, Margaret E. to Gideon P. Norman 10-15-1860
Clark, Martha to James H. Helton 1-6-1866 (1-7-1866)
Clark, Matilda C. to John T. Miller 10-6-1864
Clark, Nancy Ann to Charles Walker 10-4-1859 (10-8-1859)
Clark, Nancy J. to Wm. A. Porter 11-15-1866 (11-18-1866)
Clark, Sarah to John M. Tinel 10-3-1874 (7?-11-1874)
Clark, Sarah A. C. to Henry C. Duncan 3-12-1866 (3-15-1866)
Clark, Susan P. to John Murphey 10-11-1865 (10-12-1865)
Clark, Susan P. to John Murphy 10-12-1865 (10-13-1865)
Clavey, Vesta to Lindsey Mathis 6-11-1859 (6-12-1859)
Clemens, Mary to Saml. McCall 12-15-1863
Clouce, M. to M. Mahoney 3-19-1870 3-20-1870
Cloud, Martha M. to George Graham 8-19-1871 (8-20-1871)
Clower, Jerome? to William Long 8-14-1868 (8-16-1868)
Clower, Nancy J. to Elias Walker 3-17-1874 (3-19-1874)
Clower, Nancy L. to Jas. L. Wirick 12-9-1869 12-23-1869
Clower, Sarah J. to John M. Webb 6-5-1862 (6-8-1862)
Clowers, Mary Elizabeth to Joseph C. Johnson 3-29-1864 (4-9-1864)
Clowers, Rachel J. to Samuel G. Ball 1-10-1860
Clowers, Rachel Jane to Saml. G. Ball 1-10-1860
Cofer, Frances Malvina to Stephen A. Geasland 11-21-1858 (11-25-1858)
Cofer, Francess to Joel H. Isham 2-4-1858
Cofer, Hariet to Wm. D. Bagwell 8-6-1870 8-11-1870
Cofer, Martha W. to Thomas S. Harvey 10-26-1865
Cofer, Sarah L. to S. C. Haney 3-2-1871 (3-5-1871)
Cofer, Savannah to Geo. H. Delosier 12-4-1867 (12-5-1867)
Cofer, Susan C. to Jas. D. Tedder 10-3-1857 (10-6-1857)
Coffee, Harriet to Edwd. C. Roberts 3-13-1860 (3-18-1860)
Coker, Cinda E. to James R. Davis 2-22-1862
Coker, Elizabeth to Samuel C. Carter 4-3-1858 (4-4-1858)
Coker, Jane to John Fritts 6-3-1863 (6-4-1863)
Coldwell, Eliza M. to S. J. T. Johnson 10-13-1856 (10-14-1856)
Cole, Elizabeth to David Alley 8-1-1856
Cole, Mary to Thomas England 7-24-1860
Cole, Sarah A. to Daniel W. Fender 2-6-1856
Coleman, Sarah F. to John W. Inman 8-19-1864
Coley, Mary E. to Wiley Tutterow 8-28-1874 (8-30-1874)
Collet, Elizabeth to David Cook 7-24-1865 (7-25-1865)
Collet, Mary to George Cook 5-31-1871 (6-1-1871)
Collins, Mary to Jesse Knight 7-25-1867
Conner, A. E. to M. H. Haney 10-21-1865 (10-22-1865)
Cook, Caroline to F. B. Chapman 9-4-1862

Cook, Dicy to Sherwood Whitlock 4-10-1859 (4-21-1859)
Cook, Eliza to James McCamish 12-25-1864
Cook, Eliza J. to John Estes 9-14-1871
Cook, Eliza J. (Miss) to Thomas J. Haney 4-5-1873 (4-6-1873)
Cook, Elizabeth to J. J. Chumney 1-28-1860 (2-12-1860)
Cook, Elizabeth to William Leffew 8-19-1861 (8-22-1861)
Cook, Elizabeth to James? Roberts 4-17-1860
Cook, Emiline to James K. Taylor 5-22-1865 (5-23-1865)
Cook, Hannah C. to Samuel J. Hope 4-20-1867 (4-21-1867)
Cook, Lucretia to Jasper N. McAnally 2-5-1859 (2-14-1859)
Cook, Margaret A. to James M. Grubb 2-23-1867 (3-10-1867)
Cook, Martha to S. P. Delaney 5-15-1869 (5-16-1869)
Cook, Martha J. to James M. Scarborough 9-2-1867 (9-5-1867)
Cook, Sarah J. to John E. Parson 5-22-1872 (5-26-1872)
Cook, Visey Ann to Fielding Estes 12-18-1872 (12-19-1872)
Cooley, Elizabeth to Winfield Sopsher 7-25-1867 (7-28-1867)
Cooley, Farley Ann to Jesse Everett 7-17-1857 (7-19-1857)
Cooley, Martha to Saml. Doran 6-17-1870 6-19-1870
Cooley, Martha C. to Jesse Cooly 9-4-1868
Cooley, Mary to Thomas J. Hensley 12-5-1872 (12-8-1872)
Cooley, Mary J. to Allen Buckner 1-2-1868 (1-5-1868)
Cooley, Nancy E.(Mary?) to Daniel M. Carter 4-30-1864 (5-1-1864)
Cooley, Nancy Jane to George W. Johnson 8-23-1859 (8-25-1859)
Cooley, Rachel M. to Bayless W. Billings 8-27-1873 (8-31-1873)
Cooley, Sarah J. to Wm. F. Kile 7-27-1870 7-28-1870
Cooly, Elizabeth to John Christian 11-27-1856 (11-13-1857?)
Cooly, Nancy A. to John H. Kings 7-21-1860
Coons, Juiley? to Michael Fleming 3-23-1865 (3-24-1865)
Cooper, Letha A. to Franklin White 3-7-1867 (3-12-1867)
Cooper, M. J. to Wm. J. Cofer 5-26-1869 (5-27-1869)
Cooper, Mary E. to Taylor Chiles 7-11-1871 (7-17-1871)
Cooper, Sarah C. to Isaac Whitson 5-16-1865 (5-18-1865)
Cooper, Thursey Ann to Alfred G. Watson 2-4-1867 (2-7-1867)
Copeland, Catharine to John Belew 8-4-1862
Copeland, Elizabeth to Benj. F. Kenner 12-22-1860
Copeland, Elizabeth J. to Samuel A. Davis 1-23-1871 (1-26-1871)
Copeland, Mary to George W. Cluff 12-26-1866 (1-27-1866?)
Copeland, Ruth to Franklin B. Grubb 7-18-1865 (7-20-1865)
Copeland, Sarah Ann to John D. Belew 8-15-1865
Copland, M. J. to J. F. Linsey 11-5-1875
Corbin, Mary Jane to J. L. Keith 7-16-1870 7-17-1870
Cormany, Rachel F. A. to William R. Littleton 5-2-1857 (8-9-1857)
Couch, Lucinda to James Nelson 10-10-1864 (10-12-1864)
Couston, Sarah to William Wallace 10-27-1868 (11-2-1868)
Couvy?, B. J. to Robert Viar 8-20-1866 (not executed)
Cowan, Sarah E. to John H. Soward 9-14-1866 (9-16-1866)
Coward, Mary to James Frady 7-16-1859
Coward, Mary A. to Wayne French 7-11-1866 (7-12-1866)
Cox, Amanda D. to James Liles 8-5-1861
Cox, Caroline C. to Wm. C. Davis 9-26-1866 (9-30-1866)
Cox, Louisa to Rufus S. Breeden 8-26-1861 (8-27-1861)
Cox, Malinda to Samuel T. Briggs 11-2-1870 11-3-1870
Cox, Margaret F. to William D. Brashers 7-12-1865 (7-13-1865)
Crabtree, Mary J. to Levi Newcomb 5-21-1873 (5-22-1873)

Roane County Brides

Crabtree, Sarah Ann to James M. Carroll 6-28-1859
Crace, Nancy C. to Joseph Bradham? 6-30-1865
Crase, Elizabeth to Allen Smith 7-19-1873 (7-20-1873)
Crass, Mary G. to Rufus J. Halburt 4-7-1871 (4-9-1871)
Crawford, Malinda to John Conly 6-3-1874 (6-4-1874)
Crews, Rutha E. to William H. Letsinger 8-28-1858 (8-31-1858)
Crisp, Jane to John Niceley 3-13-1861
Crisp, Rutha to William Letner 5-12-1858
Cristenbury, Louis Isabella to William Turpen 2-29-1864 (2-25?-1864)
Cristian, Minerva to Wetherford G. Barnwell ;12-1-1856
Crocket, Margaret E. to Meredith jr. Sharp 8-29-1862 (8-30-1862)
Crockett, Sarah P. to Gideon M. Dennis 11-3-1865 (11-5-1865)
Cross, Matilda J. to Charles J. Robinson 10-23-1867 (10-24-1867)
Crouch, Emily Jane to L. M. Jenkins 2-12-1862
Crow, Caroline to Walter B. Dalton 9-22-1857
Crow, De Annah to James D. Barnett 2-22-1859 (2-23-1859)
Crow, Eliza Jane to Zachrih Cofer 8-17-1868 (8-20-1868)
Crow, Elizabeth to Samuel H. Littleton 12-5-1871 (12-7-1871)
Crow, M. C. to W. B. Underwood 10-24-1871
Crow, Margaret to James W. Robinson 12-17-1873 (12-18-1873)
Crow, Sarah C. to T. W. Weatherford 2-2-1874 (2-4-1874)
Crow, Sarah W. to Franklin K. Center 11-21-1859
Crowder, Amelia J. to Wm. A. Bacon 5-24-1865 (5-25-1865)
Crowder, Margaret to James J. Barnard 4-1-1869 (4-4-1869)
Crowder, Melinda C. to George W. Barnard 1-5-1857 (1-8-1857) *
Crowder, Nancy J. to Isaac N. Eblen 9-14-1857 (9-15-1857)
Crowder, S. K. to A. S. Bacon 5-16-1868
Crumbless, Mary to Alexander Tuck 10-6-1858 (10-7-1858)
Crumpley, Mary E. to Richard Turnbill 5-13-1859 (5-19-1859)
Crumpley, Ruth to Jonathan Edgmond 10-21-1871 (10-22-1871)
Crutchfield, Adaline to Charles Bearden 9-18-1873
Culveyhouse, Maryann to A. J. M. Miller 3-24-1864
Culvyhouse, Rosannah to Samuel P. Robinson 6-26-1858 (6-27-1858)
Cummings, Calafornia to George Morrow 1-23-1871
Cundiff, M. C. to M. V. Burns 3-3-1871 (3-5-1871)
Cundiff, Mary E. to A. E. Ford 11-8-1873 (11-9-1873)
Cunningham, Elanor W. to Rufus F. Kendrick 8-25-1860
Cunningham, Theodocia to Lemuel Burgess 7-6-1870 7-10-1870
Currier?, Nancy J. to G. W. Turpin 7-24-1867 (7-25-1867)
Currin, Susannah to James Cox 8-24-1860
Cuthbertson, Tabitha? to John M. Honeycutt 7-13-1865 (7-19-1865)
Cynthia(last name?), Mary A. to Jacob W. Foust 1-20-1875
D'Armand, Julia M. to Wiley M. Christian 3-20-1866
D'Armand, Mahala to Wm. B. Nichols 7-28-1866 (7-29-1866)
D'Armond, G. J. to F. M. Wylie 6-25-1861 (6-26-1861)
D'Armond, Maria to Wm. Lea 5-23-1868 B
Dail, Martha E. to Ellis M. Devaney 10-8-1868
Dail, Mary to A. J. McAllen 12-7-1872 (12-8-1872)
Dail, Nancy E. to James W. Peters 8-2-1865
Dalton, Elizabeth to Samul Leftgo? 9-16-1868 (9-17-1869?)
Dalton, Sarah to John Marney 11-21-1867
Daniel, Amy to George H. Lea 2-4-1860
Daniel, Amy to George H. Lea 2-4-1860 (2-1?-1860)
Daniel, Nancy E. to James M. Magill 3-1-1872 (3-5-1872)

Roane County Brides

Daniels, Elizabeth J. to Joseph E. Melton 4-19-1866 (4-21?-1866)
Davidson, Mary A. to John H. Copeland 10-2-1866 (10-4-1866)
Davis, Calie to George Ralston 4-9-1869
Davis, Elizabeth to Thos. J. Staples 5-21-1870 5-22-1870
Davis, Elizabeth to James M. Sylvey 12-14-1864 (12-29-1864)
Davis, Jane to Caleb Conner 7-16-1859
Davis, Lucinda to James G. Smith 1-14-1870 2-14-1870
Davis, Malinda to Jackson Stubbs 11-1-1858
Davis, Margaret to Thomas C. Ruggles 10-31-1867
Davis, Margaret to Wm. H. Underwood 10-24-1872
Davis, Martha to Henry Watkins 6-25-1870
Davis, Mary to Joseph S. Davis 5-16-1872
Davis, Mary to Samuel H. Johnson 2-7-1872 (2-8-1872)
Davis, Mary Ann to Hugh Evans 4-20-1872
Davis, Mary J. to Arthur Edwards 2-8-1873 (4-13-1873)
Davis, Mary J. to James McCamy 2-21-1874 (2-22-1874)
Davis, Nancy to Wm. Shubart 1-25-1873 (1-26-1873)
Davis, Nancy Ann to Lenzey Liles 8-16-1858 (8-26-1858)
Davis, Rachel to James T. Weatherford 12-21-1869 12-26-1869
Davis, Sarah M. to W. W. Fleming 3-7-1866
Davis, Selina to Charles J. Williams 9-27-1873 (10-12-1873)
Davis, Susan(Miss) to Wm. Smith 1-6-1872 (1-17-1872)
Davis, Susanah to Warren Quartermous 2-7-1857 (2-8-1857)
Davis, Virginia to John F. Medford 3-23-1864 (3-4?-1864)
Davis, Winney to Thomas Boyd 6-11-1865 (7-2-1865)
Dawson, Jane Z. to Martin V. Vann 8-1-1865 (8-3-1865)
Day, Patsy to John Whaley 7-28-1858 (8-5-1858)
Day, Sarah E. to Wm. C. King 7-13-1865 (7-20-1865)
De Armand, Susan E. to Ephraim Langley 11-7-1866 (11-8-1866)
Dean, Lucretia to Arch Pass 4-8-1874 (4-9-1874)
Dean, Martha C. to William F. Kelsay 6-30-1874 (7-1-1874)
Dean, Susan to William Webb 11-26-1862
Deatherage, Catherine to John O. Pollard 1-12-1859
Deatherage, Martha to O. B. Fuller 11-26-1867
Deatherage, Martha to Saml. Graham 8-13-1869 8-19-1869
Deatherage, Mary A. to C. C. Durham 4-22-1863
Deatherage, Nancy L. to Daniel N. Clower 5-7-1859 (5-8-1859)
Deatherage, Sarah A. to Samuel H. Williams 9-12-1867
Deatherige, Elizabeth J. to John D. Pope 1-17-1867 (1-20-1867)
Deatherige, Margaret to D. J. Coalman 12-21-1870 12-22-1870
Deatherige, Nancy C. to Albert C. Guffie 4-17-1866 (4-19-1866)
Deathrage, Mahaily to Ruben Lacy 11-3-1868 (11-4-1868)
Deavenport, Margaret S. to John H. Butler 9-1-1857
Delaney, Arminta A. to John N. A. Moore 11-9-1869 11-10-1869
Delaney, Mary J. to Robert L. Moore 7-28-1870 7-31-1870
Delany, Caroline M. to John Mounger 11-11-1874 (11-12-1874)
Delany, Mary J. to Jacob Mayton 12-24-1873 (12-31-1873)
Delcyris?, Susan E. to John C. Martin 10-1-1868 (10-4-1868)
Delezier, Malinda C. to James M. McDuffie 5-4-1860
Delezin, Enarcha W. to W. O. Ellis 7-7-1859 (7-21-1859)
Delosier, Amanda C. to Samuel J. Hendrickson 4-17-1869 (4-18-1869)
Delosier, Louisa J. to Thomas C. Blevins 8-10-1867 (8-11-1867)
Delosier, Martha C. to John N. McCoy 9-4-1867 (9-5-1867)
Delosier, Martha M. to W. D. Kelsay 12-22-170 12-22-1870

Roane County Brides

Delosier, Mary J. to Elijah Isham 1-10-1871 (1-11-1871)
Delosier, Sarah C. to Moses F. Millican 10-25-1866
Delozier, Margaret to Thos. L. Goddard 10-11-1860
Demming, Mary J. to Seth Alley 12-24-1860
Dennis, Arminda to Robt. Campbell 12-19-1865 (12-24-1865)
Dennis, Cynthia J. to Newton S. Miller 4-29-1868 (5-7-1868)
Dennis, Della M. to William Grimes 8-7-1868 (8-16-1868)
Deputy, MSary to Simpson Foster 5-17-1858
Derruitt?, Patsy to Robert N. Martin 2-12-1857
Devaney, Ann to Charles Absten 5-19-1857
Devaney, Elizabeth to W. A. Aughinbaugh 12-7-1869
Dever, Rachel C. to Hugh L. Bolden 7-9-1858
Devers, Lurina J. to William Belew 5-7-1857
Dickey, Sophronia C. to Henry A. Waller 11-12-1866 (11-15-1866)
Dickson, Lucinda to George W. Branham 11-11-1856
Diggs, Frances C. to Samuel J. Bailey 5-21-1867 (5-23-1867)
Dillinger, Martha C. to Walker Pierce 11-11-1873
Dines?, Lucinda to John Rayby 10-20-1866 (10-21-1866)
Dinkins, Eliza to Wiley Kearsey 12-19-1866 (12-20-1866)
Dixon, Malinda to James Davis 1-22-1857
Dixon, Mary D. to John N. Hill 3-25-1871 (3-26-1871)
Dixon, Providence B. to Calvin M. Liles 1-8-1866 (1-9-1866)
Dizney, Rachel A. to Thomas Johnson 10-3-1860
Dodson, Dicey to Alfred Cook 12-18-1856 (12-19-1856)
Dodson, Sarah E. to Thos. N. Upton 9-4-1874 (9-6-1874)
Donlap, M. J. to S. L. King 7-22-1868 (7-25-1868)
Dorm?, Emily to Thomas Gibson 9-13-1864
Doss, Margaret J. to C. S. Peak 6-25-1863
Dosson, Margaret M. to John Ghormley 3-20-1860
Dosson, Sarah C. to H. H. Ghormley 3-13-1860 (3-18-1860)
Doughty, A. M. to William H. Venzant 6-23-1874
Dridman?, Nancy E. to Robert Luffman 8-14-1865 (8-19-1865)
Duff, Ellen C. to Jas. P. Allen 10-2-1869 10-10-1869
Duff, Margaret A. to Robert W. Davis 11-22-1858 (11-23-1858)
Duff, Margaret E. to H. H. Shinpaugh 7-25-1866 (7-26-1866)
Duff, Martha E. to Joseph Kollick 10-6-1863
Duff, Mary E. to James D. Davis 3-10-1858 (3-11-1858)
Duker, Darcus Ann to Samuel McMillon 5-29-1858 (5-30-1858)
Dullon, Elizabeth to Benj. Luffman 2-1-1864
Dumar?, Sarah to William Wycuff 4-5-1870 4-6-1870
Duncan, Eliza P. to Hugh L. Shinpaugh 12-10-1866 (12-13-1866)
Duncan, Margaret E. to A. M. Magill 2-21-1857 (2-22-1857)
Duncan, Martha E. to Samuel A. Daniels 5-26-1866 (5-27-1866)
Duncan, Parthena to Edward Rasin 1-28-1858
Dunn, Nancy to Charles Glass 10-8-1872 (10-10-1872)
Durrett, Polly to John Fergerson 4-24-1869 (4-25-1869)
Dutton, Susannah to William M. Hall 12-9-1858
Dyer, Sarah J. to Andrew T. Cash 10-18-1865
Dyke, Susan to Caswell Henderson 12-17-1857
Dykes, Malinda to Wm. P. Proffitt 8-30-1866
East, M. J. to W. T. Bodine 8-11-1874 (8-13-1874)
East, Sallie to William Jolley 4-9-1870 4-10-1870
East, Sarah E. to J. S. Keylon 8-26-1874 (8-27-1874)
Easter, Elizabeth to Eli M. Galyon 12-18-1857 (12-20-1857)

Roane County Brides

Easter, Malinda to Frank Cook 3-21-1873 (3-27-1873)
Easter, Margaret J. to Robt. M. Wyrick 7-11-1872 (7-14-1872)
Easter, Martha to Wm. P. Nipper 8-22-1866 (8-25-1866)
Easter, Martha J. to Wm. P. Nelson 10-20-1866 (10-23-1866)
Easter, Mary to M. L. Cooke 4-6-1867 (4-7-1867)
Easter, Matilda to Jeremiah Selvige 10-10-1874
Easter, Rhoda to John S. Russell 10-4-1860 (10-7-1860)
Easter, Sarah to Benjamin F. Hensley 8-22-1866 (8-31-1866)
Easter, Susan to James Beeler 3-14-1863
Eaton, Amanda to Joshua A. Carter 11-23-1864
Eaton, Elizabeth to Geo. Smith 8-19-1863
Eaton, Elizabeth J. to Rawlings Carter 12-19-1865
Eaton, Malinda to Dennis Carroll 4-30-1870 5-1-1870
Ebbens, Lillie F. to M. L. Lynch 11-18-1873
Eblen, Amanda E. to J. W. Harvey 4-5-1869 (4-8-1869)
Eblen, Eliza to Wiley Houston Wheat 10-16-1857 (10-18-1857)
Eblen, Lucinda to Jesse F. Jordan 11-20-1857
Eblen, Martha to John V. Jordan 10-21-1857 (10-22-1857)
Eblen, Mary to Robert Wilkison 2-27-1869 (3-4-1869)
Eblen, Nancy Ann to Saml. D. Richardson 9-22-1857 (9-23-1857)
Eblen, Nancy J. to Wm. F. Littleton 1-23-1873 (1-26-1873)
Eblen, Rebecca Jane to Elijah Isham 10-6-1857
Eblen, Sarah J. to J. W. Duff 7-25-1866 (8-1-1866)
Edes, Mary J. to T. J. McDonald 10-18-1867 (10-19-1867)
Edes, Ruth S. to C. O. McLean 11-12-1866 (11-15-1866)
Edgmon, Mary to Samuel H. Walker 9-16-1873 (9-18-1873)
Edgmon, Sarah to Andrew J. Wade 9-10-1862 (9-13-1862)
Edgmond, Martha J. to Gideon P. Morrison 11-14-170 11-15-1870
Edmonds, Mary J. to Wm. H. Hout 1-6-1865
Edwards, Allice to John Marney 8-19-1869
Edwards, Catharine to Wm. P. White 9-15-1869 not solemnized
Edwards, Cornelia A. to J. A. May 6-30-1860 (7-2-1860)
Edwards, Elizabeth A.(N.?) to Eli May 10-30-1872
Edwards, Jemima to James L. Bowman 11-3-1856 (11-6-1856)
Edwards, Josephine to Joseph F. McMahan 2-6-1858 (2-7-1858)
Edwards, Mary to Samul H. Roberts 10-22-1868
Edwards, Mary E. to John Mullins 1-28-1860 (1-29-1860)
Edwards, Sarafina to Noah Fentral 4-24-1869 (4-25-1869)
Eldridge, Sarah J. to Rufus Wilson 2-19-1859
Elkins, J. Evaline to William J. Hamilton 11-24-1860
Eller, Amanda to Tho. W. Hughes 12-8-1869 12-9-1869
Elliot, Mary Jane to Elijah Hill 11-15-1865 (11-16-1865)
Ellis, Elizabeth to Henry C. Wester 9-15-1869 9-19-1869
Ellis, Hannah C. to Wm. A. Cook 12-20-1865 (12-24-1865)
Ellis, M. A. M. to J. F. Harvey 10-24-1867
Ellis, Mary E. to John T. Phillips 11-19-1866 (11-20-1866)
Ellis, Parthena to Wm. Whitlock 5-2-1874 (5-3-1874)
Ellis, Rebecca C. to William Kimbrough 8-16-1856
Ellis, Sarah to Wm. Retherford 5-13-1865 (5-14-1865)
Ellis, Sarah J. to Thomas H. Sturges 11-28-1866 (11-29-1866)
Ellis, Susan W. to John Brient 9-28-1865 (9-29-1865)
England, Mary A. to John Hill 6-11-1864
England, Mary J. to William A. Clemens 3-17-1860
England, Misorina to Willis Adkins 5-25-1861 (5-28-1861)

Roane County Brides

English, Rhoda E. to Peter H. Slagle 10-27-1868 (10-29-1868)
Enochs, Edney to Casper Miller 11-21-1874 (11-22-1874)
Enochs, Mary A. to William McCoy 3-19-1863
Enox, Rebecca to James Poland 10-25-1865
Ervin, Martha to Saml. McMillen 9-13-1873 (9-14-1873)
Erwin, Amanda to James Stringfield 1-2-1867
Erwin, Caroline M. to Henry B. Woody 11-23-1864 (11-24-1864)
Eskridge, Eliza to Daniel Martin 7-30-1870 B
Estabrook, A. M. to W. J. Hornsby 7-23-1868
Estes, Delilah to Francis M. Bates 5-1-1867 (5-5-1867)
Estes, Lucy A. to Henry Fortner 10-20-1860
Estrige, Caroline E. to Josiah Fortner 5-2-1861 (5-4-1861)
Evans, Catharine to Stephen Richison 8-19-1865 (8-20-1865)
Evans, Catharine J. to King W. Grubb 9-12-1866 (9-13-1866)
Evans, Lucinda C. to Wm. L. Edmondson 1-20-1866 (1-21-1866)
Evans, M. J. to J. P. Glover 7-13-1867 (7-14-1867)
Evans, Margaret J. to Andrew Solomon 1-10-1870 1-11-1870
Evans, Nancy to Evan Davis 4-24-1869 (5-11-1869)
Evans, Susan E. to Joseph McKinney 2-15-1859
Everett, Cynthia J. to James Clark 11-14-1856
Everett, Margaret H. R. E. to Verlian H. Thompson 8-18-1856
Everitt, Sarah J. to Samel J. Everitt 12-2-1868 (12-6-1868)
Everrett, MSary to Jefferson Alexander 11-19-1859 (11-24-1859)
Everton, Sarah to William Shoebert 5-6-1869 (5-7-1869)
Ezell, Amanda to E. Richmond 2-28-1865 (3-1-1865)
Fagan, Ann to T. J. Stewart 11-1-1870 11-2-1870
Fapp, Malinda to Hiram H. Carroll 6-16-1870
Farmer, Fanny to Martin Cox 12-12-1860
Farmer, Lucy Hale to Robert Overton 9-19-1860
Farmer, Margaret E. to Samuel W. Crow 7-9-1870 7-10-1870
Farmer, Mary J. to D. R. Littleton 12-22-1872 (12-26-1872)
Farmer, Matilda A. to Joshua Cooley 12-28-1869
Farner, Mary A. to William Carroll 4-19-1856
Farriss, Catharine to Benj. Sword? 5-26-1864 (5-27-1864)
Fauscher, Lina to Jacob Heins 3-11-1870 3-12-1870
Felts, Maranthas J. to Stephen Wells 9-7-1860
Felts, Phebe E. to James B. Pickins 10-10-1856 (10-12-1856)
Fender, Margaret A. to Archibald R. Hartman 11-27-1861 (12-1-1861)
Fields, Matilda to Lewis B. McKinney 11-27-1865 (12-12?-1865)
Fifer, Nancy J. to William L. Thompson 10-5-1859 (10-6-1859)
Finch?, Martha to J. S. E. Bane? 12-16-1859
Finder?, Winney C. to Elijah Crudgington 10-7-1856
Fink, Sarah J. to Saml. Soard 3-3-1873
Fisher, Laura to W. F. Baily 8-11-1868 (8-13-1868)
Fitts, Melvina to Dewitt C. Abbot 7-28-1857 (7-30-1857)
Fleming, M. E. to G. Taylor 5-23-1871 (5-23-1871)
Fleming, Nancy A. to Thomas Milsaps 9-26-1873 (9-27-1873)
Floyd, Mary to Pleasant Leffew 6-9-1856 (6-10-1856)
Floyd, Mary H. to Geo. Pickelsammers 12-28-1865 (11?-30-1865)
Fondered, Nancy Ann to James Bett 7-31-1865
Ford, Mary E. to George W. Green 8-5-1873
Forester, Nancy J. to Wm. Owens 6-28-1873
Forguson, Lucinda P. to G. W. Easter 9-7-1860 (9-20-1860)
Forister, Matilda F. to George W. Fuller 12-22-1860

Roane County Brides

Forrester, Elizabeth to Josiah Hughes 2-23-1863
Forrister, Catharine to Jas. W. Russell 12-15-1874
Fortner, Arty J. to Jas. E. Carroll 7-11-1864 (7-24-1864)
Fortner, Martha to William Morten 5-2-1862 (5-8-1862)
Foster, Elizabeth to Ambrose Russell 12-24-1872 (12-25-1872)
Foster, Martha J. to Wm. Petty 7-29-1867
Fouse, Margaret to James Black 1-11-1865 (1-12-1865)
Fox, Eliza Jane to Jasper Billings 1-28-1868 (1-30-1868)
Francis, Selina to Silas M. Helton 8-4-1860 (8-5-1860)
Franklin, Mahaly A. to Joseph Brandon 6-25-1873
Frazier, Metilda to Daniel Arndel 10-26-1859 (10-27-1859)
Freeh, Mary V. to Francis M. Clack 7-25-1856
Freeh, Susannah to Jacob Watt 11-22-1856 (11-23-1856)
Freelds, Sarah E. to George W. Belew 7-25-1863
Freels, Melia to Geoge Butler 9-17-1870
Freeman, Frances E. to Henry M. Bogart 1-7-1859 (1-9-1859)
Freeman, R. E. to Joseph Chaney 8-15-1874 (8-16-1874)
Frees, Mary A. to Wm. S. Crockett 5-11-1865 (5-14-1865)
French, Alzy to Saml. McCollum 8-7-1869 8-10-1869
Frith, Catharine to James Burnett 11-24-1858
Fritts, Caroline to R. A. Beaver 7-20-1869
Fritts, Ellen to Alvin J. Irons 3-7-1863
Fritts, Malinda to Chas. Johnson 4-20-1867 (4-23-1867)
Fritts, Malinda C. to W. H. McDermond 7-3-1864 (8-4-1864)
Fritts, Permelia to John D. Reeves 1-3-1866 (1-4-1866)
Fritts, Rebecca O.? to Jasper Fritts 11-20-1860
Fritts, Sarah J. to William N. Fritts 2-1-1860 (2-2-1860)
Fryar, Cynthia T. to William H. King 11-26-1867 (11-28-1867)
Fryar, Flora A. to J. F. Shelton? 8-21-1869
Fryar, Sarah E. to Wm. B. Shelton 12-1-1865 (12-7-1865)
Fuller, Elizabeth to James Clowers 10-19-1865 (10-29-1865)
Fuller, Florentha J. to Samuel B. Cook 7-25-1856 (7-31-1856)
Fuller, Margaret J. to Zachariah Amos 6-13-1866
Fuller, Margarett E. to J. N. Rowden 9-1-1868 (9-3-1868)
Fuller, Mary Emaline to Calvin Crabtree 8-4-1858
Fuller, Rhoda A. to James H. Keelin 8-7-1872 (8-8-1872)
Furgerson, Eliza to Calvin M. Brown 11-19-1872 (11-21-1872)
Furgerson, Josie to Joseph D. Bowling 10-26-1872 (10-27-1872)
Furgerson, Margaret A. to John Easter 8-20-1868 (9-24-1868)
Gage, Sarah J. to Henry H. Dennis 2-11-1870 2-13-1870
Gallaher, Amelia to Stephen Bradley 3-31-1870 4-3-1870
Gallaher, Maggie to Tho. J. Russell 5-20-1874 (5-21-1874)
Gallaher, Mary M. to P. T. McCroskey 12-22-1858 (12-23-1858)
Gallaher, Sarah E. to John F. Browder 3-11-1862 (3-12-1862)
Gallamore, Julia A. to John Miles 3-18-1871 B
Gallimore, Caroline to James Taylor 2-14-1862 (2-23-1862)
Gallimore, Nancy J. to Wiley Cockam 2-6-1861 (2-7-1861)
Gallimore, Susan to William A. Benge 5-4-1863
Gallyan, Tempy to David R. Crockett 8-2-1860
Galyon, Betsey Jane to Rufus M. Wirick 1-17-1860
Galyon, Eliza L. to F. W. Taylor 11-5-1867 (11-14-1867)
Galyon, Mary to Mark S. Miller 10-12-1859
Galyon, Sarah G. to David R. Crockett 9-19-1870 9-19-1870
Galyon, V. L. to Wm. E. Passe? 11-12-1867 (11-14-1867)

Roane County Brides

Gamble, D. E. to R. L. Hooker 4-6-1865
Gamble, Margaret E. to F. E. Apperson 12-27-1865
Gambol, Sarah A. to David R. Johnson 1-19-1865
Gammon, Mary E. to John West 3-25-1859 (3-31-1859)
Gammon, Mary M. to Samuel Right 1-14-1857 (1-15-1857)
Gammon, Mary M. to William Right 12-8-1856
Gammon, Rachel Lavica to Charles Amos Hodge 8-19-1858 (9-1-1858)
Gardenhire, Paralee to Wm. C. Rather 5-4-1874 (5-10-1874)
Gardner?, Cora? to J. E. Plumadore 10-15-1862 (10-16-1862)
Gardnierr, Caroline to B. F. Roberts 8-12-1871 (8-13-1871)
Garland, Elizabeth B. to James L. Randolph 2-26-1869 (2-27-1869)
Garland, Martha J. to George W. Fitch 10-19-1861
Garland, Mary M. to William R. Cundiff 10-27-1858 (10-28-1858)
Garner, Malinda to T. J. Farris 9-23-1869
Gerron, Amanda to John Gregory 9-25-1864
Getgood, Caroline to John Duggan 12-27-1864 (12-28-1864)
Getgood, Sarah to William Hudgins 7-5-1859
Gibbs, Susanah to Levi C. Hipps 3-19-1866
Gibson, Martha Ann to James A. Duff 1-20-1858
Gideon, Sarah J. to F. M. Kitrell 5-8-1865 (5-11-1865)
Gilbert, N. E. to B. L. Warren 2-7-1865
Giles, Martha to Samul H. Bell 1-7-1873 (1-9-1873)
Giles, Mary E. to G. M. Bowman 5-14-1864 (5-15-1864)
Gill, Eliza N. to James Prater 12-30-1863
Gillam, Rebbecca A. to Franklin Raehl? 3-4-1874 (3-5-1874)
Gillem, Elizabeth S. to Charles Bauer 7-18-1872
Gillespie, Caroline to Moses Butler 5-23-1868 B
Gillum, Letha A. to C. C. Green 9-16-1871 (9-21-1871)
Girley, Sarah L. to Wm. H. Chaney 9-2-1872 (9-5-1872)
Gitgood, Sarah to John Carmichael 5-13-1859 (6-3-1859)
Gladen, M. J. to G. W. Briant 11-20-1874
Godard, Alice to John Woolsey 3-27-1873
Godby, Emma R. to S. P. Evans 12-26-1868 (12-27-1868)
Goddard, Elizabeth R. to August B. Hacker 3-29-1856
Godsey, Phoebe to Isaac Bowling 3-12-1874 (3-13-1874)
Goldston, Sarah C. to John Johnston 1-31-1872 (1?-1-1872)
Gooden, Polly to James M. Carroll 2-4-1868 (2-6-1868)
Goodman, Elizabeth C. to M. A. Staples 2-2-1872 (2-5-1872)
Goodman, Margaret E. to William F. Miller 4-11-1856 (4-12-1856)
Goodman, Sarah to James Winchester 4-29-1868 (5-3-1868)
Gooram?, Margaret T. to Henry Isham 2-26-1867
Gottard, Dotty? to C. L. Turk 7-26-1864 (7-28-1864)
Gowings, Adaline to Tobias Gallimore 10-8-1863
Graham, Malinda E. to Anderson Godsey 11-5-1867 (11-7-1867)
Grammer, Margaret E. to Wm. Galston 2-11-1871 (2-12-1871)
Grammer, Mary to John L. Thompson 11-1-1871 (11-2-1871)
Grant, Anna to John Duncan 9-6-1873
Grant, Mary V. to Pryor L. Craigmile 4-22-1858 (4-27-1858)
Grasen, Clementine to J. L. Jones 12-30-1864 (1-2-1865)
Graves, Joann M. to Wm. A. Crow 9-18-1873 (9-19-1873)
Graves, Susan E. to M. M. Suddath 11-5-1857
Gray, Jane to George W. Greene 7-22-1859
Gray, Louisa J. to Charles Hilands 1-7-1869 (1-14-1869)
Gray, Martha J. to Lewis W. Bartonett 3-29-1869

Green, China to S. H. Jewell 11-21-1874
Green, Julia to Eli Hendrix 6-15-1872 (6-16-1872)
Green, Margaret to Barney B. King 10-7-1861 (10-8-1861)
Green, Mary to G. W. Cate 5-9-1872
Green, Nancy J. to M. D. Hodges 3-6-1874 (3-8-1874)
Green, Rebecca A. to Henry Ward 4-30-1872 (5-2-1872)
Green, Vianna to Thomas Nipper 2-1-1856 (2-3-1856)
Greene, Emaline to Wilkerson Adkisson 7-7-1866 (7-8-1866)
Greene, Jennie E. to John T. Mahoney 9-6-1870
Griffin, Mary Ann to John Fuller 8-21-1872 (8-22-1872)
Griffis, Sarah to George Burton 10-24-1874 (10-25-1874)
Griffiths, Jane to Joseph Smith 3-16-1861
Grimes, Sarah A. to Wm. J. Moore 5-7-1870 5-8-1870
Grimsley, Margaret E. to John M. Durham 1-20-1866 (1-21-1866)
Grimsley, Sarah J. to William G. Hatfield 5-1-1861 (5-7-1861)
Grooms, Laura Jane to William Mayfield 4-12-1856
Guenther, C. A. to J. A. Newton 6-19-1873
Guenther, Louise Elise to Wm. J. Hartley 10-18-1866 (11-17-1866)
Guffee, H. R. H. to John H. Shipley 1-17-1866 (1-18-1866)
Guffee, Lucinda to Lawson Cooper 8-6-1867 (8-18-1867)
Guffey, Clori S. to Joseph Bivins 3-3-1871 (3-4-1871)
Guffey, Margaret to Joseph Clower 12-26-1868 (12-27-1868)
Guffie, Elizabeth to George R. Reed 3-24-1866
Gurly, Mary to David Brown 9-7-1868
Guthrie, Arballa F. to George M. Hutsell 4-18-1864
Guy, Amanda E. to Harvey Gibson 7-14-1869 (7-16-1869)
Hacker, Elizabeth to Calvin Ball 3-23-1864 (3-24-1864)
Hacker, Elizabeth to George W. Roberts 9-22-1870
Hacker, Louisa to R. C. Martin 1-8-1868 (1-9-1868)
Hacker, Louisa Z.? to P. F. Hester 11-19-1874
Hacker, Margaret C. to Caswell W. McKinney 3-27-1861 (3-28-1861)
Hacker, Mariah to Millard F. Heder 1-1-1874
Hacker, Martha A. to Abner C. Liles 11-9-1867 (11-10-1867)
Hacker, Martha M. to Joseph Riggs 1-18-1866 (1-31-1866)
Hacker, Mary Jane to John Delany 7-4-1865 (7-6-1865)
Hacker, Pricilla to John Burns 8-8-1860 (8-10-1860)
Hackler, Alcey to Daniel Grifith 2-8-1864 (not executed)
Hackler, Rebecca A. to Martin G. Hicks 12-28-1874 (12-29-1874)
Hackney, Elizabeth W. to William Jeffries 3-20-1856 (4-10-1856)
Hackney, Margaret J. to John T. Morgan 8-30-1866
Haggard, Jane to John H. Bacon 4-7-1859 (4-10-1859)
Haggard, Margaret to A. J. Rothwell 9-19-1866 (9-20-1866)
Haggard, Mary to Charles Ellis 7-21-1871 (7-24-1871)
Haggard, Mary A. to Edward C. Shearwood 6-6-1857 (6-9-1857)
Haggard, Parthena to John Ellis 11-2-1864 (11-3-1864)
Hagler, Lottie J. to William A. Word 4-12-1870 4-17-1870
Hagler, Margaret to George Harvey 12-20-1871 (12-21-1871)
Hagler, Nancy Jane to William H. McGee 5-13-1858
Hagler, Nancy S. K. to George W. Helms 4-18-1857
Hagler, Susan to Thos. L. Hood 4-11-1867
Halcomb, Nancy J. to Jonathan Hayworth 12-19-1865 (12-21-1865)
Haley, Elizabeth to J. W. C. Wilson 7-22-1868
Haley, Margaret E. to Thomas K. Suddeth 11-22-1865
Haley, Sallie T. to J. B. King 11-10-1873 (11-13-1873)

Roane County Brides

Hall, Eliza to Daniel Smith 12-3-1856 (12-7-1856)
Hall, Elizabeth to Elisha Heath 9-10-1856 (10-20-1856)
Hall, Elizabeth to John Lane 12-9-1859 (12-11-1859)
Hall, Frances to Bruce Cook 10-13-1868 (10-15-1868)
Hall, Josephine to William Cook 10-23-1872
Hall, Malissa D. to M. V. Hall 3-2-1865
Hall, Mary to Andrew J. Vann 2-4-1863
Hall, Nancy Isabel to A. M. Williams 9-16-1858 (9-23-1858)
Hall, Nancy J. to Jas. T. Miller 2-13-1875
Hall, Rebeca D. to William Deathridge 5-28-1868
Hall, Telitha J. to George W. Littleton 9-22-1856 (9-23-1856)
Hamby, Mahala to James Underwood 10-4-1867 (10-6-1867)
Hamby, Mary A. to G. W. King 5-5-1873 (5-15-1873)
Hamer, Louisa C. to Oscar L. Thompson 4-5-1868 (4-12-1868)
Hamilton, Evaline to Henry H. Thomas 6-1-1867 (6-2-1867)
Hamilton, M. H. to A. M. Capps 3-27-1867 (4-4-1867)
Hamilton, M. J. to T. J. Wright 1-20-1872 (1-25-1872)
Hamilton, Mary M. to George Scarbrough 3-6-1874 (2?-7-1874)
Hamilton, Sarah A. to Henry W. Soward 9-15-1866 (9-16-1866)
Hamilton, Susan E. to Wm. Eastwood 4-3-1874 (4-9-1874)
Hammons, Mary Jane to Calvin Wright 8-12-1871 (8-14-1871)
Hammontree, M. J. to Thos. J. Lynn 4-2-1867 (4-4-1867)
Hampton, Elizabeth to Leonidas Harp 8-17-1873
Hampton, Louisa M. to Freeman Cables 12-17-1864 (12-18-1864)
Hanecey, Rebecca C. to James M. Crowder 10-27-1866 (11-1-1866)
Haney, S. R. to F. P. McCulley 9-17-1870 9-18-1870
Haney, Sarah to D. A. Knapp 7-24-1873
Hankins, H. N. (Mrs.) to A. B. Johnson 8-23-1869 8-30-1869
Hanley, Ella A. to Joseph J. Hembree 12-15-1874 (12-11?-1874)
Hanson, Martha J. to John Rector 10-2-1858
Hardbarger, Barbara to Luke Bell 3-18-1872 (3-21-1872)
Hardbarger, Sarah to James Kezziah 10-14-1874 (10-15-1874)
Hardbarger, Susan to Rufus Hood 10-6-1863
Hardbarger, Susannah to Rufus Hood 10-6-1863
Harless, Margaret to J. C. Clark 2-13-1874
Harmon, Columbia A. to James S. Durham 12-20-1873 (12-25-1873)
Harner, Melissa to G. P. Bacon 2-25-1870 2-27-1870
Harner, Rachel E. to James P. Hickey 3-30-1859
Harner, Susan M. to Albert N. Hinds 8-10-1866 (8-12-1866)
Harp, Lillie L. to Wm. Wilson 1-16-1875
Harris, Mary E. to William F. Ling 4-19-1870
Harris, Sarah to John Goodwin 11-22-1856 (11-23-1856)
Harris, Sarah C. to James C. J. Shubart 4-10-1871 (4-13-1871)
Harrison, Elizabeth to J. N. Clark? 8-23-1867 (8-25-1867)
Harrison, Rachel S. to Robert W. Adams 12-26-1860
Harrison, Sarah E. to M. P. Harrison 11-26-1864
Harrison?, Emilin to John? ____is 3-19-1868 (3-22-1868)
Hart, Elizabeth to Felix H. Hall 10-15-1857
Hart, Lucinda to Yocum C. Bush 5-1-1866 (5-3-1866)
Hart, Martha E. to L. H. Cook 12-16-1869
Hart, Mary Washington to Richard Allen 2-10-1858 (2-11-1858)
Hart, Sarah C. to Eli Hembree 6-27-1857 (6-28-1857)
Hartley, Abby Jane to Wiley Kittrell 5-26-1858 (5-27-1858)
Hartley, Kiziah to J. P.? Hays 11-10-1862 (11-11-1862)

Roane County Brides

Hartley, Margaret to George Bearden 11-24-1869 11-25-1869
Hartley, Sarah Ann to Wm. L. McClure 7-3-1868 (7-5-1868)
Hartsell, Hannah E. to John J. Howell 9-11-1869
Hartsell, Mollie to John Viar 10-13-1870 10-12-1870?
Hartsell, Nannie to A. P. Hutchinson 1-19-1869
Harvey, Ann to W. J. Pickel 1-5-1875
Harvey, Elizabeth to David W. Amos 9-12-1867
Harvey, Martha J. to H. H. McKinney 10-15-1864 (10-20-1864)
Harvey, Mary Jane to Peter Johnson 12-29-1863
Harvey, Nancy A. to Wm. S. Littleton 12-4-1865 (12-7-1865)
Harvey, Susan B. to William S. Crowder 10-5-1857
Harvey, Susan J. to Robt. W. Johnson 2-28-1865
Harwell, Susan to Benjamin F. Smith 8-2-1866
Hassler, Armeda A. to James R. Crow 5-18-1867
Hassler, Mary E. to Francis K. Suddath 2-20-1868
Hassler, Roena to George G. Byrd 10-24-1861
Haun, Mary L. to Isaac L. Monger 12-8-1866 (12-9-1866)
Hawkins, M. E. to R. E. Smith 10-5-1874
Haynes, Caroline to Darius Browder 2-11-1856 (2-14-1856)
Haynes, Catharine to D. W. Odum 2-29-1856 (4-1-1856)
Haynes, Hester A. V. to William R. Reed 6-2-1856 (6-11-1856)
Hays, Emiline to James Scrimpsher 5-25-1866 (5-26-1866)
Hays, Rebecca Ann to Malchi Monday 8-14-1865 (8-17-1865)
Hays, Sarah E. to A. L. Russell 4-29-1859 (5-1-1859)
Haywood, Eliza to Abraham Ellis 3-25-1873 (3-26-1873)
Heath, Lucretia J. to Stephen Dail 9-19-1868 (9-27-1868)
Hedgecock, Orleans E. to Simeon W. Anderson 7-12-1873 (7-13-1873)
Helton, Sarah M. to Nathaniel J. Smith 10-3-1864
Hembree, Nancy J. to Jacob Hester 4-9-1861 (4-11-1861)
Henderson, Fanny to John Tucker 9-12-1865 (5-13-1865)
Henderson, Mahala to Isaih Phillips 8-4-1874
Henderson, Mary A. to Francis M. Johnston 10-4-1856
Hendrichson, Martha J. to Martin Matz 8-8-1873 (8-10-1873)
Hendrixon, Nancy E. to Philip R. Dickey 1-9-1867 (1-10-1867)
Henry, Jane to William A. Enoch 8-25-1870 8-25-1870
Henry, Mary to W. F. James 3-25-1871 (3-26-1871)
Hensley, Catharine to Henry Miles 10-6-1866 (10-21-1866)
Hensley, Josephine to Thomas Hudson 12-27-1860
Hensley, Martha to G. W. Evins 5-17-1864 (5-19-1864)
Hensley, Mary M. to Robert McGoins 4-25-1873
Henson, Charity Ann to Thomas Collet 11-26-1867 (11-28-1867)
Henson, Sarah A. to Joseph Leffew 8-7-1873
Henston, Mary A. to Hugh Lackey 9-5-1864 (not executed)
Herontree?, Elizabeth to Benjamin Thompson 2-13-1869 (2-18-1869)
Herring, Dorcas to James Celp 9-20-1865 (9-21-1865)
Hess, L. S. to James Camp 6-7-1873 (6-12-1873)
Hester, Christina to George P. Barley 8-5-1859
Hester, Elizabeth to Bluford Y. Greene 10-1-1857 (10-9-1857)
Hester, Louisa to Robert S. Roberts 11-22-1856 (11-23-1856)
Hester, Margaret to Bazel Roberts 4-3-1858
Hester, Rebecca to David A. Baker 11-1-1869 11-3-1869
Heston, Sarah E. to Nelson Mathis 3-19-1869 (3-21-1869)
Hews, Catharine to John Majors 7-23-1870 7-24-1870
Hichew?, Sarah to Wm. Ables 10-6-1874 (10-8-1874)

Roane County Brides

Hickey, Annaliza to Geo. W. Majors 10-8-1866 (9?-10-1866)
Hickey, Martha J. to Geo. W. Blackwell 10-9-1856
Hickey, Mary J. to William Grimes 6-27-1873
Hickey, Mary M. to Isaac B. Witt 11-10-1871 (11-12-1871)
Hickey, Sarah J. to J. M. Witt 11-2-1872 (11-3-1872)
Hicks, Charlotte to Thomas Philips 3-10-1871
Hicks, Lottie to Daniel Grifith 2-17-1864
Hicks, Lucinda to Drury D. Green 6-25-1860
Hicks, Martha J. to James A. Lyon 2-7-1874 (2-8-1874)
Hicks, Mary E. to John Bowen 9-16-1860 (9-17-1860)
Hicks, Matilda to M. Reaves 8-15-1870 8-16-1870
Hill, Elizabeth to Calaway Adkins 12-5-1864 (12-6-1864)
Hill, Mary E. to Albert M. Owings 7-7-1866 (7-8-1866)
Hillsman, Amanda to William Carter 5-3-1869 (5-6-1869)
Hinds, Emiline to W. H. H. McCulley 9-28-1866 (9-30-1866)
Hinds, Jemima A. to Lynville Mynatt 12-30-1857
Hinds, Louisa to Nathaniel Doss 5-10-1873
Hinds, Louisa to James T. Jordan 9-11-1872 (9-12-1872)
Hinds, Margaret D. to James H. Dyke 12-18-1865
Hinds, Nancy to John A. Montgomery 6-28-1873 (6-29-1873)
Hinds, Nancy to D. C. Short 6-12-1873
Hinds, Sarah Ann to Absalom K. Rector 12-11-1867 (12-12-1867)
Hinds, Sarah E. to Jasper Crabtree 8-21-1872 (8-22-1872)
Hinds, Serena to Jas. Naramore 8-12-1869 8-15-1869
Hines, Caroline to A. P. Thompson 5-17-1865 (5-18-1865)
Hines, Rutha C. to Josiah J. Bacon 12-29-1864 (1-1-1864?)
Hitch?, Huldah Jane to Stephen Murray 9-22-1856
Hitshen, Amelia to M. G. Toucher 11-1-1873 (11-2-1873)
Hodge, Mary E. to James H. Rice 5-24-1860
Hodge, Minerva to Wm. A. Lewis 9-4-1874 (9-6-1874)
Hogue, Pearsy M. to Edmond Lawson 7-31-1865 (8-2-1865)
Hogwood, Mary to Umphrey Thacker 9-15-1873 (9-18-1873)
Holland, Rebecca J. to Charles M. Bane 6-27-1874 (6-28-1874)
Holloway, Sarah A. to Samuel H. East 12-22-1874 (12-24-1874)
Holmen, Mary Ann to D. F. Asbury 10-24-1871 (10-29-1871)
Holmes, M. C. to M. S. Miller 6-16-1868 (6-17-1868)
Hood, A. E. to F. M. Murry 12-19-1865 (12-20-1865)
Hood, Josephine B. to Smith Gibson 8-20-1872 (8-22-1872)
Hood, Rachel J. to Wm. L. Doughty 10-10-1866 (10-11-1866)
Hood, Sarah to Harvey Cates 9-27-1873 (10-2-1873)
Hope, Elizabeth E. to Wm. J. Keelin 9-27-1867
Hope, Mary E. to Wm. H. Cornwell 6-15-1867 (6-16-1867)
Hopkins, Nancy J. to James P. Bivens 10-6-1871 (10-8-1871)
Horn, Louisa to Thomas Roberts 7-8-1874 (7-10-1874)
Horne, Margaret C. to John Richardson 5-3-1866 (5-11-1866)
Horner, Emaline to John Cates 2-8-1860
Hornsby, Catherine to Alexander Deatherage 6-2-1860 (6-5-1860)
Hornsby, Elizabeth to Aaron Hart 9-8-1866 (9-13-1866)
Hornsby, Margaret to Fithrus? Woolsey 6-18-1856 (6-19-1856)
Hornsby, Polly to John Lacy 11-30-1857 (12-3-1857)
Hotchkiss, Isabella to John Anderson 4-30-1867 (5-2-1867)
Hotchkiss, Laura to John F. Lauderdale 10-9-1865
Hotchkiss, M. L. to J. R. Love 3-6-1867 (3-7-1867)
Houston, Nancy A. to Hugh Lackey 12-3-1864 (12-4-1864)

Roane County Brides

Howard, Angenira to John W. Mayton 5-23-1868 (not executed) *
Howard, Jane to Joseph Crowder 2-20-1868
Howard, Martha to Wm. Burnett 6-22-1870 6-24-1870
Howard, Martha to Henderson Davis 4-16-1870 4-17-1870
Howard, Nancy to John Wright 9-2-1856
Howard, Pheba J. to Thomas C. Keener 7-23-1870
Howard, Taupa to W. R. Webster 2-22-1867 (2-24-1867)
Howe, Elizabeth to John Smith 7-2-1862 (5-5-1862?)
Huckaby, Mary Ann to Joseph Shackelford 8-12-1865 (8-27-1865)
Huddleston, Mary J. to M. V. Whittier 9-1-1870
Hudson, Elizabeth to Ryland? Hudson 3-25-1862 (3-26-1862)
Hudson, Elizabeth to James Matlock 4-30-1859 (5-3-1859)
Hudson, Frances B. to R. M. Williams 5-3-1873 (5-8-1873)
Hudson, Frances K. to Mathias Williams 9-23-1857
Hudson, Mary A. to Henry B. Jones 3-5-1860 (3-22-1860)
Hudson, Sarah A. to Samuel P. William 10-27-1868 (10-29-1868)
Hudson, Sarah A. M. to N. F. Dannels 10-2-1871 (10-4-1871)
Huff, Emily J. to Robert R. Anderson 10-13-1859
Huff, Margaret to Samuel Anderson 4-27-1867 (4-28-1867)
Huff, Sallie E. to Samuel Reese 12-21-1866 (12-23-1866)
Huffine, Caroline to J. T. Carroll 12-2-1874 (12-3-1874)
Huffine, Martha J. to Isaac Wallace 7-5-1856 (7-6-1856)
Huffine, Mary A. to George P. Littleton 1-2-1869 (1-3-1869)
Huffine, Rachel E. to S. F. Longbottom 12-30-1874 (12-31-1874)
Huffland, Nancy to James Abner 7-20-1867 (7-21-1867)
Huffman, Amanda to John Blair 2-7-1859 (2-10-1859)
Huffman, Mary to Jacob Williams 1-27-1869 (1-28-1869)
Hughes, Martha to John A. Gideon 1-25-1868 (1-26-1868)
Hughs, R. E. to J. H. Pyatt 10-21-1874 (10-14?-1874)
Hughs?, Caroline to Elihu Potter 5-4-1860
Hulen, Charity M. to Philip Voiles 7-2-1858 (7-4-1858)
Hunt?, Sarah S. to Jackson Tinel 4-21-1856 (4-24-1856)
Hurst, Nancy to Wm. King 10-11-1865
Hutchison, S. I. to Eligah Gibson 2-23-1870 2-24-1870
Hutsell, Virginia to John Maupin 6-10-1864
Hyatt, Rebecca O. to A. W. Guffee 6-19-1871 (6-25-1871)
Ingalls, Frances A. to John O. Sullivan 1-14-1859 (1-25-1859)
Ingram, Elizabeth A. to Pleasant G. Littleton 9-13-1867
Ingram, Lucinda J. to Martin V. Stow 9-22-1859
Ingram, Mary A. to John Collet 11-14-1871 (11-16-1871)
Irons, Ellen to Jesse Terry 4-17-1869 (4-18-1869)
Isham, Mary Jane to Joseph N. Love? 9-9-1856 (9-11-1856)
Isham, Sarah F. to John E. Bailey 10-4-1866
Isham, Sarah Jane to Zadock Pierce 9-26-1867
Ivey, Mary Jane to John Philips 2-22-1860
Ivis, Martha to Asbery Kelam 2-14-1864
J----on, Lusettie to James W. Shurits 10-3-1867 (10-20-1867)
Jackson, Malinda to George W. Moore 11-4-1873
Jackson, Mary A. to W. F. Renfro 5-23-1871 (5-24-1871)
Jackson, Mary J. to John H. Johnson 6-2-1860
Jackson, Sarah to William Tinel 8-2-1858 (8-5-1858)
Jenkins, E. J. to W. M. Wells 2-14-1874 (2-15-1874)
Jenkins, Fanny to Jacob Jenkins 6-17-1867 (6-20-1867)
Jenkins, Mary to James P. Cooley 7-13-1871

Roane County Brides

Jiles, Margaret to Andrew McClellan 9-3-1870 9-10-1870
Jiles, Margaret C. to Michael Hill 8-20-1870 8-21-1870
Jiles, Mary A. to Rufus Boles 10-3-1872
Jiles, Nancy E. to John H. Nelson 1-29-1866
Johnson, Alsey J. to Asa Mathis 11-20-1856 (11-23-1856)
Johnson, Caroline to Thos. S. Whitlock 1-4-1869 (6?-6-1869)
Johnson, Clara to Uriah Kiker 1-24-1862
Johnson, Eliza J. to David C. Ambrose 9-18-1856 (9-19-1856)
Johnson, Eliza L. to Brice Coalman 11-10-1866 (11-11-1866)
Johnson, Elizabeth M. to Saml. A. Pair 10-11-1865 (10-12-1865)
Johnson, Ellen to John H. Lenard 11-17-1859
Johnson, Elly Heniger to Gilbert Thacker 11-15-1856 (11-16-1856)
Johnson, Frances E. to Robert Rich 9-14-1868 (9-15-1868)
Johnson, Hannah F.? to Francis M. Montgomery 10-29-1866 (11-1-1866)
Johnson, Letitia to D. C. H. Abbott 10-5-1870 10-6-1870
Johnson, Malinda E. to Samuel Sharp 10-23-1865
Johnson, Margaret to J. J. Cooley 2-8-1865 (2-9-1865)
Johnson, Margaret K. to William J. Ladd 2-18-1858
Johnson, Martha to John W. Grimsley 12-12-1856
Johnson, Martha J. to L. L. Abbott 9-15-1868 (9-17-1868)
Johnson, Martha K. to Joshua B. Harvey 11-6-1860 (11-8-1860)
Johnson, Mary to Willis Burchfield 4-9-1872 (4-19-1872)
Johnson, Mary to Wm. P. Proffett 10-17-1857 (10-18-1857)
Johnson, Mary Jane to Willis J. Babb 11-16-1869 11-18-1869
Johnson, Mary M. to Mark Milsaps 6-25-1873
Johnson, Mildridge F. to Samuel H. Cook 9-5-1859 (9-8-1859)
Johnson, Nancy B. to Hugh Blair 8-30-1865
Johnson, Rachel E. to William R. Herold 2-2-1860
Johnson, Rebecca to William Hornsby 11-6-1869 11-7-1869
Johnson, Sarah E. to Noah N. West 10-1-1870 10-2-1870
Johnson, Susan to James Majors 10-25-1869 10-28-1869
Johnson, Winney to John h. Brock 6-4-1866 (6-19-1866)
Johnston, Mary J. to Jonathan M. Scarborough 6-7-1872 (6-9-1872)
Johnston, Sophia S. to Robert M. Ladd 7-2-1859
Jolly, Nancy to Samuel T. Blair 1-13-1858 (1-15-1858)
Jolly, Sarah E. to G. E. Proffitt 12-19-1865 (12-25-1865)
Jones, Amanda M. to Isaac N. McKinney 10-25-1871 (10-29-1871)
Jones, Catharine to John Bruce 8-4-1866 (8-9-1866)
Jones, Eliza A. to Wm. H. Vann 11-9-1872 (11-14-1872)
Jones, Eliza G. to W. F. Roberts 12-23-1874 (12-24-1874)
Jones, Eliza N. to Geo. W. Philips 1-21-1865 (1-26-1865)
Jones, Elizabeth J. to Henry G. Young 1-31-1866 (2-1-1866)
Jones, H. H. to R. H. Hankin 9-19-1868 (9-20-1868)
Jones, Martha E. to John M. Monger 2-12-1868 (2-13-1868)
Jones, Mary to Isaih Philips 4-1874? (not executed)
Jones, Mary E. to Samuel Fitch 11-18-1857 (11-19-1857)
Jones, Melinda C. to John Scarbrough 1-25-1861 (1-31-1861)
Jones, Nancy to George W. Crabtree 10-5-1859 (10-8-1859)
Jones, Nancy to James Perkins 3-5-1866 (3-11-1866)
Jones, Sarah to Jacob Crase 1-2-1867 (1-31-1867)
Jordan, Margaret to James Hughes 8-5-1870 8-11-1870
Jordan, Martha to Marshall H. Forrister 5-4-1859
Jordan, Sarah to Allen Clark 10-10-1857 (10-12-1857)
Jordan, Selah to Henry Hinds 8-5-1870 8-11-1870

Roane County Brides

Julian, Sarah J. to J. P. Mayes 10-2-1858 (10-5-1858)
Keelin, Anna to W. R. Mullins 12-21-1866 (12-23-1866)
Keelin, Nancy A. to Thomas N. Rucker 9-7-1871
Keeling, Harriet to Coleman Fitsgerald 5-4-1869 (5-6-1869)
Keeling, Margaret to Charley Jenkins 9-10-1869 9-11-1869
Keener, Lorinda to William Holder 3-22-1861 (3-24-1861)
Kelsay, Margaret E. to Wm. H. Pope 11-4-1870 11-6-1870
Kelsay, Sarah A. to John T. Walker 10-13-1869 10-17-1869
Kelsay, Sarah E. A. M. to J. P. Edgwood 10-4-1870
Kelsey, Mary M. to James K. P. Yates 7-19-1861 (7-21-1861)
Kendrick, Mary E. to D. M. Acuff 12-23-1868 (12-24-1868)
Ketchenn, Anna M. to William A. Estes 12-6-1870 12-25-1870
Ketchum, Ann Eliza to Jas. Russell 1-19-1865
Keyton, Harriet J. to Floyd Gilleland 6-11-1874 (6-19-1874)
Kidd, Monarcky to Peter Cook 3-11-1858
Kile, Margaret E. to S. B. White 2-10-1866 (2-15-1866)
Kile, Susan H. to Wm. M. McCollum 7-28-1860 (8-2-1860)
Kilgore, Addie(Abbey) to John Nichol 12-14-1866 (12-19-1866)
Kilpatrick, Ellen to Franklin Hornsby 9-16-1874 (9-20-1874)
Kimbrough, Mattie to W. S. Roddy 6-16-1871 (6-22-1871)
Kincade, Clementine to William Guffey 12-4-1860 (12-7-1860)
Kincade, Mary S. to John R. Porter 9-23-1856
Kindrick, Elizabeth to John Montgomery 4-2-1870 5-19-1870
Kindrick, Leatha M. to Samuel J. Acuff 8-1-1859
Kindrick, Margaret A. to Isaac A. Hill 11-8-1870
Kindrick, Rebecca A. to Jas. F. Tarwater 7-31-1871 (8-2-1871)
Kindricks, Martha S. to Allen Deatherage 5-6-1872 (5-9-1872)
King, Addie E. to Jeremiah R. Friar 2-14-1868 (2-20-1868)
King, Mariah to John B. Campbell 7-21-1866 (7-25-1866)
King, Mary to George W. Wells 10-3-1865 (10-5-1865)
King, Nancy to William J. Wells 9-18-1866 (9-20-1866)
Kirby, Mollie to Columbus Turpin 9-23-1874 (9-24-1874)
Kirkland, Caroline to Albert Hicks 6-20-1872 (6-23-1872)
Kirkland, Eliza to John Casey 8-4-1874 (8-23-1874)
Kirkland, Eliza to Jacob Stewart 2-1-1873 (2-2-1873)
Kirkland, mary to James Hembree 9-1-1860
Kitchen, Sarah E. to Wm. R. Brumett 3-18-1868
Kitzay, Nancy C. to Amasa H. White 10-21-1873 (10-23-1873)
Kizziah, Nancy to Jesse Bowles 2-19-1873 (2-20-1873)
Kline, Mary A. to Jas. H. Johnston 10-9-1866 (10-18-1866)
Knoblauch, Emily A. to Charles G. Grabner 2-13-1862
Knox, Margaret T. to W. J. Burell 10-1-1869 10-3-1869
Kollie, Betsy to Wm. R. West 11-7-1868 (11-8-1868)
Kollock, Elizabeth to Jefferson Breazeale 1-30-1856 (1-31-1856)
Kries, Dora to Frank Ladd 12-24-1873 (1-1-1874)
Kyle, Eliza J. to W. C. Burnett 12-24-1870 12-25-1870
Kyle, Rachel M. to Newal W. Miller 10-3-1865 (10-5-1865)
Kyle, Rebeca Jane to Enoch Leach 4-16-1862 (4-24-1862)
Lacey, Elizabeth to Dodson Coward 12-19-1867 (12-22-1867)
Lack, Margaret J. to Jas. H. Miles 4-23-1869 (4-24-1869)
Lacy, Eliza to Harrison H. Shewbart 8-24-1860 (12-14-1860)
Ladd, Ann E. to John H. Limbo 9-9-1868 (9-10-1868)
Ladd, CAroline M. to Isaac S. T. Roberts 5-10-1860
Ladd, Caroline to Joseph Absten 4-28-1856 (not executed)

Roane County Brides

Ladd, Emily Jane to Samuel Hamilton 11-3-1866 (11-4-1866)
Ladd, Isabel D. to Marshall Moore 5-29-1857
Ladd, Margaret to John F. Patterson 12-26-1857 (12-28-1857)
Ladd, Martha to Thomas Hedgecock 1-28-1858 (2-4-1858)
Ladd, Martha to A. W. Largin 11-7-1861
Ladd, Sophia to G. W. Cardon 8-22-1867
Land, Julia Ann to Edward Choat 8-2-1866
Lane, Elizabeth to Wm. Sharp 3-25-1869
Lane, Mary A. to Thos. C. Whitlock 5-6-1865 (5-11-1865)
Lane, Rhona to Jackson Hester 10-8-1873
Langen, Celena A. to John W. Ladd 6-24-1862 (6-29-1862)
Lasley, Mary J. to Wm. J. Leffew 9-26-1871 (9-27-1871)
Latten, Margaret E. to J. W. Wallice 7-25-1867 (7-27-1867)
Laughton, Elizabeth to Isreal E. Wright 2-25-1865 (2-26-1865)
Lawhorn, Mary M. to Newton Eblen 10-17-1857
Lawson, Jane to Joseph Russell 10-25-1860
Lawson, Sarah to Thomas Ollis 2-14-1856
Lea, Barbara to James A. Erwin 11-3-1857
Lea, Eliza to Josiah Blair 12-23-1868 (1-3-1869)
Lea, M. A. to R. M. Denney 8-31-1868
Lee, M. M. to John S. Fain? 6-7-1863 (6-9-1863)
Lee, Vina E. to Geo. Fritts 1-2-1864? (1-3-1865)
Leeper, Julia Ann Malinda to C. P. Bussell 2-5-1862
Leeper, Lizzie to Martin B. Carter 2-8-1866 (2-21-1866)
Leffers, Luisa to Benj. H. McDuffe 3-27-1868 (3-29-1868)
Leffever, Sarah Jane to Wm. B. Hormsley 10-17-1867
Leffew, Elizabeth to John B. Isham 3-18-1872 (3-19-1872)
Leffew, Etherlinda to Benjamin Ellis, Jr. 2-28-1870 3-3-1870
Leffew, Nancy to Z. T. Bowling 3-5-1874 (3-4?-1874)
Leith, Betheny to William H. Liles 12-24-1866 (12-25-1866)
Lemons, Nancy C. to John Brandon 1-17-1871 (1-19-18710
Lenoir, Lizzie J. to David M. Key 6-25-1857 (7-1-1857)
Lenoir, M. L. to J. S. McDonough 3-7-1867 (3-13-1867)
Lesley, Teda? to Wm. Stout 5-9-1874
Lestner?, Elizabeth to Andrew Kain 12-28-1859 (12-29-1859)
Letsinger, Rebekah to Isaac A. Stout 4-14-1864
Lewis, Elizabeth J. to Albert McCarroll 3-5-1856 (3-6-1856)
Lewis, Francess H. to John Wallace 8-2-1858 (8-10-1858)
Lewis, Hannah to Jas. Holt 3-2-1869 (3-3-1869)
Lewis, Hannah L. to Benj. F. Bishop 5-12-1863 (5-14-1863)
Lewis, Rachel to John Marlin 5-30-1873
Lewis, Sarah to George McMillen 11-18-1872
Lewis, Sarah Ann to John Kelsay 9-24-1860 (9-27-1860)
Lewis, Susan A. to A. J. Bailey 7-29-1869 8-1-1869
Liles, Jane to Jos. H. Taylor 10-6-1874 (10-7-1874)
Liles, Rebecca F. to Sterling Ward 8-23-1873 (8-26-1874?)
Limburgh, Katrina to Ferdinand Wegner 11-13-1872 (11-14-1872)
Linn, Nancy to John Moore 7-15-1861 (7-20-1861)
Litsinger, Joanna B. to George White 3-1-1858 (3-4-1858)
Littleton, Catharine to Wm. J. Rich 11-14-1866 (11-16-1866)
Littleton, Catherine to Sanford Ingram 5-12-1857
Littleton, Elizabeth E. to Benjamin L. Huffine 1-21-1871 (1-22-1871)
Littleton, Emily C. to William Wilson 1-1-1857
Littleton, Martha A. to J. J. Butler 4-13-1869 (4-15-1869)

Littleton, Martha J. to Thos. Johnson 12-19-1868 (12-20-1868)
Littleton, Mary A. to Ephraim M. Huffine 7-26-1856
Littleton, Mary J. to Leland Jackson 10-8-1858
Littleton, Nancy A. to James P. Freeman 9-19-1871
Littleton, Stacey E. to James H. Littleton 9-12-1863
Lively, Sarah to Abner Hester 3-21-1859 (3-24-1859)
Lloyd, Anna C. to Henry jr. Liggett 10-22-1859 (10-23-1859)
Lloyd, Jennie to W. J. Moore 10-29-1873 (10-30-1873)
Locke, Sarah J. to Columbus Campbell 11-3-1869 11-4-1869
Locket, Martha W. to William B. Morton 2-9-1872 (2-15-1872)
Lockett, Catherine to N.? J. Griffith 1-4-1864 (1-6?-1864)
Lockett, Margaret A. to James M. Kenney 6-14-1872 (6-16-1872)
Lockett, Mary C. to Benjamin T. Fields 8-16-1871 (8-20-1871)
Lockett, Nancy A. to Seth Coker 10-19-1868 (10-22-1868)
Long, Anna to George Hatfield 5-3-1867 (5-8-1867)
Long, Annie M. to J. Y. Hogsett 11-20-1869 11-21-1869
Long, Johanna to William Cross 6-7-1872
Long, Sarah E. to John Amos 6-28-1867 (6-30-1867)
Long, Serena C. to Thomas J. Belamy 5-30-1870 6-1-1870
Loning?, Tennessee to J. H. Henry 12-31-1874
Looney, Lotta to James Lewis 4-15-1856 (4-21-1856)
Love, Selia Ann to John Jones 12-20-1867 (12-21-1867)
Lovelace, Nancy J. to George W. Berry 5-17-1873
Lovelace, Sarah J. to R. S. Lowery 9-25-1872 (9-26-1872)
Lovelass, Emiline to Wm. W. Guy 9-23-1864 (9-27-1864)
Loveless, Mary E. to John R. Scarborough 4-23-1859 (4-24-1859)
Loveless, Nancy to James Bishop 11-21-1866 (11-23-1866)
Lowe, Orpa to john Jones 12-20-1862 (12-22-1862)
Lowery, Elizabeth to Wm. R. Hembree 3-7-1868 (3-8-1868)
Lowery, Frances to James E. Woodruff 9-20-1860 (9-25-1860)
Lowery, Maggie E. to James W. Hartley 11-1-1871
Lowery, Martha to R. E. Allison 7-11-1863 (7-12-1863)
Loyd, Marie E. to Chas. A. Ruoff 5-3-1865 (5-4-1865)
Ludick?, Mary to Louis Hester 4-16-1869 (4-18-1869)
Lundie, Amey to Thomas Y. Reed 10-22-1857 (10-24-1857)
Lunsford, Rebecca C. to Jas. A. Babb 6-18-1869 (6-19-1869)
Luttrell, America J. E. to Daniel Shahan 8-21-1867 (8-22-1867)
Luttrell, Elizabeth to Isaac C. Grant 12-21-1857 (12-24-1857)
Luttrell, Susan to John Turnbill 1-24-1865
Lyle, Elizabeth J. to George W. Wheat 6-4-1859 (6-9-1859)
Lyles, Margaret L. to Edward C. Sherwood 2-27-1866
Lynn, Martha to James P. Riddle 1-29-1866 (1-30-1866)
Lynn, Sarah C. to Marshall C. Perry 8-20-1856
MDyer, Martha J. to Wm. S. Haun 6-18-1864
MSagill, Margaret E. to G. W. Richards 9-13-1864
Maberry, Nancy to Bernhard Hacker 7-29-1861
Maberry, Sarah E. to S. B. Suddath 9-3-1868
Magill, Mary to Robert Magill 12-5-1874 (11?-6-1874)
Magill?, Nancy Ann to Jacob B. Re____ 12-19-1859
Majors, Margaret to Thomas Scroggins 10-25-1869 10-26-1869
Mallsiore?, Martha J. to Adam Kirkland 7-29-1872 (7-30-1872)
Malone, Mary E. to James McElhancey 6-22-1858 (6-24-1858)
Maloy, Alice E. to Jas. R. Freeman 10-10-1868
Mamey, Emiline to Frank Stratford 8-24-1867 (8-25-1867)

Roane County Brides

Marcum, Elizabeth l to A. M. Duggan 12-12-1856 (12-14-1856)
Marcus, Nancy L. to Cary J. Pogue 7-31-1865
Margile?, Jane N. to John W. Hudson 3-15-1865 (4-23-1865)
Margrave, C. E. to J. M. Margrave 8-6-1868
Margrave, Mary to R. A. Mee 2-24-1866 (2-25-1866)
Margrave, Nancy C. to James E. Gibbs 1-17-1860
Margrave, Savanah E. to Thomas B. Byrd 3-6-1856
Marney, Amanda to Preston Isham 4-1-1869
Marney, Caroline to John W. Bowman 12-21-1858 (1-4-1859)
Marney, Mary S. to William T. Childress 3-24-1858 (3-25-1858)
Marney, Matilda to Henderson Bowling 10-31-1864
Marney, Nancy J. to B. F. Grammer 12-22-1870
Marthis, Martha to Levi Russell 3-13-1868 (3-15-1868)
Martin, Adelia to Wm. W. Patton 10-13-1870
Martin, Elizabeth to Canady Britt 7-31-1857 (8-2-1857)
Martin, Elizabeth to John Watts 9-11-1866 (9-13-1866)
Martin, Jane to Jasper Yarber 1-1-1863
Martin, Johanna C. to Richard Allen 8-24-1865
Martin, M. F. to G. L. D. McCelland 11-28-1868 (12-3-1868)
Martin, Malinda to Thomas Halder 12-3-1864 (12-5-1864)
Martin, Margaret M. to Richard Halder 9-21-1870 9-23-1870
Martin, Martha to John Shoat 1-4-1868 (1-5-1868)
Martin, Martha Ann to James Peters 9-1-1868 (9-3-1868)
Martin, Mary to S. P. Blair 8-31-1868 (9-1-1868)
Martin, Mary E. to John Darhuty 9-17-1868 (10-4-1868)
Martin, Nancy A. to Lindsey L. Hamby 5-9-1861 (5-10-1861)
Martin, Nancy Jane to Henry E. Borum 12-25-1858 (12-26-1858)
Martin, Polly Ann to William Dodd 5-31-1856 (6-1-1856)
Martin, Rebecca to Asbury Brooks 12-18-1856
Martin, Sallie to G. A. Guenther 2-12-1874
Martin, Sarah C. to Samuel J. Moser 8-1-1857 (8-2-1857)
Martin, Susan H. to Preston Isham 6-11-1870 6-12-1870
Martin, W. F. to A. F. Zwickes 4-6-1861 (4-7-1861)
Massey, Susan to M. B. Capps 3-30-1867 (3-31-1867)
Matheny, Nancy E. to James D.? Patterson 9-19-1866 (9-20-1866)
Mathis, Deannah E. to P. D. Roda 6-29-1861
Mathis, Eliza J. to John Pelfry 5-5-1864 (5-6-1864)
Mathis, Elizabeth to Wm. A. Dulton 5-12-1860 (5-15-1860)
Mathis, H. A. to L. L. Johnson 12-21-1867 (1-2-1868)
Mathis, Jane to James Curd 4-10-1866
Mathis, Kittie to Rufus Hardbarger 5-6-1864
Mathis, Lois L. to John M. Cully 12-13-1856 (12-14-1856)
Mathis, Martha L. to Samuel L. Dixon 6-21-1872 (6-23-1872)
Mathis, Martha L. to W. A. G. Estes 8-14-1874 (8-16-1874)
Mathis, Matilda C. to James C. Pope 9-5-1864 (5-17-1865)
Mathis, Rebecca J. to Samuel G. Hughes 7-17-1866 (7-18-1866)
Mathis, Sarah to D. A. Melton 11-24-1869 11-25-1869
Mathis, Savanah to Duke Keagan 9-19-1860
Matlock, Elizabeth to C. C. Bacon 9-18-1857 (9-24-1857)
Matlock, Elizabeth C. to Samuel E. Harvey 2-18-1874 (2-19-1874)
Matlock, Mary to Wm. Littleton 5-15-1864
Matlock, Matilda to Josiah Hughs 5-1-1856
Matney, Mary J. to Wm. M Woody 3-14-1868 (3-15-1868)
Matthews, Dianah E. to Joseph L. Hartsell 11-13-1867 (11-17-1867)

Maupins, Mary A. to Isaac Vaine? 8-9-1871 (8-18-1871)
May, Caroline to Zachrich T. Nelson 12-24-1866 (12-25-1866)
May, Lydia to Lewis Davis 2-2-1869 (2-5-1869)
May, Mary C. to W. R. Silvey 8-2-1859 (8-7-1859)
May, Permelia F. to Henry W. Burns 9-20-1860
Mayberry, Emma to John Margrave 10-7-1869
Mayo, Laura H. to James M. Harrison 12-26-1860
Mays, Delilah to Saml. Brashears 12-28-1863 (12-29-1863)
Mayton, Nancy A. to C. H. W. Brown 2-8-1869 (2-11-1869)
McAlister, Margaret E. to Jesse Hall 7-18-1874 (7-19-1874)
McAlister, Polly A. to William Brewer 4-6-1867 (4-7-1867)
McAmy?, Nancy to Raymond Reed 10-12-1874 (10-13-1874)
McAnally, Lucretia to John B. Cunningham 12-29-1866 (12-30-1866)
McAnally, mary Ann to Wm. M. Rodgers 8-2-1860 (8-10-1860)
McCaleb, Bashler to Right Hambright 9-15-1869
McCall, Candis Ann to William G. Flinn 2-2-1856 (2-3-1856)
McCampbell, Louisa V. to William L. Ramsey 6-19-1858 (6-23-1858)
McCamy, Malinda to John W. Silvy 8-19-1874 (8-20-1874)
McCarrol, Caroline to Robert L. Pitman 1-29-1861 (1-31-1861)
McCart, Elizabeth to John M. Easter 2-28-1868 (3-1-1868)
McCart, Mary to Chas. Benegyr 9-17-1867 (9-18-1867)
McChristian, Artis to David Clark 10-31-1864 (11-1-1864)
McClanahan, Rebecca A. to John W. Byram 9-11-1868 (9-15-1868)
McClenden, Mary to Thomas P. Scarbrough 11-2-1858
McClendon, Elender to Robert M. Scarbrough 10-29-1858
McClure, Elizabeth E. to Jessee A. Nalley 10-2-1867 (10-6-1867)
McClure, Vianna to Robert Moore 9-9-1868 (9-10-1868)
McCollister, Martha to J. C. Bates 8-3-1869 8-4-1869
McConnell, Angaline to William Crumley 7-4-1860
McConnhell, Nancy A. to Pinckney F. Crook 6-19-1860 (6-20-1860)
McCray, M. B. to J. J. Harrison 6-18-1870 6-23-1870
McCulley, Cynthia J. to John Temple 7-16-1869 7-19-1869
McCulley, Delila to Francis M. Gage 4-16-1856 (4-17-1856)
McCulley, Elizabeth to J. B. Atwood 12-28-1864 (12-29-1864)
McCulley, Mary to George sr. Fuller 2-27-1867 (2-28-1867)
McCullin, S. L. to Alson White 10-25-1865 (10-26-1865)
McCully, Sarah E. to Robert A. Bink 4-24-1861 (4-25-1861)
McDaffro?, Rhoda C. to John C. Fritts 10-4-1859
McDaniel, M. E. to Samuel B. Eskridge 12-26-1866 (12-27-1866)
McDaniel, Martha to John A. Snow 2-23-1858 (2-25-1858)
McDonald, Mary Ann to James W. Duncan 1-30-1866 (2-1-1866)
McDuffee, Eliza J. to Benj. F. Billingsly 12-23-1856 (12-24-1856)
McDuffie, Kizziah to John Leffew 12-30-1857
McDuffie, Melissa A. to Daniel C. Stone 9-25-1856
McEwen, Joanna C. to Thomas C. Center 8-31-1857 (9-1-1857)
McEwen, Lizzie to Thomas Lauller 12-12-1863
McEwen, Matilda H. to George Netherland 12-26-1865
McEwen, Tempy to Jesse P. Campbell 3-7-1859 (3-29-1859)
McGee, Nancy J. to Philip Wilson 12-20-1866 (12-21-1866)
McInally, Martha J. to Jas. A. Furgerson 3-14-1867
McInally, Mary A. to James C. Voiles 3-23-1865 (3-26-1865)
McKinley, Ann to Crabtree Denham 2-9-1874
McKinney, Artalissa to James W. Watson 1-18-1859
McKinney, Martha J. to Benj. L. Hendrickson 7-2-1860 (7-12-1860)

Roane County Brides

McKinney, Mary to Joseph S. Green 1-2-1868
McKinney, Mary E. to Wm. J. Watson 1-29-1865
McKinney, Nancy J. to John Nelon 11-12-1872 (11-14-1872)
McKinney, Rebecca to Basil Hester 5-14-1857
McKinney, Sarah F. to Hesekiah Davis 4-6-1865
McLey, Sarrah Jane to John J. Overton 3-3-1863? (3-2?-1863)
McNutt, Mary A. to Wm. G. Lloyd 4-9-1867
McPeters, Lizzie to J. R. Basket 6-13-1868
McPhearson, Mary to Jacob M. Ewings 9-19-1859 (9-29-1859)
McPhearson, Parthena to Jas.? P. Pearson 3-1-1861 (3-5-1861)
McPhearson, Susan J. to James Martin 7-26-1859
McPherson, Elizabeth to F. L. B. Johnson 4-2-1866 (4-3-1866)
McPherson, Margaret to Thomas J. Gipson 10-12-1867 (10-15-1867)
McRea, Emily to Joseph Huffine 1-19-1869 B
McReynold, Moin Ann to Henry M. Shubird 8-24-1857 (8-25-1857)
McSherman, Rhoda to Joseph L. Erskins 2-8-1870
Medlin, A. A. to C. L. Rice 7-16-1870 7-17-1870
Mee, Amanda A. to Elkaney Hilton 7-6-1874
Mee, Mary E. to J. H. Taylor 1-28-1874 (1-29-1874)
Mee, Nancy C. to William Furry 4-29-1874 (5-3-1874)
Melton, Jane to Richard Cox 12-11-1865 (9?-12-1865)
Melton, Nancy to Henry Edwards 2-18-1865 (3-5-1865)
Melton, Sarah E. to Wm. Hembree 11-9-1864
Micael, Elizabeth J. to George W. Guy 1-2-1867 (1-3-1867)
Miles, Adaline to John W. Young 8-6-1860
Miles, Lydia to Saml. Bazel 9-3-1874 B
Miligan, M. J. to L. W. Sigman 6-14-1864
Miller, Barbara to Aaron Russell 8-17-1865
Miller, Caroline to William Cates 12-29-1859
Miller, Catharine to W. F. Luffman 12-14-1872 (12-19-1872)
Miller, Elizabeth to Hiram Bailey 4-17-1861
Miller, Elizabeth to James R. Porter 3-7-1868 (3-8-1868)
Miller, Elizabeth to John Walker 5-3-1862
Miller, Elly M. to Benjamin G. Bulling 1-16-1867 (1-21-1867)
Miller, Margaret to J. M. Blankenbicker 9-1-1865 (9-8-1865)
Miller, Margaret to Robt. M. Harvey 2-22-1865 (2-24-1865)
Miller, Margaret E. to Austin Reynolds 3-18-1856 (3-20-1856)
Miller, Mary C. to John Cate 9-21-1863
Miller, Mary J. E. to James A. Smith 8-12-1865 (8-13-1865)
Miller, Matilda to Wm. H. H. Mayton 8-15-1857 (8-16-1857)
Miller, Nancy Jane to Daniel Cate 5-19-1865 (5-21-1865)
Miller, Rachel to Joseph W. Rose 4-2-1864 (4-3-1864)
Miller, Sarah E. to R. A. Tinnell 1-7-1870 1-9-1870
Miller, Sarah W. to Edward F. Culvahouse 1-17-1868 (1-19-1868)
Miller, Talitha C. to Houston A. Markis? 2-7-1872 (2-8-1872)
Millican, Eliza C. to Jas. M. Aytes 8-17-1867 (8-18-1867)
Millican, Malvina C. to Stephen C. Mathis 3-22-1856 (3-23-1856)
Millican, Martha E. to Stephen Bowlin 7-19-1856
Millican, N. E. to T. J. Bagwell 7-15-1869 7-16-1869
Million, Elizabeth M. to Gideon M. Sharp 9-24-1858 (9-26-1858)
Millions, Martha A. to W. H. Butler 1-26-1865 (1-29-1865)
Milsaps, Lurena J. to Wm. E. Sherwood 9-5-1871 (9-7-1871)
Minsey, Mary J. to William Whitlock 6-10-1858
Minton, Elizabeth to Wm. Fisher 8-28-1865

Roane County Brides

Minton, Julia A. J. to John W. Holder 2-20-1865 (2-23-1865)
Minton, Keziah to Edward Culveyhouse 5-10-1869 (5-11-1869)
Minton, Mary L. to D. B. Webster 9-27-1869 9-29-1869
Minton, Nancy J. to William Giles 9-3-1860 (9-4-1860)
Minton, Sarah to James L. Day 7-7-1865 (6-8-1865)
Mitchell, Elizabeth J. to Presley W. Nave 6-26-1861 (6-27-1861)
Mitchell, Sarah G. to Wm. L. Knox 2-2-1869 (2-3-1869)
Monday, Martha N. to Wm. T. Bell 11-29-1873 (11-30-1873)
Monday, Susan L. to John F. Bowles 7-16-1870 7-31-1870
Mongen, Elizabeth to Wiley P. Miller 6-29-1867 (6-30-1867)
Mongen, Susanah to James F. Breazeale 5-1-1866 (5-3-1866)
Monger, Ann to C. M. Waller 12-31-1866
Monger, Sarah J. to John L. Burnett 5-29-1869 (5-30-1869)
Montgomery, Eva to B. M. Eblen 9-30-1874 (10-1-1874)
Montgomery, Martha Jane to George T. Wilson 8-17-1861 (8-19-1861)
Montgomery, Mary A. to John W. Waller 5-10-1860
Montgomery, Mary Jane to John C. Haley 2-23-1866 (2-28-1866)
Montgomery, Sarah to B. Hensly 3-9-1860 (3-15-1860)
Montgomery, Sarah E. to James Cole 12-27-1862
Moore, Amanda M. to Amos C. Greene 3-12-1864
Moore, Annie to Wm. J. Erving 8-28-1874 (8-30-1874)
Moore, E. W. to Houston Wheat 1-5-1857
Moore, Elizabeth to Benjam Smith 9-8-1868 (9-13-1868)
Moore, Martha J. to D. H. Narramore 3-3-1874 (3-8-1874)
Moore, Martha J. to Ransom Vials 6-9-1860 (6-10-1860)
Moore, Mary E. to George L. Forrister 5-31-1856 (6-3-1856)
Moore, Mary Jane to James Cook 11-20-1858 (11-21-1858)
Moore, Matilda E. to Lenoindas Horne 9-8-1870
Moore, Susan to John E. Sturges 10-30-1872 (10-31-1872)
Mooton, Mary A. to Jackson Mayton 7-11-1868 (7-12-1868)
Moreland, Elender to Arch Fitts 2-2-1857 (2-3-1857)
Moreland, Elizabeth to Wesley Amos 12-17-1856 (12-18-1856)
Moreland, Frances C. to John E. Basket 2-21-1865
Morgan, Cordelia to Joseph Green 11-28-1872
Morgan, Feriba to Asa Howard 12-30-1858
Morgan, Mary to F. M. Brown 6-17-1874
Morgan, Sarilda B. to Wm. M. Pickel 8-7-1865 (8-16-1865)
Morris, Caroline to J. W. Lankford 1-15-1873 (1-19-1873)
Morris, Elizabeth J. to Winfield Hicks 12-3-1866 (12-4-1866)
Morris, K. M. to M. T. Price 7-24-1873
Morris, Louisa Hand to Danl. Thompson 7-2-1860
Morris, Sarah (Mrs.) to James Reed 12-1-1870
Morris, Sarah E. to William D. Gowins 3-18-1861 (3-20-1861)
Morris, Sarah E. to Miles Langley 9-21-1869 9-26-1869
Morris, Serulda to John H. Narimore 9-1-1857 (9-3-1857)
Morrison, Malinda J. to C. C. Wilkey 8-16-1865 (8-17-1865)
Morrison, Margaret to John R. Hendrix 2-22-1868 (2-23-1868)
Morrison, Mary Ann to Nicholas Sante 8-5-1856 (8-7-1856)
Morse, Elizabeth to James H. Buren? 5-24-1861 (5-25-1861)
Moses, Martha to Benjamin Fritts 3-1-1871
Moss, Mary to James Farmer 2-14-1866 (2-18-1866)
Motney, Line to Frank Keeton 12-5-1874 (12-7-1874)
Mourfield, Martha to Columbus M. Duncan 1-17-1857 (1-18-1857)
Mullins, Giszeal? to Wm. G. Ward 1-1-1872 (1-2-1872)

Roane County Brides

Mullins, Jane? to James Shoat 8-4-1864
Mullins, Matilda to George Carroll 1-20-1866
Mullins, Nancy J. to Wm. J. Weese 11-2-1865 (11-5-1865)
Munday, Mary to Mathew Sheets 5-19-1874 (5-23-1874)
Munday, Nancy C. to W. T. Griffin 10-27-1873 (10-30-1873)
Munger, Nancy C. to Robert H. Alexander 12-10-1866 (12-13-1866)
Munsey, D. C. to Berry H. Johnson 11-16-1865 (11-23-1865)
Murphy, Lucinda J. to Elkany Brogden 10-17-1868 (10-18-1868)
Murray, Margaret E. to A. O. Carden 1-11-1866 (1-15-1866)
Murray, Margaret H. to John Gardener 12-14-1858 (12-25-1858)
Murray, Sarah to John S. Cash 9-11-1865
Myers, Rachel to Robert Heaton 3-26-1867 (3-27-1867)
Myers, Sarah P. to Casper F. Bowers 8-19-1871 (8-20-1871)
Mynatt, Polly Ann to John J. Hukey 8-26-1856
Narramon, Mary to Robert Preston 8-23-1856 (8-25-1856)
Narramore, Amanda A. to Jas. . Hamby 12-14-1869 12-15-1869
Narramore, Eliza J. to Daniel J. McIver 3-30-1867 (4-4-1867)
Narramore, Elizabeth to Asa Adams 11-18-1861
Narramore, Elizabeth to John J. Overton 2-1-1860
Narramore, Margaret to Alex. H. Brown 9-23-1869
Narramore, Martha to John Taylor 1-10-1859
Narramore, Surreloa to Samuel Hart 11-13-1869 11-14-1869
Narramore, Tabitha J. to John B. Morrone? 12-6-1865 (12-7-1865)
Nealy, Sarah to Moses Pitts 10-9-1871 (10-12-1871)
Neergard, Mary Jane to William M. Hall 12-20-1866
Neil, Margaret to Philip Humphreys 9-1-1865
Nelon, Sophronia to James Underwood 8-5-1874 (8-6-1874)
Nelson, Mahaley to John Kizer 3-7-1859 (3-8-1859)
Nelson, Mary to Geo. Hacker 3-9-1865 (3-12-1865)
Nelson, Mary E. to Joseph Liles 5-19-1866 (5-24-1866)
Neorgrard?, Henrietta A. to Joseph A. Muecke 12-12-1872
Newcomb, Sarah A. to James C. Kitchner 9-9-1869 9-12-1869
Newman, Jane to Chas. Moore 4-21-1865 (4-27-1865)
Nicely, Elizabeth to Robt. Crudgington 7-27-1859
Nichol, Margaret to Livingston Lavender 12-18-1866
Nichol, Sarah to William Fisher 12-14-1866 (12-20-1866)
Nichols, Mary to D. R. McDuffee 9-29-1869 9-30-1869
Nicholson, Anna to Jacob Fritts 2-12-1874
Nicholson, Charlotte to Pleasant Vance 11-30-1873 (12-1-1873)
Nicholson, Emiline to James M. Coley 8-15-1867
Nicholson, Martha to Seborn Hood 2-6-1874 (2-7-1874)
Nicholson, Mary to Saml. Bainbridge 7-21-1865
Nicholson, Susan to Seborn Hood 5-7-1870 5-8-1870
Niece, Martha A. to J. L. Roe 8-5-1870 8-7-1870
Niece, Mary to A. I. Childress 4-16-1870 4-17-1870
Nipper, Eliza to Napoleon St. John 2-11-1864
Nipper, Naomia C. to William Crawford 10-17-1857 (10-18-1857)
Nipper, Rhoda S. to M. W. Miller 10-6-1856 (10-8-1856)
Nipper, Sarah J. to John W. Flinn 7-28-1869 7-29-1869
Nixon, Ann E. to William Barnette 5-22-1862
Norman, Eliza to Wm. J. Deatherige 5-11-1871 (5-14-1871)
Norman, Maria to Abraham Lacey 11-18-1867 (11-22-1867)
Norman, Martha to Preston C. Estes 9-7-1859 (9-11-1859)
Norman, Permelia to T. J. Mathews 8-6-1864 (8-7-1864)

Roane County Brides

Norman, Sarah C. to John M. Deatheridge 2-17-1868 (2-20-1868)
Odem, Amanda J. to John G. Redman 10-10-1866 (10-11-1866)
Odem, Emily E. to Wm. Sliger 6-4-1866 (6-6-1866)
Odom, Harriet L. to Thomas F. Sliger 12-21-1860
Odom, Mary E. to Wm. Gross 2-24-1869 (2-5?-1869)
Odonall, Bridget to Thos. W. Cooper 5-5-1864 (5-6-1864)
Oliphant, Harriet to Washington Ballard 4-6-1857 (4-9-1858?)
Oliphant, Mary Jane to John C. Matlock 11-15-1858 (11-18-1858)
Oliver, Marcella to Isaac G. Crawford 8-18-1873 (8-19-1873)
Ollis, Elizabeth to Jordan Stringer 2-14-1856
Ollis, Sarah to William R. Webb 6-26-1856 (6-29-1858)
Ollison, Betsey J. to Otter Peirce 7-3-1869 (7-4-1869)
Olliver, Elizabeth to William K. Griffeth 12-15-1858
Oneal, M. J. to W. T. Gentris 1-3-1865 (1-5-1865)
Ophatits, Mary to George Gallimore 9-30-1858
Osborn, Mary C. to John J. Blair 9-9-1861 (9-17-1861)
Osborne, Martha J. to David W. Siler 5-30-1862 (6-4-1862)
Overton, Dorcas to Jessee Tindle 4-3-1868 (4-5-1868)
Owings, Eliza C. to Enoch J. Kendrick 1-1-1862 (1-2-1862)
Owings, Eliza J. to Benjamin Jordon 1-7-1870 1-16-1870
Owings, Martha A. to Thomas J. Brown 12-11-1867 (12-12-1867)
Owings, Truthena to Albert Pinyan 5-21-1867 (5-26-1867)
Page, Mary Ann to Haskew Stamper 2-29-1860
Pain, Martha A. to J. H. Smith 3-15-1870 3-16-1870
Palmer, Mary M. to Henry C. Nichols 1-29-1866 (1-30-1866)
Parker, Margaret C. to James L. Neill 8-22-1860 (8-23-1860)
Parker, Mary E. to Tho. J. Miller 1-16-1860?
Parker, Mary E. to Thos. J. Miller 1-11-1860 (1-17-1860)
Parker, Sarah Ann to Greenberry Schrimpsher 12-24-1868 (12-25-1868)
Parker, Tempy J. to Mark S. Miller 10-12-1859
Parks, Ann E. to John W. Carroll 9-25-1873 (9-28-1873)
Parks, Mary to Jesse Tinel 3-29-1873
Parks, Mary E. to Martin F. Ward 7-12-1872 (7-13-1872)
Parmley, Mariah? to William D. Barbour 6-21-1856 (6-22-1856)
Parmley, Seraphina to Newton A. Adams 6-24-1862
Pass, Mary Ann to Elbert Huffman 5-10-1873
Pasty, Matilda C. to Stephen H. Stone 10-14-1865 (10-19-1865)
Patterson, Almeda S. to Deaderick Kries 9-10-1874
Patterson, Eliza J. to John Parks 9-19-1872
Patterson, Martha J. to Jonathan N. Rodgers 1-17-1859 (1-27-1859)
Patton, Mary E. to John Ellis 10-15-1866 (10-16-1866)
Patty, Elizabeth to Jesse Johnson 10-13-1863
Pearson, Lucinda to Anthony Smith 12-28-1870 (12-29-1870)
Peatt, Rebekah to Jeremiah Brown 3-3-1864 (3-4-1864)
Peatt?, Elizabeth to John Brown 7-6-1867 (11-7-1867)
Peirce, Martha to Joseph Clak? 12-5-1874 (12-6-1874)
Pelfry, Mahala J. to John N. Qualls 10-4-1872 (10-5-1872)
Pelt?, Tolly Ann to Sanders McClendon 6-4-1858
Penex, Sarah C. to Gustave Zwicker 2-7-1874 (2-8-1874)
Penix, Mary Malinda to James Bennett 6-2-1865
Percy, Mary J. to G. W. Hinds 2-8-1871 (3-12-1871)
Perkins, Kizziah T. to Robert King 2-16-1857
Perry, Eliza to Wm. B. Mifflin 3-8-1873 (3-9-1873)
Perry, Elizabeth M. to William F. Belvin 3-26-1859 (3-27-1859)

Roane County Brides

Perry, Nancy to Alvis V. Hicks 2-5-1859 (2-6-1859)
Peters, Mary to James E. Johnson 7-2-1866 (7-5-1866)
Peters, Sarah J. to John N. Haggard 2-2-1865 (2-9-1865)
Peters, Tabitha M. to Jas. M. Cook 2-14-1865
Phelps, Margaret J. to Hugh J. Hackney 3-11-1857 (3-15-1857)
Phifer, Eliza C. to Rufus B. Brown 11-3-1865 (11-19-1865)
Phifer, Martha A. to Aron P. Tallent 11-30-1857 (12-3-1857)
Phifer, Mary E. to J. E. Hamby 10-11-1865
Phifer, Sarah A. to Jackson W. Smith 2-20-1865 (2-21-1865)
Philips, Adeline to James H. Johnston 2-12-1856
Philips, Amanda to Jas. Smith 1-19-1865 (1-21-1865)
Philips, Margaret to Henry Whisenhunt 6-16-1857
Philips, Martha J. to Wm. Magill 12-21-1864 (12-22-1864)
Philips, Mary A. to Newton M. Sellers 2-11-1856 (2-12-1856)
Philips, Rachel R. to John Brock 9-28-1865
Philips, Susan to George W. Effingham 4-5-1856
Philips, T. L. to J. B. Rudder 8-12-1873 (8-13-1873)
Phillipie, Elizabeth to Washington Van 4-2-1869
Phillips, Julia A. to Nathaniel McKinney 10-23-1866
Phillips, M. P. to James T. McCristian 5-10-1864 (5-12-1864)
Phillips, Sarah to Gooden Webster 4-19-1865 (4-21-1865)
Phillips, Sophia to John F. Williams 5-30-1860
Philpot, Margaret E. to John H. Duff 12-21-1867 (12-29-1867)
Pickel, Anna A. to John J. Holt 10-4-1866
Pickel, Bethilda A. to Isaac M. Freels 11-3-1866 (11-15-1867?)
Pickel, Eliza to Levi V. Mays 3-29-1865 (4-3-1865)
Pickel, Emily J. to James M. Jones 8-28-1867
Pickel, Mary P. to Sanford N. Littleton 10-6-1873 (11-2-1873)
Pickel, S. J. to J. C. Hembree 1-4-1875
Pickel, Sarah K. to E. L. Duncan 10-14-1865 (10-17-1865)
Pickle, Eveline? to Andrew J. Good 12-19-1859 (12-22-1859)
Pierce, Martha C. to Jason Miller 5-28-1870 5-29-1870
Pierce, Matilda A. to M. J. Fritts 6-12-1869 (6-20-1869)
Pierce, Misouri A. to Rufus A. Davis 5-12-1870 5-4-1870?
Poland, Amanda to Allen Philips 6-12-1872
Poland, Sarah to Allen Philips 1-2-1874 (1-4-1874)
Ponder, Eliza to James Moss 5-23-1863
Pool, Mary to Wm. M. Collet 8-2-1873 (8-7-1873)
Pope, Elizabeth J. to James Jones 2-11-1868
Pope, Nancy J. to Joseph M. Kelsay 12-17-1867 (12-19-1867)
Porter, Maggie J. to P. J. Doremus 8-14-1866 (8-16?-1866)
Porter, Mary A. to Thos. J. Lewis 2-1-1869
Porter, Mary B. to Nelson C. Redman 10-20-1860
Porter, Mary S. to James W. Woods 6-6-1862 (6-8-1862)
Potter, Mary A. to Jonathan Scarbrough 8-11-1871 (8-13-1871)
Potter, Nancy to Volentine Ponder 3-9-1858 (3-10-1858)
Potter, Rachel to Henry Haggard 11-25-1869 11-23-1869?
Pottier, Callina to H. C. Haggard 5-14-1864
Powell, Eliza N. to Joseph Turpin 6-27-1871 (7-6-1871)
Powell, Elizabeth to Jasper Vann 2-8-1859 (2-9-1859)
Powell, Louisa J. to Elihu L. Hembree 11-16-1867 (11-17-1867)
Powell, Melvisa to Hugh L. Beard 8-4-1865 (8-5-1865)
Powell, Nancy J. to Ransom Fritts 8-17-1859
Powell, Sarah to Jeremiah Fritts 8-17-1859

Roane County Brides

Powers, Barthy to Hardin Hope 2-12-1864 (2-14-1864)
Prater, Mary A. to Augustus W. Beale 1-30-1866 (2-21-1866)
Pratt, Rachel M. to J. J. Beaver 12-19-1868 (12-3?-1868)
Price, Fanny A. to M. B. Mullins 1-26-1871
Price, Martha J. to John Ford 7-10-1874 (10-4-1874)
Price, Matilda to John Doherty 4-11-1865
Price, P. A. to J. B. Edmonds 6-30-1869 (7-1-1869)
Price, Sarah to Mitchell V. Rose 1-27-1859 (2-2-1859)
Price, Talitha to Wm. H. Stephens 4-7-1866
Proffitt, Sarah E. to B. W. Clark 8-9-1867 (8-11-1867)
Pulham, Louisa C. to John E. Dunham no dates (with 9-1864)
Pursley, Mary to William P. Henderson 8-9-1856 (8-19-1856)
Pyatt, Eliza to Jas. W. Lea 4-22-1867
Pyatt, Louisa to Hiram V. Frost 7-26-1873
Pyatt, M. H. to Samuel O. Cunningham 9-10-1874 (9-12-1874)
Qualls, Catharine to James K. Copeland 2-8-1869 (2-11-1869)
Qualls, Margaret to Wm. L. Butler 12-23-1856 (1-31-1856?)
Qualls, Mary to Samuel Cates 1-7-1856
Qualls, Rachel to Samuel Baily 9-13-1869 9-19-1869
Qualls, Rachel E. to George Parks 2-17-1874 (2-20-1874)
Qualls, Rebecca E. to Andrew L. Derossett 5-30-1856 (6-1-1856)
Qualls, Sarah to George W. Henson 6-21-1859
Qualls, Sarah to George W. Wright 6-7-1865
Query, Olla to George G. Short 5-16-1874 (5-17-1874)
Raby, Lucinda to William C. Guffee 9-18-1858 (9-19-1858)
Ragh, Mary C. to J. H. Adams 9-20-1865
Ragles, Catharine to A. J. Evans 12-26-1866 (12-27-1866)
Rainey, Fanny to William Lollis 9-1-1858
Rainey, Susan to John Bennett 5-24-1862
Ramsay, Lucy M. to Allen Myres 2-14-1868
Ramsy?, Mary E. to D. J. Collins 7-31-1867
Raney, Phebe to John Farmer 4-17-1857 (4-19-1857)
Rankins, Nancy C. to S. H. Jones 8-18-1866 (8-21-1866)
Rather, Susan C. to William S. Freels 8-10-1870] 8-11-1870
Rausin, Sarah A. J. to Absalom Melton 12-13-1870 12-15-1870
Ray, M. E. to G. W. Lowery 3-1-1867 (3-3-1867)
Ray, Sarah Ann to Lafayette Garland 1-11-1868 (1-12-1868)
Rayborn, Mary to Richard Driskill 3-29-1866
Rayborn, S. A. to John H. Wright 12-13-1866 (12-14-1866)
Rayborn, Susan to Ricahrd Newman 7-19-1856 (7-21-1856)
Raybourn, Elizabeth J. to Samuel Eblin 9-23-1863 (9-25-1863)
Rayder, Nancy to Michael Cagan 2-3-1866 (3-3-1866)
Reader, Martha J. to Geo. W. Clark 12-7-1867 (12-8-1867)
Reagan, Ann E. to Thos. A. Eblen 2-18-1867 (2-19-1867)
Reagan, Telitha to James W. Walker 9-20-1856 (9-21-1856)
Rear, Mary to James M. Christian 11-13-1860
Recror?, Elizabeth to James W. Doke 9-29-1865
Rector, Amanda to Pleasant Chiles 4-3-1857
Rector, Louisa to John Ward 12-14-1869 12-15-1869
Rector, Margaret F. to John Smith 1-12-1871 (1-22-1871)
Rector, Mary to John N. Carden 1-1-1856
Rector, Nancy S. to William C. Hill 10-30-1866 (10-31-1866)
Redfearn, Nancy A. to James W. Stockton 9-9-1857 (9-12-1857)
Redman, Sarah J. to Reuben A. Webb 9-20-1873 (9-21-1873)

Roane County Brides

Reed, Hannah to Jacob Jeffers 12-18-1872
Reed, Lavina T. to Jas. C. Knox 5-25-1869 (5-20?-1869)
Reed, Nancy to James L. Clower 5-3-1856 (5-4-1856)
Reed, Nancy to Jacob M. Cook 11-11-1861 (11-14-1861)
Reed, Sarah Ann to Jacob Stewart 1-16-1874
Reed, Tempy to Jefferson Crabtree 8-28-1862
Reeder, Mary C. to James Brackett 2-25-1861 (2-26-1861)
Reeves, M. O.? to Wm. J. Howard 8-15-1870 8-16-1870
Reileo, Maria to Oscar De Konnoritz 5-1-1872 (5-3-1872)
Reiney, Mary to James Solomon 10-28-1867 (10-29-1867)
Reins, Sarah to John Newman 2-13-1865
Renfro, Harriet L. to Thomas Keeling 5-4-1869 (5-6-1869)
Renfroe, Elis. A. to Alexander Keelin 11-17-1874 (11-19-1874)
Rentfro, Annis to James Buckland 4-22-1857 (4-30-1857)
Rentrfro, Sarah to Samuel M. Giles 9-19-1867 (9-22-1867)
Retherford, Rebecca E. to John A. Fuller 8-5-1857 (8-16-1857)
Rhea, Sarah E. to Samuel A. Rodgers 5-7-1863 (5-10-1863)
Rich, Emaline to James Fumbill? 12-5-1857 (12-16-1857)
Rich, Louisa to George W. Fritts 1-17-1866 (1-19-1866)
Rich, Lucinda to John Byrum 10-13-1858 (10-16-1858)
Rich, Nancy C. to Wm. Fritts 12-20-1865 (12-21-1865)
Rich, Rebecca to Henry Bailey 2-20-1866 (2-22-1866)
Richardson, Nancy J. to James Mounger 3-4-1874 (3-5-1874)
Richerson, Columbia A. to R. L. Pierce 4-20-1865
Richmond, Nancy to Wm. Lockett 5-24-1866
Riley, Sarah to Joseph J. Kinnick 8-11-1868 (8-13-1868)
Robbs, F. M. to Geo. W. Abels 6-22-1867 (6-23-1867)
Robbs, Mary E. to Langston Bacon 10-9-1858 (10-10-1858)
Robbs, Sarah C. to W. H. Tarwater 12-31-1872 (1-1-1873)
Roberson, Sarah to James Greene 1-31-1861
Roberts, Catharine to Thomas Hacker 4-30-1874
Roberts, Elizabeth to James Bronson 7-31-1872 (8-1-1872)
Roberts, Elizabeth to Hiram J. Buller 10-24-1859
Roberts, Elizabeth to John Hacker 9-4-1858
Roberts, Emaline to Campbell Wilkie 2-16-1864
Roberts, Jane to Francis A. Hicks 7-21-1870
Roberts, Lidia M. to John Coker 2-7-1865 (2-16-1865)
Roberts, Louisa to Stephen B. Abstent 1-7-1861 (1-9-1861)
Roberts, Louisa to Andrew J. Sutton 7-19-1858 (7-19-1858)
Roberts, Margaret to Saml. H. Crow 11-7-1872
Roberts, Marinda to James Stone 7-6-1865
Roberts, Mary to William Wright 1-1-1864 (1-5-1864)
Roberts, Mary E. to Joseph D. Turner 8-7-1858 (8-12-1858)
Roberts, Nancy to Tho. McInally 9-1-1870
Roberts, Rebecca to Joseph Brown 10-10-1868 (10-11-1868)
Roberts, Rebecca to James McCrary 3-9-1865
Roberts, Rebecca A. to Smith P. Burns 9-3-1860 (9-6-1860)
Roberts, Sabrie to Alfred Hacker 10-31-1864
Roberts, Sarah Ann to William J. Hicks 12-7-1859 (12-8-1859)
Roberts, Sarah E. to Dalmon A. Tuterrow 3-13-1872
Roberts, Sarah M. to Jas. W. McNutt 8-8-1865
Robertson, Barbara P. to James B. Kelley 8-31-1874 (9-2-1874)
Robertson, Betsy Jane to George W. Russell 6-15-1858 (6-17-1858)
Robertson, M. J. to George Whelock 8-10-1863

Roane County Brides

Robertson, Margaret T. to G. W. Hester 11-5-1867 (11-14-1867)
Robertson, Mary to James m. Henderson 9-7-1861 (9-10-1861)
Robertson, Mary J. to George W. Cole 7-20-1861 (7-25-1861)
Robinson, Betsey A. to Tho. R. Evans 2-22-1869 (3-2?-1869)
Robinson, Cornelia to C. W. Williamson 5-2-1871
Robinson, Elizabeth to Thomas Davies 9-3-1870
Robinson, Elizabeth A. to James D. Miller 10-22-1867 (10-24-1867)
Robinson, Elizabeth J. S. to Rufus M. Hudson 11-26-1864 (12-1-1864)
Robinson, Hannah to James M. Mosier 11-6-1858 (11-7-1858)
Robinson, Lucinda to John C. Carroll 8-25-1865 (8-30-1865)
Robinson, Mary Ann to W. B. Paul 3-2-1870 4-3-1870
Robinson, Mary Jane to Moses T. Campbell 9-9-1858 (9-10-1858)
Robinson, Mary O. to C. O. Libby 2-24-1871 (3-5-1871)
Robinson, Rebecca to Thomas S. Henderson 11-6-1865 (11-7-1865)
Robinson, Sarah to John L. White 10-16-1867 (10-17-1867)
Robinson, Sarah C. to Wm. B. Hope 4-10-1862
Robinson, Sarah Jane to Wilson Carter 3-30-1866
Roday, Selah Ann to George Nodes 8-6-1864 (8-7-1864)
Roddie, Harritt to Byrd Pope 3-21-1868   B
Rodgers, Mary E. to William A. Enocks 1-18-1859 (1-20-1859)
Roehl?, Amanda to John Rose 4-8-1874
Rogers, Caroline to Jasper Yarber 10-24-1865
Rogers, Catharine to John Scarborough 12-30-1865 (1-4-1866)
Rogers, Mary Jane to M. L. Gibson 10-14-1865 (10-18-1865)
Rogers, Nancy A. to Geo. W. Stinett 8-17-1865 (8-19-1865)
Rose, Eliza to James Sharp 7-26-1873 (8-26-1873)
Rose, Margaret Ann to Wm. M. Tate 8-31-1860 (SB 1864?)
Rose, Margaret Ann to Wm.? M. Tate 8-31-1864 (9-1-1864)
Rose, Martha A. to John B. Peterman 3-3-1866 (3-4-1866)
Rose, Sarah E. to William P.? Tate 10-6-1871 (10-8-1871)
Rosier, Clarissa to Charles Redferren 8-14-1856 (not endorsed)
Row, Nancy to Emanuel Thornton 8-7-1858
Rowe, Margaret to Harvey Scott 1-30-1858 (1-31-1858)
Rowe, Rachel to Richard Nelson 1-1-1861 (1-4-1861)
Rucker, Julinda E. to John McCarroll 6-16-1860 (6-17-1860)
Rucker, Thena to JSames L. Clower 8-14-1868 (8-16-1868)
Ruggles, Abigail to James A. Props 4-9-1856 (4-10-1856)
Ruggles, Elisebeth H. to George W. Melton 12-3-1864 (12-4-1864)
Russell, CLythia D. to John H. Webster 2-2-1872 (2-4-1872)
Russell, Charlotte B. to James M. Hinds 7-30-1861 (8-1-1861)
Russell, Eda P. to John Mathis 9-14-1872 (9-19-1872)
Russell, Elizabeth to I. M. Edmonds 2-28-1870
Russell, Elizabeth Ann to Wm. Lollis 4-7-1865 (4-9-1865)
Russell, Jane to E. K. Brown 6-27-1866 (6-28-1866)
Russell, Lavinia S. to Jacob A. Tibbs 6-15-1858 (6-14?-1858)
Russell, Lotty to Elbert Huffman 1-26-1860
Russell, Lucy A. to Benjamin F. Underwood 8-31-1861 (9-4-1861)
Russell, Mary A. to Jackson Grubb 7-2-1860 (7-8-1860)
Russell, Mary C. to William H. Easter 3-25-1873 (3-27-1873)
Russell, Milly to William Howard 9-29-1860 (10-1-1860)
Russell, Sarah to G. W. Kyle 4-6-1874 (4-17-1874)
Russell, Sarah C. to James H. Wirick 9-25-1873 (9-28-1873)
Rutherford, J. E. to Philip Hughes 12-20-1873 (12-25-1873)
Rutherford, MaryC. to George Washam 3-27-1864

Roane County Brides

Rutherford, Nancy J. to Francis Galyon 12-31-1868
Rutor?, Malinda to George Faulkner 5-1-1858 (5-3-1858)
Sams, Ann to George Kyle 9-11-1860 (9-13-1860)
Sams, E. C. to Thomas A. Goury? 12-14-1868 (12-15-1868)
Sams, E. C. to Joseph M. Rice 1-25-1865 (1-26-1865)
Sams, Mary C. to N.W. Whitlock 1-27-1864 (2-11-1864)
Sanders, Mahala to D. S. Webb 11-3-1869 11-4-1869
Sane?, Frances to William Farris 3-6-1860
Saunders, M. J. to Rufus M. Carter 12-22-1868 (12-27-1868)
Scales, Rebecca to Jasper Eldridge 5-14-1869 (5-16-1869)
Scarbrough, Georgiana to Andrew McElroy 7-25-1872
Scarbrough, Mahala D. to James M. Clough 7-31-1872 (8-1-1872)
Scarbrough, Malinda J. to John W. Briddle 3-19-1874 (3-22-1874)
Scarbrough, Margaret R. to Edward Cates 12-21-1871
Scarbrough, Mary E. to Chas. E. Clough 12-5-1874 (12-6-1874)
Schooler, Sarah to Nelson Nothern? 4-22-1862
Scott, Louisa E. to George Scott 8-27-1868 (8-30-1868)
Scott, Nancy J. to James Greene 2-2-1867 (2-3-1867)
Scott, Sarah J. to Joseph M. Browning 5-23-1871 (5-24-1871)
Scott, Sarah May Cora W. to William Randolph 4-25-1868
Seabert, Nancy to John F. Grubb 4-10-1861 (4-11-1861)
Seiber, Julia to Wm. J. Shackelford 7-20-1872 (7-21-1872)
Seiber, Malinda to Jasper M. Hoskins 8-30-1871 (9-1-1871)
Seiber, Malinda to Chas. W. Taylor 2-4-1867 (2-8-1867)
Seiber, Margaret A. to John W. Davis 10-25-1874 (10-29-18740
Seiber, Mariah to Samuel Martin 12-27-1869 12-28-1869
Seiber, Pheabe to Ananias McKinney 12-18-1865 (12-24-1865)
Seiber, Rutha to William Copland 8-27-1860
Seibor, Martha J. to Geo. W. Coaker 12-17-1867 (12-19-1867)
Sellars, Ada to J. L. McKinney 11-21-1874 (11-22-1874)
Sellars, Mary to Jas. A. Cassady 12-21-1867 (12-22-1867)
Sellars, Mary H. to George W. Ball 1-31-1867
Sellars, Matilda (Mrs.) to Robert Waller 11-8-1873 (11-9-1873)
Sellars, Sallie to Thomas Smith 9-10-1873 (9-11-1873)
Sellers, Harriet J. to Smith Brady 1-29-1856 (1-30-1856)
Selvage, Melinda C. to William Brogdon 3-17-1860
Selvage, Sarah J. to W. J. Wilkerson 4-24-1865 (4-31?-1865)
Selvege, Mary to James Smith 5-7-1864 (5-6?-1864)
Selvey, Serilda J. to Edward W. Currier 2-12-1864 (2-14-1864)
Selvey?, Martha to George Phillips 4-27-1864
Selvidge, Caroline to Robert Martin 3-4-1857 (not endorsed)
Selvige, H. T. to Albert P. Leffew 9-16-1871 (9-17-1871)
Senoir?, Laura to Henry A. Chambers 1-25-1867 (1-13?-1867)
Shackelford, Alice to Wm. Martin 4-26-1865
Shackelford, Barbara J. to Joseph E. Buns? 9-12-1862
Shackelford, Mary to John E. Graves 11-8-1866
Shackelford, Mary A. to John Selvage 8-2-1864
Shaham, Martha to George Wilkerson 7-17-1857 (7-19-1857)
Shahan, Elizabeth to Jas.? Collins 1-16-1868
Shahan, Emma to James Thompson 2-3-1875
Shahan, Mariah to Henry C. Wilkerson 8-1-1863
Sharp, Amanda M. to J. L. Humphrey 8-25-1870 8-28-1870
Sharp, Cynthi J. to W. R. Caroway 9-12-1868 (9-15-1868)
Sharp, Eliza to Z. Shackelford 2-24-1870

Roane County Brides

Sharp, Elizabeth to Wm. O. Mulinix 2-25-1873
Sharp, Jane to John Childs 3-13-1869 (3-17-1869)
Sharp, Jemmima C. to Robert Webster 12-18-1871 (12-21-1871)
Sharp, Louisa to Francis M. Fisher 12-25-1858 (12-28-1858)
Sharp, Marylin to Shade Tow 10-26-1866 (11-1-1866)
Sharp, Nancy I. to Smith? Pope 11-4-1870 11-10-1870
Sharp, Orlena to Albert Lane 4-6-1865 (4-16-1865)
Sharp, Ruth E. to John S. Jones 12-16-1873
Sharp, S. M. to S. C. Brown 2-2-1875
Sharp, Sarah to John H. Bradshaw 8-13-1864 (9-1-1860?)
Shell, Jane to Daniel Helton 12-18-1866
Shelton, Elizabeth N. to Joel Dotson 12-6-1860
Sherwood, Kate C. to Isaac Turpin 6-7-1865 (6-8-1865)
Sherwood, Laura E. to T. J. Crawford 4-15-1874
Shields, Mary E. to John A. Williams 3-1-1867 (2?-5-1867)
Shinpaugh, Elizabeth C. to John Stansbury 11-4-1861
Shinpaugh, Mary Jane to Wm. P. Tuterow 7-25-1866 (8-2-1866)
Shoat, Sarah to Jackson Moss 2-27-1866 (3-1-18660
Shoate, Margaret to Clingen Hartley 9-11-1873 (9-12-1873)
Short, Charlotte to Flaven Demars 5-5-1870 5-8-1870
Short, Deanah to Lewis Roberts 3-17-1866 (3-18-1866)
Short, Loriet to Thomas A. Chapman 6-20-1857 (6-22-1857)
Short, Mary to J. S. Robbs 10-17-1874 (10-18-1874)
Short, Nancy R. to Geo. W. Frazier 11-7-1860
Shote, Betsey to Samuel Shote 3-25-1873
Shouse, C. J. to John A. Lowery 9-2-1868 (9-3-1868)
Shubart, Lydia to Wm. Lasey 9-8-1860 (9-9-1860)
Shubert, Fanny to David Jinkins 4-11-1859
Shuburt, Eliza to Wm. B. Whaley 7-25-1866 (8-5-1866)
Shuburt, Elvira to Griffin Thomas 5-12-1871 (5-18-1871)
Silvey, E. A. to James H. Baker 4-14-1874 (4-16-1874)
Silvey, Malinda D. to Michael A. May 9-26-1872
Silvey, Mary F. to Jesse Hacker 4-22-1874 (4-23-1874)
Silvey, Nancy G. to W. M. Roberts 5-6-1865
Simons?, Mary T. to Georg W. Carmichal 10-24-1868 (10-25-1868)
Simpson, Henrietta to Andrew Wilson 4-13-1865
Simpson, Martha L. to James Parker 7-29-1873 (7-30-1873)
Simpson, Mary to Robert Sherwood 6-28-1861
Slack, Eliza to Andrew McCaleb 4-3-1856
Sliger, Margaret L. to B. M. Locke 2-18-1871 (2-26-1871)
Sliger, Sarah E. to Martin M. Hicks 9-9-1872 (9-12-1872)
Small, Eliza J. to Arthur S. Mathis 3-2-1858
Smalley, Amanda to William H. Huffine 10-6-1857 (10-8-1857)
Smalley, Charity to James Jones 1-2-1873
Smalley, Elizabeth J. to Wilson Rose 9-15-1858 (9-16-1858)
Smalley, Jane to James M. Huffine 8-4-1864
Smalley, Malinda to James E. Rose 8-22-1865
Smalley, Sarah to Jesse J. Patty 2-18-1856 (2-21-1856)
Smart, Cyntha to Fritts Myres 8-12-1868 (8-13-1868)
Smicegood, Mary to George Isham 4-10-1869 (4-11-1869)
Smith, A. W. to M. L. Moore 4-25-1874 (4-26-1874)
Smith, Caroline P. to James A. Corry 2-13-1861 (2-14-1861)
Smith, Dicy to Joseph Roberts 10-17-1860 (10-18-1860)
Smith, Dora A. to J. C. Bullen 4-12-1871

Roane County Brides

Smith, Elender to Robert Woody 12-13-1857
Smith, Elisabeth to John C. Hammonds 12-26-1874 (12-31-1874)
Smith, Elizabeth to James Bradley 4-4-1859 (4-7-1859)
Smith, Jane to William Miller 12-17-1866 (12-20-1866)
Smith, Jane to Squire Wilson 7-16-1870 7-17-1870
Smith, Lucy A. to Bird Pickel 10-8-1867 (10-17-1867)
Smith, Margaret to William Lackey 11-5-1867
Smith, Margaret A. to Richard Oliver 4-26-1862 (4-29-1862)
Smith, Martha Ann to Hesekiah Woodey 4-10-1866 (4-12-1866)
Smith, Martha Caroline to Elisha T. Ingram 5-26-1857
Smith, Martha J. to George W. Ellis 8-26-1856 (10-21-1856)
Smith, Martha M. to James W. Moore 9-14-1866 (9-20-1866)
Smith, Mary to james H. Johnson 2-10-1866 (2-15-1866)
Smith, Mary Ann to Samuel Browder 1-18-1858 (1-21-1858)
Smith, Mary Jane to Jonathan Hulen 4-30-1859 (5-1-1859)
Smith, Mary S. to David J. Ingram 9-25-1865
Smith, Matilda C. to Geo. G. Hardin 12-16-1867 (12-19-1867)
Smith, P. Melinda to John Langen 6-14-1862 (7-3-1862)
Smith, Pheby L. to Wm. G. Arnett 6-6-1857 (6-7-1857)
Smith, Sallie P. to D. M. Boyd 10-13-1869
Smith, Sarah to A. J. Ingram 1-22-1866 (1-25-1866)
Smith, Sarah E. to Wm. Haney 12-18-1872 (12-19-1872)
Snow, Mary to Thomas F. McDaniel 8-22-1860 (?-3-1860)
Snow, Mary to John Morris 12-25-1858 (12-30-1858)
Snow, Sarah E. to Thomas L. Lewis 12-5-1866 (12-6-1866)
Solomon, Martha to John Gray 6-13-1868
Solomon, Martha J. to William Priddy 10-3-1859 (10-4-1859)
Solomon, Nancy A. to G. W. Raney 9-8-1866 (9-9-1866)
Somerville, Maggie C. to H. M. Wilder 5-29-1871 (5-30-1871)
Soward, Catharine to Wm. Blackburn 5-2-1871 (5-4-1871)
Soward, Mary Ann Jane to William H. G. Campbell 4-5-1857 (4-6-1857)
Soward, Orfin to Stewart Weese 3-6-1860 (3-8-1860)
Sparks, Mary A. to Francis Andrew 1-18-1869
Sparks, Sarah Jane to Willson N. Dewitt 9-23-1856 (9-25-1856)
Sperling, Mary to Jesse Pass 12-22-170
Spurling?, Narcissa E. to Wm. H. Frank 8-27-1867 (8-28-1867)
Stalcup, Lorena E. to John H. Fritts 10-9-1866 (10-11-1866)
Stalcup, Rebecca to Isaih Dickinson 4-19-1866 (4-22-1866)
Staley, Elizabeth N. to Wm. A. Gray 6-21-1869 (7-18-1869)
Staley, Mary Ann to Amos Hart 5-9-1866 (5-10-1866)
Staples, Alsa to John Eaton 11-9-1865
Staples, Delilah C. to Joel D. Hembree 4-22-1868 (4-23-1868)
Stark, Elizabeth to James H. Fender 3-28-1859 (4-6-1859)
Stencil, Sarah A. to E. B. Short 1-11-1869
Stephens, H. M. to John A. Tankless 9-4-1862
Stephens, Louisa to Abraham Curd 3-17-1866 (3-18-1866)
Stevens, Charlotte M. to Wm. F. Brown 5-6-1873 (5-18-1873)
Stevens, Lorinda to James C. Ketchum 8-12-1874 (8-4?-1874)
Stevenson, Alice J. to Samuel S. Hutsell 9-12-1872
Stewart, Polly E. to J. A. West 5-2-1874 (5-3-1874)
Stewart, Rebecca to Ben Ellit 2-29-1868 (3-1-1868)
Stewart, Susannah to Ulrich Herin 3-14-1857 (3-15-1857)
Stinecipher, Lucinda to Jas. Cunningham 9-21-1874 (9-24-1874)
Stinecipher, Mary M. to Wiley H. Richmond 3-1-1869 (3-4-1869)

Roane County Brides

Stinecipher, Nancy M. to Daniel T. Coker 10-10-1874 (10-11-1874)
Stokes, Polly A. to W. A. Work 4-7-1874 (4-9-1874)
Stolling, Margaret to Charles Bisplinghoff 7-22-1858 (7-23-1858)
Stout, Elisabeth to John Burnett 10-22-1874 (8?-22-1874)
Stout, Mary Ann to John Massey 3-3-1868
Stowers, Malinda to Robert Cook 8-22-1858 (8-26-1858)
Stringess, Nancy to Wiley Goldston 6-16-1862 (6-17-1862)
Stubbs, Telitha to Wm. H. Clough 9-2-1871 (9-3-1871)
Stuffels, Elizabeth to T. B. Grand 8-13-1867 (8-15-1867)
Sturgess, Eliza to Joseph Fritts 11-3-1863
Sturgess, Sarah to Richard White 1-18-1858
Suddath, Evaline to George M. Stanfield 11-25-1858 (11-30-1858)
Suddath, Nancy L. to William T. Rice 9-1-1857
Suddeth, Julia to Emanuel Montgomery 5-1-1872 B
Sullins, Elizabeth to Z. T. Bargers 12-21-1870 12-22-1870
Summers, S. A. to J. B. Smith 7-6-1869 (7-7-1869)
Surrett, Martha to C. M. Atwood 8-8-1874 (8-9-1874)
Susey, Sarah E. to James W. Golston 11-20-1871 (11-23-1871)
Susir?, Margaret A. E. to Thos. Costen 9-18-1860 (9-20-1860)
Suvall, Catharine to David Bowles 10-8-1864
Swaner, Mahala to Stephen Seiber 12-5-1867
Swicegood, Mary E. to Andrew J. Hall 1-11-1867
Swicegood?, Martha J. to John H. Leffew 8-22-1867
Sylvey, Charlotte to George Qualls 12-2-1870 12-4-1870
Sylvey, Eliza Jane to Joseph Hacker 3-31-1866 (4-1-1866)
Sylvey, Elizabeth to Calvin Seiber 12-15-1865
Sylvey, Louisa to A. J. Cheatham 5-10-1873 (5-11-1873)
Sylvey, Mary to Geo. W. Byrd 1-31-1865
Sylvey, Susan Ann to George Edwards 11-20-1869 11-23-1869
Talent, Amanda to G. W. Byrd 9-22-1869
Talent, Malinda to Alexander Williams 7-20-1870 7-23-1870
Talent, Margaret A. to J. P. Russell 8-8-1864
Taliaferro, Nancy to Henry Green no dates (with 1870) B
Taliaferro, Samantha C. to A. J. Lillard 11-9-1866 (1-29-1867)
Tally, Sallie A. to J. T. Shipley 2-18-1871 (2-19-1871)
Talor, Sarah A. to John Casey 12-25-1856
Tankersly, Hilah M. to Calvin Price 7-26-1871
Tap, Manerva to Wm. Hudleson 10-13-1865 (10-16-1865)
Tapp, Adaline to Leroy R. Hudelston 9-15-1862
Tapp, L. C. to James Bly 8-2-1873 (8-4-1873)
Tarwater, Maggie E. to E. M. Bales 5-19-1874 (5-27-1874)
Tate, Margaret to George W. Gideon 2-6-1866 (2-7-1866)
Tate, Margaret E. to John J. Weese 10-12-1870 10-13-1870
Tauscher, Matilda to M. H. Stansbury 8-6-1873 (8-7-1873)
Taylor, Angeline to Wiley Carnell 6-27-1856
Taylor, Eliza F. to G. M. Littleton 1-28-1875
Taylor, Eliza J. to Lemuel Guinn 12-28-1868 (12-31-1868)
Taylor, Jane to James H. Stubbs 6-18-1873 (7-6-1873)
Taylor, Louisa C. to H. R. Stansbury 9-17-1873
Taylor, Mary Ann to W. H. King 9-12-1870
Taylor, Mary C. to A. J. Smith 9-10-1868 (9-11-1868)
Taylor, Mary R. to John M. Russell 7-16-1866 (7-19-1866)
Taylor, Matilda Y. to Samuel Marney 2-9-1858 (2-14-1858)
Taylor, Nancy to John Gallimore 7-5-1860

Roane County Brides

Taylor, Nancy F. to William Donaldson 1-14-1858 (3-2-1858)
Taylor, P. C. to James Scarbrough 3-10-1868 (3-15-1868)
Taylor, Sarah to Richard Rector 7-3-1871 (7-4-1871)
Tedder, Catharine to Lewis Cofer 12-28-1872 (12-29-1872)
Tedder, Mariah L. to Morgan B. Hawkins 10-20-1863 (10-30-1863)
Tedder, S. C. to Lewis F. Aliston 1-13-1872 (1-14-1872)
Tedder, Sarah A. to Joseph A. Shadden 6-20-1867 (6-21-1867)
Teller, Jane to Richard Claybrooks 8-20-1863 (8-23-1863)
Temple, Mary E. to Jacob M. Cobb 6-14-1867 (6-23-1867)
Temple, Nancy to James M. Galyon 11-19-1866 (11-23-1866)
Thacker, Celia J. to William Ray 9-2-1872 (9-8-1872)
Thacker, Elizabeth to James Currier 9-19-1866 (9-20-1866)
Thacker, Ruth to Thomas Turpin 7-29-1874
Thomas, Elizabeth P. to John H. Isbel 3-24-1868
Thomas, Margaret to James Ortin 9-16-1856
Thomas, Mary to Moses Chester 1-11-1868 (1-12-1868)
Thomas, Mary A. to M. E. Smith 4-9-1870 4-10-1870
Thomas, Mary Ann to Lewis Williams 6-17-1872 (6-22-1872)
Thomas, Sarah to Thomas Aiken 11-1-1866 (11-7-1866)
Thompson, Amanda to Samuel Finchum 10-9-1867 (10-13-1867)
Thompson, Caroline to C. N. Pleming 6-7-1873 (6-16-1873)
Thompson, Catharine to Lewis Howard 12-31-1872
Thompson, Frances to J. H. Davis 4-26-1872 (5-5-1872)
Thompson, Josephine to John L. Isham 9-14-1872 (9-15-1872)
Thompson, Martha to Josiah Smith 8-24-1867 (11-25-1867)
Thompson, Nancy to Hezikah Miller 9-4-1868 (9-6-1868)
Thompson, Nancy C. to Amos B. Clifton 12-14-1874 (12-17-1874)
Thompson, Nancy C. to George W. Melton 10-7-1873 (10-9-1873)
Thompson, Rebecca A. to John L. Lewis 2-23-1867 (2-24-1867)
Thompson, S. A. to J. H. Pool 7-19-1873 (7-20-1873)
Thompson, Sarah A. to John B. Brice 9-17-1866 (9-20-1866)
Thrailkill, Nancy to Jesse Hammons 12-20-1860
Thrailkill, Nancy A. to John Cox 5-11-1870 5-12-1870
Thralekill, Elizabeth to Daniel Cross 9-1-1870
Tilley, E. T. to C. C. Wilkey 9-17-1874
Tindle?, Mary E. to Jason Allen 2-17-1869 (2-18-1869)
Tinel, Eliza Jane to John J. Miller 12-27-1865 (12-28-1865)
Tinel, Sarah Jane to Gideon Capps 1-17-1867
Tinker, Celicia to Martin M. Hix 8-10-1869 8-12-1869
Toilett, Mary J. to John F. Smith 4-8-1858
Tolleferro, Emma E. to Washington B. Rose 12-3-1867 (12-5-1867)
Toney, Mary J. to William Francis 5-15-1861 (5-16-1861)
Toney, Mary Jane to William France 3-20-1857 (3-23-1857)
Treadaway, Malinda to Major Halloway 9-24-1872 (9-25-1872)
True, Lucinda Jane to James N. Bilderback 3-8-1856 (3-12-1856)
Truet, Elizabeth to Alexander Rose 8-25-1869 8-26-1869
Turnbill, Margaret to Johnson G.? Huling 11-9-1867 (11-10-1867)
Turnbill, Mary B. to Thomas J. Cate 11-30-1864 (not executed)
Turner, Sarah to Geo. D. Wright 9-25-1856 (10-2-1856)
Turpin, Elizabeth A. to A. Mack Maham 7-9-1874 (7-10-1874)
Turpin, Nancy J. to Benjamin Curnier? 3-12-1867 (3-14-1867)
Tuterow, Martha A. to John A. Syler? 1-10-1871 (1-12-1871)
Tuterow, Teresa A. to James Wells 11-29-1864 (11-30-1864)
Tuterrow, Mary to Hiram Bailey 5-3-1871

Roane County Brides

Tuton, Eveline to Newton C. Sharp 11-8-1867 (11-10-1867)
Tutterrow, Sue R. to J. D. Carter 3-2-1869 (3-11-1869)
Underwood, Amanda to James Frederick Ruoff 4-19-1859
Underwood, Caroline to Joseph A. Short 11-11-1871
Underwood, Eliza to D. M. Bell 5-1-1874
Underwood, Eliza J. to W. H. Cunningham 7-12-1872 (7-14-1872)
Underwood, Elvira to C. V. Wilkey 10-14-1865
Underwood, Jane to Wilson Maples 6-1-1865 (6-4-1865)
Underwood, Lydda to Claiborne Goins 4-21-1865 (4-22-1865)
Underwood, Martha C. to Jacob Simpson 5-7-1867
Underwood, Mary to Saml. Dugger 4-12-1860
Underwood, Mary E. to J. W. Worsham 6-26-1869 (6-27-1869)
Underwood, Nancy to Robert Cardwell 8-6-1860
Underwood, Nancy J. to Yerby Adkisson 3-24-1857 (3-26-1857)
Underwood, Sarah to Robert Dupee 9-23-1862
Underwood, Sarah E. to Irvin L. Philpot 10-17-1866 (10-18-1866)
Underwood, Sarah J. to Nathan Whittenbury 2-9-1857 (2-10-1857)
Usra, Matilda to Wm. Brown 7-28-1866
Van, Elizabeth to Rufus Duff 9-4-1862 (9-18-1862)
Vann, Eliza C. W. to John W. Jones 12-16-1869 12-19-1869
Vann, Isabel to Wm. Worsham 5-9-1874 (crossed out) B?
Vann, Louisa E. to Jas. A. Scarbrough 12-14-1874 (12-20-1874)
Vann, Martha J. to David D. Dickey 5-28-1860 (5-29-1860)
Vann, Maryakette to Wm. L. Narrimore 2-9-1864 (2-10-1864)
Vann, Sarah to John Y. Cook 2-26-1873 (2-27-1873)
Vaughn, Adeline to Joseph Jones 8-1-1866 (8-2-1866)
Vaughn, Nancy to Marion Ledford 9-15-1866 (9-16-1866)
Vaux, Victoria to J. G. W. Gerding 3-10-1863 (3-17-1863)
Wade, Malinda to Daniel J. Cardin 2-28-1862 (3-2-1862)
Wade, Sarah to Wm. Crabtree 3-3-1866 (3-4-1866)
Wakefield, Sarah to Caleb J. Ellis 8-30-1871 (8-14-1871)
Waldrip, E. to James Row 8-9-1866 (8-10-1866)
Walker, Elizabeth to Henderson Deatherage 2-19-1863
Walker, Elizabeth to Ephraim Guffee 12-26-1862
Walker, Esther T. to James W. Fox 3-1-1869
Walker, Margaret S. to Samuel Mamey 1-6-1872 (1-11-1872)
Walker, N. J. to Jas. H. Billingsley 8-24-1869
Walker, Nancy A. to W. B. Adkisson 4-28-1870
Walker, Nancy A. to John M. Clark 11-21-1870 11-24-1870
Walker, Queen V. to Lorenzo F. Holland 10-1-1872 (10-3-1872)
Walker, Sarah E. to Wm. Ervin 12-9-1864 (12-12-1864)
Walker, Susan E. to James H. Cook 8-24-1861 (8-25-1861)
Wallace, Levina to B. A. Haskins 3-29-1864
Wallace, Louisa to Samuel French 11-12-1866 (11-15-1866)
Wallace, Martha A. to John Ervin 10-19-1860
Wallace, Nancy Ann to Elisha Rose 2-20-1867
Waller, America to Peter W. Goodin 12-1-1856 (12-17-1856)
Waller, Eliza to Samuel L. Taliaferro 9-14-1871
Waller, Keziah C. to Wm. M. Scarbrough 9-1-1871
Waller, Margaret to George P. Waller 2-15-1867 (2-17-1867)
Waller, Martha C. to Wm. M. Rayburn 5-13-1868 (5-14-1868)
Waller, Mary C. to Joseph N. Cardwell 3-25-1871 (3-26-1871)
Waller, Matilda to George W. Balew 9-24-1862
Waller, Sarah A. to Joseph A. Hinds 12-8-1860 (12-10-1860)

Roane County Brides

Waller, Sarah K. to John C. Jones 8-6-1859
Waller, Savannah M. to Wm. J. Jones 9-17-1869
Walls, Elizabeth to James Davis 9-24-1866 (9-25-1866)
Walls, Elizabeth to William Phillips 9-22-1859 (9-26-1859)
Walls, Mary A. to Larkin Brock 12-14-1872 (12-15-1872)
Walls, Sarah C. to Isaac Coward 1-22-1869 (1-24-1869)
Walton, _____ A. to David? Sherwood 7-20-1864 (7-28-1864)
Ward, Frances A. to William Scott 9-20-1867 (9-21-1867)
Ward, Margaret to Robert M. Magill 5-21-1870 5-22-1870
Ward, Mary A. to Peter P. Easter 2-19-1872 (2-20-1872)
Ward, Phinnette J. to James Woody 2-7-1868 (2-9-1868)
Ward, Tennessee A. to Thomas Boling 6-20-1874 (6-21-1874)
Ward, Ves to Monroe Utley 12-21-1869 12-22-1869
Warren, Mary M. to William Moreland 12-15-1860
Wasson, Rachel S. to John H. Rowden 12-9-1864 (12-15-1864)
Watenbarger, Elizabeth to Benj. Roach 1-29-1861
Watson, Mariah E. to Wm. J. McMinnas? 1-14-1870 1-19-1870
Watson, Minerva to Joseph King 5-8-1857
Watt, Elizabeth to Genl. T. Carter 10-28-1864 (10-30-1864)
Watt, Martha to Enoch McCall 11-26-1873 (11-27-1873)
Watt, Sarafina to D. C. White 5-2-1872 (5-31-1872)
Watts, Julia Ann to Benjamin F. Wiggins 9-4-1858
Watts, Leathy E. to Columbus McCarroll 2-6-1860
Watts, Mary Elizabeth to Leonidas F. Wiggins 1-31-1866 (2-1-1866)
Watts, Mary W. to Jas. A. Hampton 5-24-1870 5-25-1870
Weaver, Esther to William Brown 12-28-1867 (1-2-1868)
Webster, Jane to Eli May 4-29-1861
Weece, Mary to George Frank 5-14-1868
Weese, Nancy Ann to James Parks 6-20-1856 (6-21-1856)
Weese, R. A. D. to J. M. Barnard 12-21-1870 12-22-1870
Welcker, Elizabeth to Andrew J. Lackey 8-13-1867 (8-15-1867)
Wells, Hester A. to D. J. Farmer 10-10-1874 (10-11-1874)
Wells, Jane to Robert Varner? 6-8-1861 (6-9-1861)
Wells, NSancy to Geo. Washington 5-14-1864 (5-16-1864)
Wells, Sarah to R. M. Hart 8-19-1869
Weneter, Louisa D. to John C. Nelson 2-25-1859 (2-6-1859)
Wensch?, Ailan? M. to Therson Seinknecht 12-23-1869
West, Louis to Moses N. Stewart 5-2-1874 (5-3-1874)
West, Mary A. R. to John F. Lawson 10-12-1872
West, Rachel to Richard Findly 1-23-1868 (crossed out)
West, Sarah to Jas. Roberts 1-27-1865 (1-28-1865)
Wester, Alice to R. S. Kindrich 1-1-1870
Wester, Catharine A. to Henry C. Mills 9-1-1865
Wester, Maggie J. to John H. Wright 3-19-1874
Wester, Mary Ann to Hiram Gibson 4-12-1860
Wester, Rachel L. to James M. Sturgess 3-26-1859 (4-10-1859)
Wester, Sarah to Esau Raybourne 8-1-1862 (8-3-1862)
Wester, josephine M. to John M. Wester 2-20-1867 (2-25-1867)
Wetherford, Elizabeth C. to Abraham Goodman 11-15-1860
Wetherford, Mary to Wiley Z. Goddard 4-21-1859
Whaley, Margaret L. to Jos. K. Miller 9-18-1867 (9-26-1867)
Whaley, Mary Jane to Columbus Sharp 9-24-1867 (8?-26-1867)
Whaley, Sarh E. to John Mannon 12-22-1868 (12-24-1868)
Wheat, Margaret C. to William B. Tudor 2-22-1860

Roane County Brides

Wheat, Mary to Jefferson Hamilton 12-2-1860 (12-4-1860)
Wheat, Minerva C. to Jno. Rayborn 11-13-1869 11-14-1869
Whelock, Margaret to Joseph Parker 8-15-1863
White, Grizzelle to J. L. Mullings 3-16-1861 (3-17-1861)
White, Lydia E. to James P. McCarroll 1-4-1858 (1-6-1858)
White, M. E. to John Gardner 6-30-1860 (7-1-1860)
White, Margaret to Alexander Gosset 1-15-1869 (1-16-1869)
White, Margaret (Mrs.) to James R. Crow 10-23-1871 (10-25-1871)
White, Sarah to Berry Roach 11-4-1865 (11-9-1865)
White, Sarah to John P. Waller 1-25-1868 (1-26-1868)
Whitlock, Catherine to John Frank 10-4-1860 (10-6-1860)
Whitlock, Elizabeth to John T. Baldwin 12-16-1873
Whitlock, Naomi J. to James F. _____ 1-5-1860 (1-8-1860)
Whitlock, Rebecca A. to Samuel H. Barnett 10-31-1859 (11-8-1859)
Whitlock, Sarah to James Hickey 2-10-1863 (2-11-1863)
Whitlock, Sarah to John Hurley 9-20-1864
Wiggins, Catherine M. to William Washam 5-3-1857 (5-7-1857)
Wiggins, Margaret N. to Hugh H. Scapehart 1-10-1856
Wiggins, Sarah to Frank Stafford 10-18-1870
Wilhoit, Mary to John T. Griffis 4-6-1867 (4-7-1867)
Wilhoit, Serena to John A. McKenzie 3-30-1867 (3-31-1867)
Wilkerson, Mary J. to John M. Montgomery 11-25-1867 (11-29-1867)
Wilkerson, Matilda to Thos. J. Cate 2-22-1865 (3-31-1865)
Wilkey, Martha to T. C. Wright 12-27-1871
Wilkey, Mary to Pleasant Wilson 11-26-1868
Wilkey, Rachel M. to Marshall H. Forrester 10-5-1865
Wilkey, Rachel M. to Marshall H. Forrester 10-5-1865
Wilkey, Rebecca to Benjamin Cash 3-19-1872
Wilkey, Susan to Samul T. Crenshaw 12-19-1868
Wilky, Melviny to J. W. Malone 7-27-1865
William, Lucinda to Douthet Huffman 11-4-1857 (11-7-1857)
Williams, Annie E. to Thos. A. Donelson 9-22-1868 (9-23-1868)
Williams, Bettie J. to Isaac M. Luffman 7-27-1869 7-29-1869
Williams, Campbell to Evan Ladd 11-8-1873
Williams, Cloaan F. to Geo. W. Shackelford 6-28-1867 (7-4-1867)
Williams, E. E. to Henry Burns 3-4-1865 (3-5-1865)
Williams, Fanny to Julian F. Barger 9-18-1868 (9-20-1868)
Williams, G. G. to N. L. Blair 9-16-1864 (10-6-1864)
Williams, Joshua A. to John P. Stgall? 7-23-1866
Williams, Julia A. to Evan Evins 2-17-1869 (2-18-1869)
Williams, Martha A. to Calvin F. Faris 1-20-1869 (1-21-1869)
Williams, Mary A. E. to James M. Williams 10-24-1856
Williams, Mary C. to James Gallimore 1-12-1871
Williams, Mary E. to Saml. S. Ballard 4-24-1860
Williams, Nancy Jane to Josiah Sullins 4-5-1866 (4-8-1866)
Williams, Susan to George Anthony 8-22-1860
Williamson, Cynthia A. to Samel Silvey 11-9-1872
Willson, Margaret L. to Samuel L. Cole 11-26-1856
Wilshire, Emma to James D. Roberts 5-20-1872 (5-23-1872)
Wilson, Amanda to James Carter 11-20-1874 (11-21-1874)
Wilson, Anne to Obediah Mathis 2-11-1864
Wilson, Arminda A. to D. C. Sparks 3-23-1870 3-24-1870
Wilson, Callie to James Gray 4-27-1872 (4-28-1872)
Wilson, Christiana to Joseph N. Love 4-24-1872 (4-25-1872)

Roane County Brides

Wilson, Cynthia L. to Wm. J. Agee 12-15-1859
Wilson, Julia Ann to William B. Edwards 10-13-1858
Wilson, L. L. to J. S. Webster 11-15-1873 (11-16-1873)
Wilson, Lucinda G. to Robt. M. Kelly 11-7-1865 (11-9-1865)
Wilson, Lutitia to Jesse J. Patty 6-1-1858 (6-4-1858)
Wilson, M. A. to A. M. Swicegood 12-27-1871 (12-28-1871)
Wilson, M. J. to S. H. Johnson 8-7-1869
Wilson, Malinda C. to Rufus Cox 10-6-1860 (10-7-1860)
Wilson, Margaret to John White 7-21-1863
Wilson, Margaret to John White 7-22-1863
Wilson, Mary to James H.? Brock 9-25-1861 (9-26-1861)
Wilson, Mary to Thomas Green 5-5-1864
Wilson, Mary C. to J. A. Billingsly 11-28-1868 (11-29-1868)
Wilson, Mary E. to Jason A. Helton 12-23-1857 (12-27-1857)
Wilson, Nancy L. to Ephraim France 11-16-1873 (11-23-1873)
Wilson, Rebecca C. to William A. Wright 2-23-1866 (2-27-1866)
Wilson, Sallie J. to Abraham May 7-22-1871 (7-27-1871)
Wilson, Sarafine to Spencer Davis 9-10-1874 (9-11-1874)
Wilson, Sarah A. to Major W. Wilkerson 8-26-1858
Wilson, Sarah J. to Wm. J. Edwards 2-21-1868 (2-23-1868)
Winchester, Elizabeth J. to Fernando C. Boyd 6-1-1860
Wineter, M. C. to C. F. Bauer 3-8-1873 (3-9-1873)
Winters, L. J. to D. J. Bell 6-28-1872 (6-29-1872)
Wintin, Nancy J. to Rufus A. McClure 2-5-1856
Winton, Arrabella J. to John W. Mann 7-24-1861 (8-1-1861)
Winton, Fanny A. to Samuel L. Kerr 12-19-1859 (12-22-1859)
Winton, Julia C. to G. W. Hardin 7-27-1861
Winton, Mary to John M. Pickle 5-18-1869 (5-25-1869)
Winton, Rheoda A. to Thos. G. Moss 9-24-1868
Wirick, Elizabeth J. to John J. Shields 8-18-1870 8-18-1870
Wirick, Margaret to Richard Haney 8-8-1867
Womble, Mary J. to John Y. Tipton 11-14-1871
Wood, Elizabeth to Caleb James 5-3-1870 5-5-1870
Woods, Martha J. to Thos. Saunders 12-6-1864 (12-8-1864)
Woody, Delila to David C. Kelsey 3-26-1858 (3-28-1858)
Woody, Elizabeth to Josiah Cooley 11-3-1862
Woody, Elizabeth to J. F. Ivey 7-1-1872 (7-25-1872)
Woody, Mary E. to Henry Fry 12-22-1869 12-23-1869
Woody, Mary R. to A. J. Shelton 4-10-1866 (4-14-1866)
Woody, Nelli to John George 12-15-1860
Woody, Sarah to William Scarborough 12-27-1866
Wooten, Cynthia to John P.? Easter 3-9-1872
Wooten, Susan M. to Mumford Fields 9-23-1876 (9-24-1876)
Work, Eliza J. to Elihu R. Owings 2-11-1859 (2-20-1859)
Wormsley, Sarah C. to Jas. T. Martin 1-10-1872 (1-11-1872)
Wray, Elizabeth to Wm. P. Newcome 12-24-1868 (12-27-1868)
Wright, Adaline A. to Jesse S. McKinney 3-24-1869 (3-25-1869)
Wright, Cealea Ann to Samuel sr. Selvy 1-5-1863
Wright, Eliza to John Wright 10-14-1865
Wright, Emma C. to Wm. T. Worsham 10-20-1867
Wright, Esther M. to Newton O. Neal 1-8-1862
Wright, Isabella to Jasper Pitman 10-7-1859
Wright, Margaret to Hiram Babb 6-23-1857
Wright, Martha M. to John J. Hellums 1-14-1873 (1-16-1873)

Roane County Brides

Wright, Mary to Wm. C. Allen 12-27-1856 (1-25-1857)
Wright, Mary to Edmond Phillips 9-26-1859 (9-27-1859)
Wright, Mary E. to Saml. M. Wilson 8-20-1874
Wright, Mary F. to Lemuel Guinn 1-1-1866 (1-4-1866)
Wright, Sally Ann to Granville Pittman 12-18-1859
Wright, Sarah to Jackson Hester 4-9-1874
Wright, Sarah C. to Amos Marney 2-20-1867 (2-21-1867)
Wright, Sarah J. to John J. Nichol 11-24-1864
Wright, Tabitha to George Ollis 3-16-1860
Wyatt, Eliza N. to Chas. D. Smith 11-5-1870 11-9-1870
Wyatt, Nancy J. to B. R. Rudder 7-27-1874 (8-6-1874)
Wycuff, Mary to John Thomas 2-16-1869
Wyrick, Nancy E. to William M. Renfro 1-24-1872 (1-25-1872)
Yancy, Eliza to Frederick Seiber 9-14-1866 (10-30-1866)
Yarber, Caroline to William Meroney 12-3-1862
Yarber, Dice to Richard Currier 3-3-1873 (3-4-1873)
Yarber, Rebecca to Edmond Moss 8-11-1865 (8-12-1865)
Yokely, Hannah E. to Albert H. Taylor 2-12-1869 (2-1?-1869)
Yost, Amanda to John Tyler 2-24-1869 B
Yost, Margaret A. to Samuel J. Dearmond 1-30-1858 (1-31-1858)
Young, Eliza to Samuel E. Wright 7-12-1859 (7-13-1859)
Young, Elizabeth S. to Wm. T. Lowrey 10-26-1865
Young, Mary M. to George W. Bishop 4-14-1873 (4-17-1873)
Young, Nancy to Thomas B. Breazeale 10-11-1860 (10-14-1860)
_____, Mary K. to Robert K. Byrd 7-23-1861

www.ingramcontent.com/pod-product-compliance
Lightning Source LLC
Chambersburg PA
CBHW081940170426
43202CB00018B/2960